STANDING BEAR IS A PERSON

STANDING BEAR
IS A PERSON

➔ ←

The True Story of a
Native American's Quest for Justice

STEPHEN DANDO-COLLINS

DA CAPO PRESS
A Member of the Perseus Books Group

Designed by Brent Wilcox
Set in 10.75-point Fairfield Light by the Perseus Books Group

Library of Congress Cataloging-in-Publication Data

Dando-Collins, Stephen.
    Standing Bear is a person : the true story of a Native American's quest for justice / Stephen Dando-Collins.
        p. cm.
    Includes bibliographical references and index.
    ISBN 0-306-81370-X (hardcover : alk. paper)
    1. Standing Bear, Ponca chief. 2. Ponca Indians—Kings and rulers—Biography. 3. Ponca Indians—Relocation. 4. Ponca Indians—Claims. 5. Ponca Indians—Legal status, laws, etc. I. Title.

E99.P7S833 2004
978.004'9752539'0092—dc22

2004014783

First printing, 2004

Published by Da Capo Press
A Member of the Perseus Books Group
http://www.dacapopress.com

Da Capo Press books are available at special discounts for bulk purchases in the U.S. by corporations, institutions, and other organizations. For more information, please contact the Special Markets Department at the Perseus Books Group, 11 Cambridge Center, Cambridge, MA 02142, or call (800) 255-1514 or (617) 252-5298, or email special.markets@perseusbooks.com.

1 2 3 4 5 6 7 8 9—08 07 06 05 04

CONTENTS

ACKNOWLEDGMENTS

This book began in the 1970s with a curiosity to learn more about Standing Bear and the Poncas after I read a brief chapter about their struggles in Dee Brown's *Bury My Heart at Wounded Knee*. In the 1990s my research gathered pace. The more I learned, the more the story haunted me. In recent times the project has garnered a host of supporters. My special thanks go to the Ponca tribe of Nebraska, in particular Chairman Mark Peniska and special projects coordinator Shaune Bell for her patient collaboration. Also to the Omaha tribe of Nebraska and Iowa, in particular Chairman Donald Grant, and to the dedicated Richard Chilton of the Omaha Tribal Historical Research Project. My sincere thanks also go to the Ponca for welcoming my wife and me to their annual powwow. I'm also greatly indebted to John Gottschalk, publisher of the *Omaha World-Herald* newspaper, the modern-day successor to T. H. Tibbles's paper, and his hard-working assistant Donna Grimm, for their detailed assistance.

To Marnie Cochran and Bob Pigeon at Perseus Books, thank you for seeing the potential of Standing Bear's story and for steering me down the focused path. My grateful thanks too go to my New York literary agent, Richard Curtis, who has guided and encouraged me and championed my work—our collaboration has been one of the joys of my life. But the greatest joy of my life is my wife, Louise, who has shared all the joys and disappointments of the writer's life with me for many years, and who, like me, abhors injustice. One of Louise's friends calls her Mrs. Sparkle; she does indeed put a sparkle in my every day.

INTRODUCTION

Should you ever venture to northern Oklahoma and visit a little metropolis near the Kansas state line called Ponca City, population 25,000, you will see an Indian chief who stands twenty-two feet tall and weighs four thousand pounds. You will be looking at a bronze statue of Standing Bear, or Machunazha as he was known in his own tongue, clan chief of the Poncas, the small Native American tribe for which the city is named. The statue, proudly dedicated by the city fathers in 1996, is the work of sculptor Oreland C. Joe. Ironically, this is the last place Standing Bear ever wanted to be.

In 1879, so determined was Standing Bear not to live here beside the Arkansas River in Oklahoma, he took the U.S. government to court, creating a legal case without precedent in U.S. history. Standing Bear and his people wished to live and die on the land of their birth, a thousand miles away in northeastern Nebraska, rather than in the Warm Land, as the Poncas called Oklahoma, the alien place to which the U.S. Army had marched Standing Bear and the Ponca tribe at the point of a bayonet two years earlier.

Before the Standing Bear case went to court, few Americans had ever heard of the small Ponca tribe. Suddenly the story grabbed the headlines across the country, and the name Standing Bear was on millions of lips. As editorial writers from New England to California told their readers, the outcome of the case could not only change the fate of the peaceable Poncas but terminate the forced removal of all Native Americans from their traditional lands and end the Indian reservation system, the system at the heart of government policy for westward expansion of the United States.

This is the story of that case, and its repercussions. An adventure story. A love story. A unique human rights story. It is also the story of an unusual coalition of players who paved Standing Bear's path to U.S. district court in April 1879—an army general who was considered America's greatest Indian fighter, a crusading newspaper editor who was once a gun-toting frontier preacher, a young attorney who had a brilliant idea but doubted the case could be won and another lawyer who hadn't appeared in court in sixteen years, and a shy Indian princess who became world famous. The tale you are about to read has all the hallmarks of a Hollywood epic, but it is very much a true story.

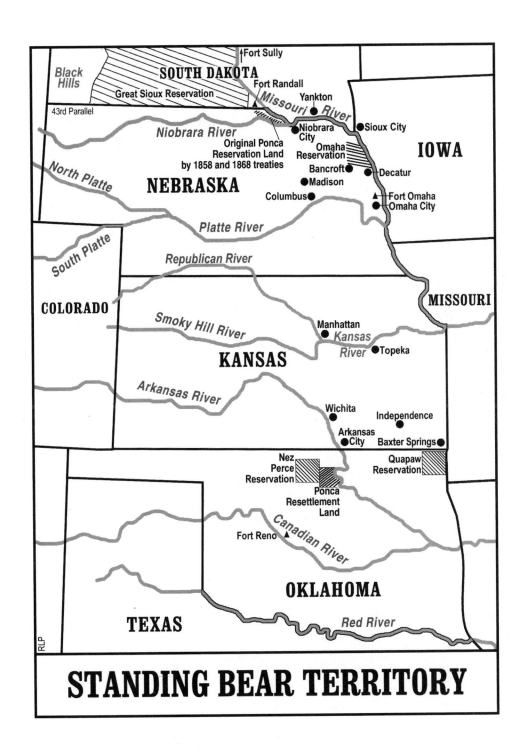

STANDING BEAR TERRITORY

✧ PART ONE: THE CAUSE ✦

If we can do something for which good men will remember us when we are gone, that is the best legacy we can leave.

General George Crook,
U.S. Army (1879)

Chapter 1

THE PRINCESS AND THE GENERAL

I T WAS LATE in the afternoon of March 29, a Saturday in the early
spring of 1879. Thirty-two-year-old Lieutenant John Gregory Bourke,
West Point graduate, Medal of Honor winner, and aide-de-camp to
Brigadier General George Crook, commander of the Military Department
of the Platte, slowly made his way across the parade ground at Fort
Omaha, Nebraska, toward the general's headquarters.

Bourke, a man of medium height and solid build who sported a bushy
mustache beneath a prominent nose, glanced over his shoulder with
deep-set gray eyes to two Indians in European dress who followed on his
heel. Bourke allowed the pace to be dictated by the solid man of
medium height who came immediately behind him—Iron Eye, paramount chief of the Omaha tribe. The fifty-seven-year-old chief walked
with a labored limp. Years before, Iron Eye lost a leg to a surgeon's knife
after stepping on a rusty nail, and the white doctor provided him with a
wooden substitute. Although the false leg slowed him down when he
was on his feet, he was a horseman without peer. Behind the chief came
his eldest daughter, Bright Eyes, a diminutive twenty-four-year-old who
wore a dark ankle-length dress and had her hair neatly tied back. Bourke
knew that the Omahas weren't comfortable in the heart of the U.S.
Army post, having come down off their reservation near Decatur in
northeastern Nebraska without government permission, but he also knew
that they had come on a mission. Without a word and with blinkered

determination, the pair traipsed along behind the lieutenant, across the fort's parade.

When it was built in 1868 as Sherman Barracks, Fort Omaha was a typical U.S. Army frontier post of its day. In design it was like most other forts, with low wooden buildings surrounding a vast square parade ground. When the Indian treaties of 1868 finally established the borders of the Indian reservations of Nebraska, several Omaha businessmen banded together to buy the sixty-four-acre site several miles outside their town. Then they had friends in Washington press the federal government to purchase it for the location of the army fort that would be built in the area to watch over the reservations and protect Omaha, the largest city in the new state of Nebraska. They sold the land to the War Department at a handsome profit. The post subsequently built on the site was thrown together so roughly and cheaply that now, just eleven years later, Fort Omaha's army surgeon condemned his rotting, vermin-ridden, wooden base hospital as too unhealthy for use, and General Crook declared the guardhouse unfit for habitation by prisoners. The fort's headquarters building was so run-down that the War Department had given the go-ahead for the construction of a new headquarters, and work was to begin within weeks.

Bribery, inflated government contracts, and shoddy workmanship typified the way things were done during the tumultuous administration of Abraham Lincoln's ultimately impeached successor, Andrew Johnson, and the two scandal-prone terms of President Ulysses S. Grant. Now, in 1879, two years after the tightest election in U.S. history, President Rutherford B. Hayes was in the White House. He was a reforming Republican who vowed to put an end to the scandals and corruption that had pervaded the government since the War of the Rebellion (as the Civil War was then known) ended in 1865. In some respects the Hayes administration changed the way the government did business, yet a number of the problems Hayes inherited were the result of policies that he endorsed. One of those problems, involving reservation Indians in the Department of the Platte, was about to take center stage in a way that no one in Washington or Nebraska could ever have anticipated.

A few minutes before, Lieutenant Bourke had been summoned to the fort gate that would one day bear his name and informed that Chief Iron Eye and his daughter had come in off their reservation after riding a hundred miles on fast Indian ponies, and were asking for an interview with General Crook. Bourke felt certain their visit involved the twenty-six members of the Ponca Indian tribe under the leadership of clan chief Standing Bear who were camped in three temporary lodges on the parade ground near the fort's main entrance.

The Poncas had been morose ever since a detachment from the 9th Infantry Regiment brought them in to Fort Omaha two days earlier. Since their arrival they had stayed in the lodges—two of which were created by linking pairs of their wagons with a covering of hides. Then they brooded. To most of the soldiers at the post, the Poncas "had a fit of the dumps," as Bourke later put it.[1] After more than a decade dealing with Indians in several American states and territories, the lieutenant was of the opinion that all Native Americans shared two common racial traits—notions and the dumps. In the first case, he observed, an Indian would get an often irrational notion in his head, which nothing and no one could change. In the latter case, Bourke would see one or more tribesmen lapse into a morbidly dejected state, for a day or for weeks on end.[2] From what Bourke had heard, these Poncas on the parade at Fort Omaha had every reason to be down in the dumps—they were exhausted, many of them were sick, they were homeless, they were mourning the death of their chief's son, and they were under military arrest.

Lieutenant Bourke led Chief Iron Eye and his daughter up the wooden steps and into Fort Omaha's headquarters building. Bourke, originally with the 3rd Cavalry Regiment, had served General Crook as his ADC for the past nine years, joining him when Crook commanded the army's Arizona Department and never leaving his side through the general's successful campaigns to subdue the renegade Apaches under Cochise and Geronimo, then accompanying him to Nebraska when Crook was given command of the Department of the Platte in 1876. Now the loyal lieutenant escorted the three Omaha Indians into General Crook's office.

Smiling warmly, Brigadier General George Crook came around from behind his desk and grasped the Indian chief's hand. Fifty-year-old George Crook was an imposing figure. More than six feet tall, he was solidly built. His blond hair was cut short, his mustache and beard neatly trimmed. His side whiskers, or sideburns (after Civil War general Ambrose Burnside who made them fashionable), were thick and bushy in the Burnside style.

According to John Bourke, General of the Army William T. Sherman described General Crook as the greatest manager the U.S. Army ever had, as well as its greatest Indian fighter.[3] George Crook was also the most unorthodox general the U.S. Army ever had. Son of a tanner and a low-ranking graduate of West Point Military Academy in 1852, Crook abstained from tobacco, only drank tea or coffee when in the wilds (he dunked his hardtack in it), and on the rare occasions he consumed alcohol it was just a spoonful of whiskey.[4] In his pursuit of personal physical fitness he lifted weights before breakfast. An expert woodsman and tracker, he was a passionate ornithologist who stuffed rare animals and birds for a hobby. A crack shot, he often slipped away to hunt and fish alone. For twenty-six years he had studied the language, customs, and psychology of the Indian tribes he fought, tracked, and parleyed with in Oregon, Idaho, Colorado, Utah, Washington, California, New Mexico, Arizona, Nebraska, Montana, and Dakota Territory. "Association with the natives," John Bourke said of General Crook, "enabled him to constantly learn their habits and their ideas and in time to become almost one of them."[5]

During his first nine years in the army Crook was as inveterate an Indian fighter as any man in uniform. He carried a stone arrowhead in one thigh as a permanent souvenir of an 1857 skirmish with the Pit River tribe of California, during which he killed his first Indian, but not his last. Yet, since the carnage of the Civil War, Crook's attitude had changed. Over the past decade or so he had achieved more through negotiation with the tribes than any of his predecessors had via military offensives. His unorthodox approach and his determination to avoid bloodshed whenever possible, together with a determination to treat Native Americans as human beings rather than animals, brought him many detractors, both inside and outside the army. He considered the Indian the "intellectual peer" of any white man and was determined to deliver on any promise he made to the Indians.[6]

Fortunately for Crook, he had the backing of the people who counted, men who recognized his skills. His immediate superior, General Phillip Sheridan, was Crook's former classmate and roommate at West Point and later his chief during the Civil War. From Chicago, Sheridan commanded the army's Division of the Missouri, of which Crook's Department of the Platte was a part. It was Sheridan who had coined the saying "the only good Indian is a dead Indian."[7] But he was astute enough to see that Crook had the very rare and very useful ability to win the trust of Indians.

George Crook had an even more influential supporter in Washington— President Hayes. The men were longtime friends. Both were originally from the state of Ohio, of which Hayes had been governor for eight years, and Hayes had served under Crook as a Union army regimental and divisional commander during the Civil War. Hayes admired and respected Crook, writing, in 1864, "General Crook is the best General we have served under," and later, "General Crook has won the love and confidence of us all."[8]

Crook had allies in the U.S. Congress too. Men such as thirty-six-year-old William McKinley, another Ohio native (who later became the twenty-fifth president of the United States), who was at this time a congressman for Ohio. McKinley knew Crook well, having served as one of his staff officers during the Civil War when Crook commanded a cavalry brigade and the Army of West Virginia with distinction. According to John Bourke, McKinley considered Crook "the brains of the Army," mirroring a sentiment expressed earlier by Hayes.[9]

As long as George Crook continued to deliver results on the frontier, his supporters in the corridors of power continued to overlook his eccentricities, which included a penchant for mules rather than horses. He brought his favorite mule, Apache, up from Arizona with him, and rode him on active duty for years. George Crook disliked military uniforms and usually wore civilian dress while on duty. In Arizona, his canvas suit and sun helmet, which gave him the appearance of an archeologist, gave rise to the name the Apaches attached to him, Chief Tan Wolf. The Sioux of Dakota

Territory called him Three Stars, although no one knew why. A U.S. Army brigadier general only wore one star, and Crook rarely wore a uniform of any kind, let alone one bearing insignia of rank. This March day in 1879, Three Stars Crook wore a plain civilian suit as he greeted Iron Eye.

Crook had known Iron Eye for the past three years. He liked him, respected him, trusted him, and the feelings were mutual. Iron Eye was not a man of striking stature. He was a little overweight and had a double chin, but he possessed an intelligent round European face and penetrating eyes. His thinning dark hair, untidily long, was slicked down with grease. He wore white men's clothes and affected white men's ways. His Indian mother, Watunna, had married Joseph La Flesche, a French trader working for the Hudson's Bay Company. In addition to his Indian name, Iron Eye, he took his father's European name, Joseph La Flesche. He also gave his children European names. His eldest boy, Woodworker, was Francis La Flesche, or Frank as he was called by those who knew him. Iron Eye's eldest daughter, Bright Eyes, was Susette La Flesche, and his other surviving children by two wives were named Rosalie, Marguerite, Susan, Lucy, and Carey La Flesche.

Chairs were provided for the Omaha pair by the general's longtime orderly, Private Andrew Peisen. As John Bourke watched Iron Eye and his eldest daughter being seated in front of the standing general, he would have expected Iron Eye to speak in his native Omaha tongue while his daughter translated; although the chief spoke good French, he only possessed basic English.

As Bourke knew, Susette Bright Eyes La Flesche was a fluent English speaker who had excelled at the Presbyterian Mission School on the Omaha reservation and later spent several years at a finishing school for white girls, the Elizabeth Institute for Young Ladies, in Elizabeth, New Jersey. A little time before, she had been appointed principal of the government school recently established on the Omaha reservation. Overcoming acute shyness, she flourished in the role. Bourke considered her a "lady of excellent attainments and bright intellect."[10]

The soft-spoken General Crook, looking on his guests with perceptive blue eyes, invited the chief of the Omahas to speak. In his native tongue, and translated by his daughter, Iron Eye announced that he had come to speak for Standing Bear and his fellow Poncas, the prisoners on the parade. The general gave an impassive nod, indicating the chief should continue. But it was the young woman who now did the talking, in English.

Miss La Flesche was a neat package. Little more than five feet in height and slim, she had a boyish face with a well-defined nose, mouth, and chin, and expressive dark eyes that were indeed bright when she became passionate—"sparkling black eyes," one acquaintance noted.[11] Unlike her bronze-skinned father, her complexion was pale, European. She wore her hair parted in the middle and drawn tightly back in a bob in the style of conservative white women. Her black dress was sober and unpretentious in the best Presbyterian fashion. Though her English vocabulary was excellent, her sentence construction betrayed her childhood experience of speaking Omaha exclusively until she was eight. Anyone meeting her without knowing her background would probably have thought her, by appearance and speech, to be of European origin. French or Spanish perhaps.

Until this point in her life, she would have taken such an assumption as a compliment. Although she had been raised on the reservation as an Omaha, she had white blood on both sides of her family. Apart from her father's La Flesche connection, her maternal grandmother, Voice of the Waters, an Omaha-Iowa mix, had married John Gale, surgeon at Fort Atkinson on the Missouri. Christened Yosette by the Presbyterian missionaries who founded her school but taking the name Susette, Iron Eye's eldest daughter grew up under church influence believing that she and her people must adopt the ways of the whites, must civilize, must assimilate, to prosper.

Where possible she spoke English and always went by her European name. Only among her family did she accept the use of the name Bright Eyes—Inshta-theamba as it was rendered in the Omaha tongue. Bright Eyes was her "at home name," she said.[12] In the future, she would gain notoriety and ultimately international fame as Bright Eyes, even being called a princess because she was the daughter of the ruler of an American Indian nation (a title she hated). Eventually she accepted that she could not escape her native name and that she could actually use it as a tool in her people's cause, and she resigned herself to accept the universal use of Bright Eyes. But much was to transpire before that happened.

It took a great deal of pluck for the shy young woman to present herself in front of a general, even if it was in the company of her protective father. But pluck was something she had plenty of, as she had demonstrated before now. Two years previously, when she had arrived back at the Omaha reservation from private school in New Jersey, she had applied to teach at the reservation's new government school. In response she had been told that she must pass a written examination and receive a teaching certificate from the School Committee of Nebraska. So Bright Eyes asked the Omaha reservation's resident Bureau of Indian Affairs agent, Jacob Vore, for permission to leave the reservation to attend the examination. He refused.

Determined not to take no for an answer, Bright Eyes slipped off the reservation and took the examination anyway. She duly passed and was awarded her teaching certificate. But the authorities made her wait two frustrating years; finally she not only was employed at the mission school but was appointed its principal. Bright Eyes was not concerned that she was only paid $20 a month, half what a white teacher earned. She would have paid the government for the privilege of teaching the young people of her tribe.

Now, nervously at first, and focused intently on the standing general, the young Omaha woman began to tell George Crook a story, speaking from the heart. She would have brought along wads of notes written in neat and methodical schoolmarm style, since she was a great one for keeping detailed records, but she didn't need them—the tale she had to tell was printed indelibly on her mind, if not her soul.

Even though some of what Bright Eyes had to impart was already known to him, the general did not interrupt her. George Crook was a good listener. His officers knew that whether they were giving him a report or making a submission, the general would take in their every word without a single interjection, comment, or change of expression.

And so it was that, with Chief Standing Bear and his followers just outside the window on the parade ground, prisoners, Susette Bright Eyes La Flesche began to tell a story of the Ponca people, the Omahas' near relatives. A story of tragedy and injustice.

Chapter 2

THE STORY OF INJUSTICE

LONG AGO, THE Ponca and four related tribes—the Omaha, the Osage, the Quapaw (also called the Akansa), and the Kaw (also known as the Kansa)—lived along the Atlantic coast of North America in Virginia and the Carolinas. In the fourteenth or fifteenth century, the five tribes migrated inland, and sometime before 1500 the Ponca and the Omaha separated from the other tribes and settled in what was to become Minnesota. Under pressure from the aggressive Dakota people (or the Sioux as the whites came to call them), these two tribes moved further west and south, settling for a time in southwestern Minnesota and the Black Hills of South Dakota before being pushed down toward the Nebraska region by the Sioux.

The Ponca tribe settled near the junction of two waterways, the wide Missouri and a river they called the Niobrara, or the Swift Running Water. This new homeland straddled the border of what later became the states of South Dakota and Nebraska, but in 1879 it was in the Dakota Territory. Their cousins the Omahas settled further to the south, along the Missouri in eastern Nebraska. There around the Swift Running Water, for generations to come, the Ponca people lived in peace and happiness.

White explorers Lewis and Clark passed through the region in the summer of 1804 on their epic trek to the Pacific Ocean. They camped at the mouth of the Niobrara and found the Poncas to be a small, friendly tribe with permanent riverbank villages of cone-roofed houses built from sod.

Like the Omaha, the Ponca people farmed corn for most of the year and went after buffalo in the summer on an annual hunt. The hunts provided meat to eat and hides and sinew and bone for shelter, clothing, and implements, as well as an opportunity for young men to show their prowess as hunters. And so it was for the next sixty-four years.

Several times between 1817 and 1865 the Poncas signed treaties of peace with the government of the United States, with the treaties of 1858, 1859, and 1865 reserving portions of the traditional Ponca land for the tribe's exclusive and permanent use. The Poncas gave up much of their land to the U.S. government in return for an assurance in writing that the government would aid and protect the tribe.

The 1859 treaty caused great consternation among the Poncas when it was learned that the white surveyors sent to redraw the boundaries of the reservation had included their traditional burial grounds and best cornfields beside the Niobrara in the land ceded to the government, something they had never agreed to and would never agree to. This was corrected in the treaty of 1865, when the small but important tract containing the burial grounds and cornfields was officially returned to Ponca ownership.

Apart from these treaty dealings with Washington, no white man bothered the Ponca tribe, and the Ponca tribe bothered no white man. Fewer than a thousand men, women, and children in all, they lived in peace and solitude on their little reservation, having nothing to do with the skirmishes that the region's larger Sioux, Cheyenne, Comanche, and Arapaho tribes were having with the U.S. Army in the 1860s.

Everything changed in 1868. In that year, through a clerical error in Washington, the U.S. Congress assigned the territory occupied by the Poncas to the Sioux. The Ponca tribe spent the next eight years fighting off Sioux raiding parties of forty and fifty warriors at a time and trying to convince Washington to correct the blunder. In one of those devastating raids alone the Sioux drove off half the Poncas' many hundreds of ponies.

In the mid-1870s things went from bad to worse for the Ponca tribe, again through no fault of their own. Raids by their old enemies the Brulé Lakota Sioux had become so bad that the Poncas signed a paper, which the

Indian Affairs Bureau took to Washington, asking for permission to move down to the reservation of their cousins the Omahas, at least until the government stopped the Sioux raids. In its wisdom the U.S. Congress—the Great Council as the Indians called it—chose not to support the request with legislation. The Poncas solved that particular problem by persuading the Brulé to agree to a truce, and life became less hazardous for the Poncas as they farmed their fields without needing to keep a rifle close by.

The other problem, also involving the Sioux, was not as easy to solve. Gold had been discovered in the Black Hills of Dakota. Thousands of white gold miners swarmed onto the Sioux and Cheyenne reservations. Instead of enforcing the treaties that guaranteed this land to the Indians, the government was largely inactive or, worse, gave military protection to white prospectors trespassing on Indian land. The Gold Rush invasion was the last straw to the Sioux and Cheyenne. The U.S. government did not even keep its treaty promise to build a school for every thirty children on the Sioux reservation—not a single school had been built. Sioux and Cheyenne tribes banded together under Sitting Bull, Red Cloud, and Crazy Horse to resist the white invasion.

In reply, in the summer of 1876 Washington sent in three army columns. One of these columns, led incautiously by the impatient, brash, overconfident Lieutenant Colonel George Armstrong Custer, stumbled onto at least 5,000 warriors encamped on the Little Big Horn River on June 25, 1876. Custer and 266 men of the 7th Cavalry Regiment were killed in the ensuing battle. George Crook knew all about this operation. He had been leading one of the other columns, and days before the Custer fight he had fought a battle on the Rosebud River against Crazy Horse, before pulling back. Hounding the renegades later that year with a mixed force of cavalry and Indian scouts, Crook "broke the Cheyenne and helped break the Sioux."[13]

The Ponca and Omaha tribes heard rumors about these fights on the Rosebud and Little Big Horn but thought little of it. They continued to lead their quiet, inoffensive lives, not realizing the reaction throughout the United States to Custer's defeat by the Sioux and Cheyenne—near panic in many quarters. As the Poncas and Omahas were to learn, public hysteria led Congress to decree the forcible removal of a number of northern tribes, who were resettled on reservations well to the south in what was called Indian Territory—present-day Oklahoma. The Poncas, who had played no part in the Custer fight, were erroneously associated with the Sioux. The Poncas, who had never ever raised a hand against the white man, were included on the list for relocation.

One Sunday in the late autumn of 1876, Reverend Samuel D. Hinman, an Episcopal missionary who had been working among the Sioux to the north, arrived at the largest of the three Ponca settlements, near the junction of the Missouri and Niobrara rivers, and prepared to conduct a service in the reservation's mission church. This settlement was called the Agency Village because an agent of the Bureau of Indian Affairs was permanently stationed there. The Ponca church and schoolhouse were also sited here. Of the smaller Ponca settlements, the Point Village was eight miles away on the Niobrara River, near the white town of Niobrara City. A little way south of the Agency Village lay Hubdon Village.

Just twenty Poncas were practicing Christians, converted eight years before when an Episcopal missionary lived among them for upward of two years. But two hundred Poncas regularly turned up to Sunday services, which were usually conducted by a white teacher named May.[14] And there, 180 of them would sit stony faced and silent through the hymns and sermons. Up to seventy-five Ponca children also went to the mission school during the week.[15] Although few were Christians, their parents wanted the little ones to learn how to speak and read and write the white man's language—this, they knew, was the way of the future. But this particular Sunday the Poncas heard a sermon unlike any they had ever heard before.

Reverend Hinman, who was known to and respected by the Poncas, told the tribe that soon they would be taken by the U.S. government to the south and never allowed to return to their homes here. Hinman said that he was sorry for the Poncas, but he could not do anything to help them; he could only pity them. He urged the tribe to do what was right and to trust in God. The Ponca people left the church following the service in a state of consternation.

Runners were sent around all the houses of the Agency Village and to the other villages on the reservation to pass on the news. From every corner the cry came back that the Poncas would not leave the home of their fathers and go to some strange land. In an attempt to learn more, the ten worried elders of the tribe sat down cross-legged in a circular council with Samuel Hinman and plied him with questions. But the minister declared that he only knew that someone had ordered that the Poncas be taken down south. Then Hinman went away, and for a little time it seemed that his warning was false.

Then, one day in early January 1877, Edward C. Kemble, an official with the Bureau of Indian Affairs in Washington, arrived at the Ponca settlement without warning. Kemble, a weedy, mustachioed man, was a newspaper editor in California for two decades before becoming one of the first roving Indian Affairs inspectors in the 1870s. When Inspector Kemble summoned the Ponca leaders to a meeting in the mission church, they came: White Eagle, the old paramount chief, and the chiefs of the nine Ponca clans—the Black Bear People, the Many People, the Elk People, the Medicine People, the Buffalo People, the Snake People, the Ice People, the Sons of White Men, and a small clan whose name would be lost over time. This ninth clan, with a total of fifty-five members, was led by a lean, normally quiet-spoken man in middle age by the name of Standing Bear who lived at the Point Village. His clan would soon become known simply as Standing Bear's People.

Inspector Kemble informed the chiefs that the U.S. government had decided to move all 752 Ponca people to a new reservation. Paramount chief White Eagle, tall and straight, with a long face and nose, asked where this new reservation was located, and Kemble informed him that it was in the Indian Territory, some six hundred miles to the south (future Oklahoma), a place the Poncas had never heard of. White Eagle shook his head; his people had lived and died here for generations. Here they had buried their ancestors, and to leave would be to desert their fathers and their grandfathers.[16]

Kemble then produced a piece of paper that he said the Poncas had signed two years before, asking to be removed to Indian Territory. This was the 1875 request to be granted asylum with the Omahas, but the interpreter at the time had bungled the translation—in English the request asked for removal to "the native people's country," which Kemble said meant Indian Territory, not the Omaha reservation.[17]

In response, a speech was made by one of the clan chiefs—Standing Bear. He told Kemble that this was the Poncas' land, that they had never sold it to anyone or asked to go to Indian Territory. They had harmed no man, they had kept to their treaty with the United States government. And there on the land of their fathers they would continue to live, and die.[18]

Kemble persisted, telling the chiefs that the land in the Indian Territory was much better than that here in Dakota Territory, and that the government would pay them for their old land. Chief White Eagle responded that he would only consider leaving if he personally received a letter from the Great Father, as the Indians called the U.S. president, a letter telling him that the Great Father wanted the Poncas to move.

Inspector Kemble retreated to the nearest telegraph office and wired Indian Affairs in Washington for instructions. A telegram soon came clicking back along the wire to Kemble—Indian Affairs Commissioner John Quincy Smith instructed his inspector to take White Eagle and the other Ponca chiefs down to Indian Territory so they could see it for themselves and choose their own location for a new reservation. Once the site was chosen, Kemble would take the chiefs to Washington to meet the president and sign a relocation agreement.

Kemble returned to the Poncas with this message, which he said came directly from the Great Father. To make it sound as if the Poncas had an element of free will in the exercise, Kemble told White Eagle that when he went to Washington, he could tell the Great Father which land in the Indian Territory he liked and which he didn't like. But this was not a decision White

Eagle was prepared to make on behalf of his people. It was the Ponca way for such important things to be decided in council, where every chief could speak for or against the proposed course of action. Kemble was left tapping an impatient foot as White Eagle met with the leaders of the Ponca clans.

Sitting cross-legged in a circle, White Eagle, Standing Bear, and his eight other clan chiefs discussed the matter, with each man stating his view. After a time, a consensus was reached—the Poncas should at least consider the Great Father's offer, and the chiefs should view this new land. They felt that if they agreed to at least go down and look at the country in the Indian Territory, "all the trouble would be ended."[19]

On Saturday, February 2, 1877, Kemble and the Indian Affairs agent to the Poncas, the recently appointed James Lawrence (who was described as "a young fellow" and was probably in his twenties), set off for Indian Territory.[20] With them went White Eagle and the clan chiefs Standing Bear, Standing Buffalo, Big Elk, Little Picker, Sitting Bear, Little Chief, Smoke Maker, White Swan, and Lone Chief (the son of a French trader and a Ponca mother also known as Antoine Le Claire).[21]

To interpret, Kemble and Lawrence took along Lone Chief's nephew, Charles Le Claire. Le Claire, called Charlie by the whites, had mixed blood like his uncle and had received a school education. Charlie and Agent Lawrence were longtime friends, and Lawrence had given Charlie the paid position of Indian Affairs interpreter at the Ponca reservation because Charlie had been instrumental in Lawrence being appointed agent.[22]

As they were about to set off, the chiefs told Kemble that they wanted to stop at the Omaha reservation on the way to talk to their cousins the Omahas—no doubt to seek the opinion of the Omahas on this matter of relocating to Indian Territory. But Kemble would not allow it.[23] To avoid any chance of the Poncas talking to their cousins the Omahas, Kemble took the party by wagon to Yankton, then capital of Dakota Territory, on the far bank of the Missouri. There Kemble purchased "civilized clothing" for the chiefs—shirts and vests in the main; most of them retained their Indian leggings and moccasins. At Yankton the party was joined by

Reverend Hinman, who had been asked by the Indian commissioner to accompany the chiefs south and help convince them to agree to relocate.[24] They then boarded a train for the journey south—a trip inside a railroad carriage being a novel and daunting first for the Indians.

When they reached Independence City in southeastern Kansas, Kemble transferred his charges to wagons for the next leg of the journey, to the Osage reservation. It straddled the border between Indian Territory and Kansas, not far away. The Poncas were welcomed by their cousins the Osages, who themselves had been relocated from southeastern Kansas to Indian Territory not many years before. But the Ponca chiefs were not impressed by the condition of the Osages: "They were without shirts, their skin burned, and their hair stood up as if it had not been combed since they were little children."[25] They still lived in round earth lodges like the Poncas once had before they progressed to wooden cabins. Privately the Osages warned the Ponca chiefs not to consider settling down in the Indian Territory—it was "bad land," they said.[26] Accompanied by Osage guide William Conner, the party headed for Indian reservations a hundred miles away.

Several tribes from the southeastern United States had been forcibly removed to the Indian Territory in the 1830s—the Cherokees, Creeks, Chickasaws, Choctaws, and Seminoles. Within the past decade, northern tribes such as the Arapaho, Southern Cheyenne, Quapaw, and Kaw had also been relocated here by the government. It was southeast to the Quapaw and Kaw reservations in the northeastern corner of Indian Territory that Edward Kemble took the Ponca chiefs on their tour of inspection.

Day after day they bumped around the desolate Indian Territory. Even in winter the Ponca chiefs found the rocky, hilly terrain they were shown to be hot and inhospitable. "The Warm Land," the Indians called it. Clan chief Standing Bear found that when he kicked the dry earth, there were stones underneath. This was not land where corn or wheat or potatoes would grow in abundance. This land did not compare with the Poncas' lush green homeland. Standing Bear came to the bitter realization that Kemble had lied to the chiefs about Indian Territory.

At the camps of the relocated Quapaw and Kaw, the Poncas came across Indian brothers who were miserable and indolent. As they spoke with the migrants in their shared tongue, they discovered that much sadness lingered in the tipis, for the people, especially the children, were dying from a variety of illnesses, including malaria. Old White Eagle and several others fell ill themselves after the party was lashed by a storm that lasted almost a week.

Undaunted, Kemble and Lawrence dragged the chiefs on an arduous tour of prospective sites, but the Poncas were unimpressed. They could see that this Indian Territory was a dry, dusty, broken land, a land of rocks. Its few low trees were unhealthy. The tribes that had already been relocated here were poor, sick, and unable to do much for themselves. The Poncas on the other hand were industrious farmers whose own land in the north was fertile and productive. The chiefs were unanimous in their opinion—this was no place for the Ponca people. The chiefs were also unanimous in their disappointment with these white men for attempting to move them to this terrible place. Seeing their growing unhappiness, Kemble brought the chiefs up to Arkansas City in southern Kansas. This inland steamboat port near the junction of the Arkansas and Walnut rivers was the last white settlement in Kansas before the border with Indian Territory less than thirty miles away. Here Kemble checked his party into the Central Avenue Hotel.[27]

The presence of the Ponca chiefs aroused quite a stir in Arkansas City. A city in name and aspiration only, it was a small nine-year-old frontier outpost whose fortunes depended largely on the needs of the Indian reservations in Indian Territory. Using government money, the Indian Affairs Bureau agents and their employees at the nearer reservations bought stock, seed, hardware, building materials, food, and transport in Arkansas City and spent a good part of their wages in the stores and saloons there. The flow-on affect boosted the local economy. The more tribes the government brought to Indian Territory the greater the likelihood the railroad would be extended from Wichita and Arkansas City would prosper. As a result, the possibility of the Ponca tribe being resettled in the Indian Territory excited the imaginations and expectations of the town's businesspeople.

With everyone in the district curious about these Indians—the next potential pot of gold for the town—an enterprising local businessman saw a way to immediately profit from the visit of the Ponca chiefs. Since the Civil War, portrait photography had become all the rage across America, and professional photographers had a constant stream of customers wanting their pictures taken for posterity. I. S. Bonsall, city clerk of Arkansas City, also ran the town's photographic studio, and he convinced Inspector Kemble to herd his Ponca charges in front of his glass plate camera on the day of their arrival—Tuesday, February 20.

The town's postmaster, Nathan Hughes, also ran a business on the side—he was publisher and editor of one of the town's two weekly newspapers, the *Arkansas City Traveler*. In his February 21 edition of the *Traveler*, editor Hughes, who had written that the Poncas were tall, well-built men, informed his readers that copies of the photograph of the Ponca chiefs would be available for purchase from Bonsall's Photograph Gallery within a few days. In that photograph, while interpretor Charlie and a white—Hinman, Kemble, or Lawrence—look quite pleased with themselves, White Eagle, Standing Bear, and the other chiefs look decidedly unhappy.

After a night's rest in Arkansas City, Inspector Kemble informed the chiefs in the hotel dining room that he now wanted to show them more Indian Territory sites, well to the south. But almost three weeks of this torturous exercise had been enough for the Ponca chiefs. White Eagle said he was ready to go to Washington to see the Great Father. Standing Bear and the others concurred.

Still Kemble urged the chiefs to come with him to see more prospective sites. But White Eagle said that he wished to tell the Great Father that he had not seen any land in the Indian Territory that he liked and so the Poncas would keep their own land in the north. But Kemble was not giving up. He now told White Eagle that he would take the chiefs to see the president only if they agreed to resettle their people in the Indian Territory. White Eagle countered that if Kemble wouldn't take him to see the Great Father, then he should take the chiefs home to their own country.

The temper of the Indian Affairs representative flared. Angrily, Kemble declared that he would not take White Eagle to see the president. And, he said, the president had not instructed him to take the Ponca chiefs back to their own country. This staggered White Eagle and his fellow chiefs, as Kemble had intended. White Eagle asked what he should do, if Kemble would neither guide the chiefs to Washington nor take them back to their homes in the north. Kemble probably only smirked in response, confident he had the Poncas over the proverbial barrel.

Poncas were accustomed to speaking their minds and to speaking truthfully. They naively expected the representatives of the godlike Great Father they dealt with to do the same. Now the chiefs realized the Great Father had not personally invited them to Washington, and White Eagle accused the inspector of not talking straight.[28]

Kemble snarled back that if the chiefs did not agree to choose land in the Indian Territory, then he and Lawrence would leave the chiefs where they were, to starve. They would not take them back north. The chiefs responded that it would be better that ten of them died here in this terrible place rather than the whole tribe. Kemble and Lawrence stormed away, with Kemble declaring that if the chiefs wanted to stay there and die they could.[29] Fuming, Kemble led Lawrence and Reverend Hinman upstairs.

The chiefs, stunned by this exchange, suddenly had visions of being stranded in this strange land and dying here without ever seeing their families again. The shattered White Eagle was close to tears at this point. But then he remembered that he was a man and pulled himself together.[30]

The shocked chiefs discussed their predicament in the Central Avenue Hotel dining room. All agreed that the Great Father could not have caused this situation; it must have been all Kemble's doing. It was also agreed that they had no choice but to walk home. Standing Bear now rose to the occasion. He reminded the others that the government still owed the tribe money it had promised them. The Indian Affairs men had money. Standing Bear sent interpreter Charlie Le Claire upstairs to Kemble and Lawrence to tell them that if they would not take the chiefs home they should at least give them some of the money that was owed them to pay their own way home. Charlie came back down with the reply—the Indian Affairs men would not give them one cent.

Standing Bear sent Charlie upstairs with another message. If they took the chiefs to Washington and the Great Father told them personally that the Poncas must come to Indian Territory, then Standing Bear supposed that they would have to agree to relocate. The reply came back that the Great Father had nothing to do with the matter and Kemble and Lawrence weren't taking the chiefs anywhere. They could stay there and die as far as they were concerned.

Again Standing Bear sent Charlie upstairs with a message—if the Indian Affairs men would not take them back home nor give them money to get home, then at least they could give them a paper to show to white men along the way, identifying the Indian party as "friendly," as opposed to hostiles on the loose, and authorizing their journey. Standing Bear knew that by U.S. law, Indians traveling off their reservations either had to be escorted by Indian Affairs officials or soldiers or had to possess a written pass from a government officer. Kemble replied that he and Lawrence would give the chiefs nothing, not even a paper.

Standing Bear and his colleagues now decided they would go home on foot, all six hundred miles or more, without food, without money, without authorization. But two of their number, Lone Chief and Little Chief, were much too old and frail to walk the distance; both were almost blind. The others agreed that they would not be able to carry the old men on their backs all the way back to the Swift Running Water. So Standing Bear sent the two old chiefs up to Kemble and Lawrence with Charlie and another message—if the able-bodied chiefs must walk home they would, but the Indian Affairs men must care for the two old men. Before sending them upstairs, Standing Bear had instructed the elderly pair to stay with Kemble, Lawrence, and Hinman no matter what. This time there was no reply from Kemble, but the old men did not come back down. It was now nine o'clock at night. The argument that had been going on between Kemble and the chiefs for many hours had at last come to an end, but without a resolution.[31]

Exactly what happened next is open to dispute. The Ponca chiefs unanimously claimed that Kemble and his associates abandoned them at Arkansas City. Kemble later declared that the chiefs had run off, and he informed the *Arkansas City Traveler* that they had left the town to walk home that same night, having "started at midnight."[32] But the chiefs' version is likely the more accurate one.

Next morning, according to the accounts of both Standing Bear and White Eagle, they and the six other younger chiefs awoke at the Central Avenue Hotel to discover that Kemble, Lawrence, Hinman, Charlie, and the two old chiefs had gone. It eventuated that Kemble had decided that if the Poncas wouldn't choose land in the Indian Territory, then he would choose it for them. While Agent Lawrence took the interpreter and two elderly chiefs to Independence to wait for the inspector to join them, Kemble and Reverend Hinman rode back to Indian Territory and summarily chose a site on the Quapaw reservation as the best place for the relocation of the Ponca tribe.

Kemble quickly penned a letter to Commissioner Smith recommending the chosen site and then returned to Arkansas City to post the letter and pick up the eight stubborn chiefs, expecting them to be chastened and humbled after being left to their own devices in a strange place for several days. But he discovered to his dismay that Standing Bear and his colleagues had called his bluff. With a total of $8 between them and with just the clothes on their backs and a blanket each, and with barely a word of English between them, the eight chiefs had set off to walk all the way home.

Kemble wired Washington that most of the Ponca chiefs had run off. Soon the U.S. Army and government representatives all the way from southern Kansas to Dakota Territory were receiving telegrams from the War Department and the Bureau of Indian Affairs warning them to be on the lookout for the Ponca chiefs. The chiefs, it was announced, had absconded from official custody.

Standing Bear and White Eagle later told of a hellish trek from Kansas to the Niobrara. It was winter, and the further north they went the deeper the snow became. Within the first ten days the leather moccasins on the men's feet wore away, and they had to walk in the snow with bleeding bare feet. Staying away from towns, roads, and rail lines to avoid arrest, the chiefs traveled across the prairies. Standing Bear said that at night they mostly slept in the open, sometimes in haystacks if they could find them, wrapped in their blankets, huddled together, trying to keep each other alive in the intense cold, and every night expecting to freeze to death. For food, Standing Bear said they found old ears of corn that had dried in the fields, and they pounded the corn with stones. After fifty days, they reached the Oto reservation in southern Nebraska, toward the end covering just a few painful miles a day.

The Indian Affairs agent at the Oto reservation gave the exhausted chiefs food and questioned them at length, expressing surprise at the way they claimed to have been treated by Inspector Kemble and promising to tell Washington their side of the story. According to White Eagle, the agent warned the chiefs that he had received a telegram from Washington ordering him not to give them food, shelter, or help of any other kind if they showed up at the Oto reservation.

For ten days the chiefs rested up with the Otoes, who sheltered them, fed them, replaced their moccasins, and gave them ponies and provisions for the remainder of the journey home. The Poncas gratefully thanked the Otoes for their comfort and aid, and again set off for home, this time aiming for the Omaha reservation in northern Nebraska before making the final leg of the trip to the Niobrara.

Their cousins the Omahas welcomed the chiefs when they reached the Omaha village at the junction of the North and South Blackbird Creeks— Joe's Village, the whites called it, in reference to Chief Iron Eye's "American" name, Joseph La Flesche. At Iron Eye's large, two-story wooden house, the eight chiefs told their story to a concerned Iron Eye, who had more than a passing interest in the Poncas. One of the Ponca chiefs, White Swan, who also went by the name Frank La Flesche, was Iron Eye's brother. Like Iron Eye, White Swan was an Omaha with Ponca blood. He had married a Ponca woman and lived and raised a family among the Poncas. Another attentive listener was Iron Eye's twenty-two-year-old daughter Bright Eyes, who had recently arrived home from school in the East.

After the chiefs sadly told their story, Bright Eyes and her father agreed that the president and the American people should know about the unjust treatment the Poncas had received. Bright Eyes took out pen and paper and wrote a statement from the chiefs, in English, telling of their ordeal. Then she wrote a telegram from the chiefs to the American president in Washington, asking him whether it had been on his authority that his men had taken the Ponca chiefs down to Indian Territory before threatening them because they did not choose land there. "Please answer," the chiefs' telegram concluded, "as we are in trouble."[33]

When push came to shove, Sitting Bear was apparently too afraid to put his name to either the statement or the telegram. To be on the safe side, in case the documents went astray, Bright Eyes penned copies of both, which she kept in a safe place. Then the other seven chiefs continued on to the Niobrara on horseback, and Bright Eyes, who had been raised a Presbyterian, took Standing Bear to see the reservation's Presbyterian minister of the past ten years, Reverend William Hamilton, who lived three miles from Joe's Village.

After Bright Eyes explained the Ponca problem to Hamilton, he called in John Springer, "an educated Omaha" and member of Hamilton's flock, provided money and horses, and told Springer to take Standing Bear across the Missouri River to Iowa.[34] There Springer was to send the chiefs' telegram to the president and then give their statement to the editor of a Sioux City newspaper known to Hamilton and urge him to print it. Standing Bear and Springer quickly set off, followed the Missouri north, and crossed the river. From Sloan, Iowa, they dispatched the telegram to Washington, before continuing on to Sioux City, where they saw the newspaper editor.

Once they had completed their tasks, Springer gave Standing Bear money to get home, wished him well, and then returned to the Omaha reservation. As Springer had instructed him, Standing Bear bought a Sioux City and Pacific Railroad ticket to Yankton and took a train north. Yankton, on the banks of the Missouri not far from the mouth of the James River, was within a day's walk of the Niobrara once Standing Bear had gotten himself across the Missouri.

In the streets of Yankton he caught sight of Agent Lawrence and Reverend Hinman, but they didn't spot him. He slipped unnoticed from the town, crossed the Missouri, and walked home to the Ponca reservation, where he rejoined his anxious wife, children, brothers, and sister. All the other Ponca leaders, including the two elderly chiefs, had safely arrived ahead of him.

The Ponca chiefs' telegram to the president was never even acknowledged. There is no telling whether it ever reached its destination; it may have only gone as far as the Bureau of Indian Affairs. Meanwhile, a favorable article based on the chiefs' statement appeared in the March 31 edition of the *Sioux City Daily Journal* under the headline "Weary and Footsore: The Poncas Tell the Story of Their Grievous Wrongs." The story was subsequently picked up and run by the *Niobrara Pioneer* on April 5.

In the meantime, Inspector Kemble had been recalled to Washington for consultations with Commissioner John Quincy Smith. On the Niobrara, some thought all this business about moving to Indian Territory was now ended.

→ ←

Back in Washington, Edward Kemble was taken by Indian Affairs Commissioner Smith to report to Smith's boss, Zacharia Chandler, the Interior secretary. Chandler was leaving office in weeks and would be replaced by an appointee of the new president, Rutherford B. Hayes. Chandler decided to leave the Ponca problem to his successor as Interior secretary, German-born Carl Schurz.

On paper, the bearded, bespectacled Secretary Schurz appeared to be a potential ally of the Ponca people, but he became one of their greatest foes. An antigovernment revolutionary as a college student at the University of Bonn, Germany, Schurz was imprisoned but made a daring escape and fled to the United States in 1852. A liberal idealist, he joined the antislavery movement and became actively involved with the Republican Party. For his part in organizing support for Abraham Lincoln's presidential nomination, Schurz was appointed U.S. ambassador to Spain in 1861. With the outbreak of the Civil War he returned to the United States and joined the Union army, becoming a brigadier general. The actions of his troops at the Battles of Chancellorsville and Gettysburg were criticized, but Schurz himself came out of the Civil War with an untarnished reputation. First a newspaper editor, then a U.S. senator from Missouri for six years to 1875, he was given the Interior portfolio by President Hayes expressly to clean up Indian Affairs.

The Bureau of Indian Affairs, administered by the War Department until 1849 before coming under the Interior Department, had become rife with corruption at all levels. At the reservation level, many BIA agents had been pocketing large amounts of the funds allocated to the feeding, housing, and education of the Indian tribes in their care. Meanwhile, land speculators, merchants, bankers, and railroad contractors had their greedy noses in the trough, making fortunes as the West was opened up to settlement and the Indians were pushed off their lands. They were aided and abetted by corrupt Washington officials and politicians on the take. In return for kickbacks, Indian Affairs administrators gave BIA construction and supply contracts to cronies who undersupplied and overcharged as a matter of course, providing poor-quality goods to the tribes at top dollar. Politicians who suppressed inquiries into bureau activities and voted through Indian bills that favored business interests received the support of wealthy party bosses who controlled congressional seats. Anticorruption reformers coined a name for the greedy businessmen and corrupt politicians who played this game—the Indian Ring.

The Indians protested, of course, but as wards of the state they had no rights, no vote, no representation. Their protests had gone largely unheard for years. Even from inside the government establishment the Indian Ring was difficult to combat. For years, General George Crook had been complaining about corruption in the system, but for the most part he had been ignored or deflected by his superiors. Like other honest men, he would have had high hopes of a new broom sweeping away corrupt practices when the administration of his friend Rutherford Hayes came into office.

Interior Secretary Schurz's reforming brief from the White House had been primarily a financial one. Indian Affairs had been hemorrhaging money for years, and President Hayes gave Schurz a very clear directive—cut BIA expenditures. At the same time, Schurz had to administer the removal of tribes to Indian Territory as Congress dictated. The Poncas' refusal to budge from the Niobrara was a small but annoying thorn in Secretary Schurz's side.

After taking office on March 12, Schurz wasted no time acting to resolve the lingering Ponca problem. Having interviewed Inspector Kemble, the new Interior secretary contacted his counterpart at the War Department, George W. McCrary, acquainting him with the problem he was having with the stubborn little tribe in the Dakota Territory. The two secretaries knew each other well. When Schurz had been a Republican senator, McCrary served in the House of Representatives as a Republican member from Iowa. Secretary McCrary agreed to give Indian Affairs full army support in the Ponca affair and passed an instruction to that effect to the army's commanding general, Civil War hero William T. Sherman. Schurz then sent Inspector Kemble back to Nebraska with orders to shift the Poncas, one way or another.

→ ←

In April 1877, Inspector Kemble arrived back on the Niobrara. He and Agent Lawrence wasted no time calling for a council with the Poncas. This time, all the men of the tribe took part in the council, although only the chiefs spoke.

Before the inspector could address the council, Standing Bear came to his feet. Pulling his red council blanket around his shoulders, he asked

why the Indian Affairs men had come to the Ponca reservation when they
had not been invited. He informed Kemble that the Poncas wanted nothing to do with him and had no interest in selling their land to them. He
advised both Indian Affairs representatives to go away and not come back
until they had a letter from the Great Father, and cash in hand, if the government truly wanted to buy Ponca land. Then, he told them, if the Poncas wanted to sell their land, they would. If they didn't, they wouldn't. He
finished up by telling the two Indian Affairs men to leave at once.[35]

Around the circle, men grunted their approval of Standing Bear's position. Beside Standing Bear, his younger brother Big Snake rose to his feet.
In his thirties, Big Snake was a huge man who stood head and shoulders
above the tallest member of the tribe. He was a gentle giant who had a
reputation in the tribe as a peacemaker. But now Big Snake folded his
arms and glared at Kemble and Lawrence. Intimidated by Standing Bear's
words, Big Snake's physical presence, and the unity of the tribe, the Indian Affairs men departed in a rage. The council broke up with many Poncas feeling better than they had in a long time now that Standing Bear had
stood up to the white men.

After Edward Kemble wired Washington about this latest impasse, he
received a short, sharp telegram from Interior Secretary Schurz: "Press the
removal."[36] Kemble decided to take off the gloves.

Next morning, Standing Bear was rudely awakened when Bluecoats,
soldiers from Fort Randall thirty miles up the Missouri, dragged him from
his bed in front of his wife and children. He was chained and hauled from
his house. Outside, he found that Big Snake had also been arrested. The
two of them were put on horses and taken to Fort Randall.[37] They were
brought before a panel of eight army officers and informed that four written complaints had been lodged against them. Asked what he had to say
in his defense, Standing Bear told the officers the story of the journeys to
and from Indian Territory. The officer in charge, appalled by the story,
promised to wire Washington to see what could be done for the Poncas,
which he did, without result. The brothers were then put in detention, to
give them time to reflect on their options.

Standing Bear and Big Snake were returned to the Ponca reservation just in time for a new Ponca council with Kemble and Lawrence. This time a white lawyer appeared and spoke long and passionately of the Poncas' right to remain on their land. Standing Bear and his fellow chiefs didn't know this man. Solomon Draper was an attorney who edited the *Niobrara Pioneer* in nearby Niobrara City. He spoke on behalf of the businesspeople of the town who considered the Poncas quiet, unthreatening neighbors and preferable to the Sioux. While the Poncas were grateful for his attempt to help them, in the end Kemble lost patience with Draper and refused to let him continue speaking. The inspector then informed the Poncas that the time for talking had passed. They must all go to Indian Territory, and that was that. The leading Ponca chiefs, just as determined, defiantly told Kemble that they would not go, and the council came to an abrupt end.

But the chiefs were not unanimous. There were men Standing Bear described as "half-breeds," men he did not get on well with who were close to Agent Lawrence. Lone Chief and nine other "half-breed" elders had begun to speak in favor of going to Indian Territory. In the third week of April these men packed their relatives and their belongings into 46 wagons, and 170 of them left the reservation with Agent Lawrence, heading for Indian Territory, overcoming attempts by other members of the tribe to block the path of their wagons as they left. Chief White Eagle later testified that Kemble had promised money to those who went south with Lone Chief.[38] This attempt to destroy the tribe's unity did nothing to soften the resolve of the rest of the chiefs to stay put.

Retreating yet again, Kemble wired Washington with the news that he had convinced part of the tribe to head south but the majority of the Poncas were still sitting stubbornly on the Niobrara. Interior Secretary Schurz had no time for men who only partly fulfilled his orders. He instructed Commissioner Smith to send a more effective officer to deal with the Poncas.

In May, Inspector E. A. Howard arrived on the Ponca reservation to take up where his predecessor had left off. The abrasive Howard, a former Union army major, had apparently been chosen because he accepted no nonsense from anyone. Howard immediately directed White Eagle to convene a council of his chiefs, which the government's man would address. Standing Bear again took his place in the council circle with his fellow chiefs, interested to learn what this new man sent by the Great Father would say.

A four-hour conference followed, but at the end of it Inspector Howard stood up and asked a terse question—would the Poncas remove to Indian Territory of their own volition, or would he have to use force to make them go? The chiefs did not reply. Howard stomped unhappily from the meeting, mounted up, and rode away.

In the general's office at Fort Omaha, Lieutenant Bourke had been listening intently to Bright Eyes as she told her story. His sympathy for the Poncas had been aroused. As he would later write, he saw a far from benevolent motive behind the Interior Department's determination to shift the benign little Ponca tribe. "They had a reservation which," he said, "unluckily for them, was arable and consequently coveted by the white invader."[39] In fact, the rich, dark alluvial soil along the Niobrara that supported communal Ponca farming produced "the finest Indian corn on the Plains."[40]

Toward the end of the second week in May, Inspector Howard returned to the Niobrara along with Agent Lawrence, who had handed the "half-breed" Poncas over to Inspector Kemble at Columbus, Nebraska, for the remainder of their journey south. A sudden thunderstorm had ominously preceded Howard's arrival. This time he brought Bluecoats with him; many Bluecoats—four detachments of cavalry and one of infantry from Fort Sully and Fort Randall, under the command of a captain.[41] This time there would be no discussion, no negotiation, and no toleration of resistance.

Around noon, Standing Bear was coming in from the fields where he, one of his brothers, and another member of their clan had been plowing. His children were in school at the Ponca reservation schoolhouse near the agency—the residence and office of Indian Affairs agent Lawrence at the Agency Village. Standing Bear had almost reached his house in the Point Village, where his wife, Susette Primo, whose lineage was part Ponca, part white, was cooking lunch. The smell of freshly baked bread would have been wafting out from their two-room forty-by-twenty log home.

Standing Bear was proud of that house. He had felled and hauled the trees, fashioned the logs, and built his family's home with his own hands. It was a slow process because he had never done such a thing before, and there was no one to teach him how. But he had seen the fine big house that his friend Chief Iron Eye had built on the Omaha reservation—the first frame house built by a Plains Indian—and he had learned from his example. After that, Standing Bear built himself a stable and cattle sheds. Emulating him, all the other Ponca men also replaced their old earth lodges with log houses they built themselves.

Now a lone horseman came cantering up to Standing Bear. It was Charlie, the interpreter, and he delivered devastating news. Soldiers had come to the Agency Village, he said. They had come to make war with the Poncas, if they did not go to Indian Territory. The officer in charge of the soldiers had given an order that every Ponca head of household was to load up all his possessions and take them to the agency. This was to include their farm implements, their household items, their livestock, their grain; everything that could be moved. Standing Bear knew that it was pointless trying to resist the soldiers—he was no longer a young man, the tribe had few rifles, and there were too many Bluecoats.

Unhitching his eight horses from his plows, Standing Bear harnessed them to his wagons. It took him three days to take all he owned to the agency—four cows, three steers, four hogs, twenty-one chickens, two turkeys, plows, axes, hatchets, saws, hoes, pitchforks, five wagonloads of corn, one hundred sacks of wheat, and all his household items, including a table, chairs, two beds, even the two stoves from his house. Two years later, Standing Bear would still be able to list every single item. It was estimated at the time that the buildings, land, stock, and goods and chattels taken from Standing Bear were worth in excess of $4,000—at a time when a journalist in Omaha earned $15 to $25 a week and a good house could be rented in the city for $25 a month.[42]

While Standing Bear was bringing his possessions to the agency, all the other Ponca men were doing the same, coming from north and south with their loaded wagons. Any Ponca who failed to comply saw the soldiers take his possessions away. In the presence of a large number of soldiers the Poncas filled evacuated houses near the agency with their belongings and then glumly watched the soldiers lock up the houses.

Inspector Howard now assembled the Ponca men. They sat in a large council circle as Howard told them that they could keep their horses and their wagons, but now they must all start for Indian Territory. Standing Bear was defiant. He told Howard that he would not go to Indian Territory. If he must, he would go and live with his friends the Omaha tribe, he said. Howard told him that he should go to Indian Territory and see how the first part of the tribe—the "half-breeds"—were living down there. If the Poncas didn't like what they saw, then he would let them come back up to live with the Omahas.[43]

Although White Eagle was inclined to think this a reasonable offer under the circumstances, Standing Bear didn't trust this inspector any more than he had trusted his slick-tongued predecessor, Kemble. He sat there, contemplating refusing to move. But his wife, Susette, a tall, "comely,"[44] and "highly intelligent" woman, came and whispered urgently in his ear.[45] Susette had relatives in the party that had already gone down to Indian Territory, and she told Standing Bear not to resist but to go south as the soldiers ordered, as she wanted to go see her relatives in the Indian Territory. Although she didn't tell Standing Bear this, she also would have wanted to prevent the soldiers from putting a bullet or a bayonet in her husband. While Inspector Howard addressed the Ponca menfolk, soldiers

had spread out, with bayonets fixed, around the edge of the village, surrounding it. Standing Bear bowed to his wife's wishes, and when a soldier
took him by the arm and pulled him to his feet, he did not resist but went
unhappily to his wagons and horses and prepared to go.

The troops moved through the village's collection of log houses like a
slow, inexorable flood, forcing the terrified women and children from their
homes while other soldiers held back the Ponca men. Driven before the
bayonets ("just as one would drive a herd of ponies," White Eagle said
later) and with women and children crying, they were forced to the Niobrara, which had risen during a storm, and made to cross.[46] The men too,
with 72 wagons and 500 horses, were forced to ford the surging river, un-
loading the wagons and carrying the contents across, to link up with the
women and children from all three Ponca villages and pack the wagons
again on the other side. As they were supervising the crossing, several of
Howard's troopers got into difficulties and were swept from the backs of
their horses by the fast-moving torrent. Without hesitation, Ponca men
dove into the river and rescued the soldiers.

Thunderstorms raged for several days, making travel impossible, so that
the Poncas had to huddle in and under the wagons. On Saturday, May 19,
the sky cleared and at 10:00 A.M., Inspector Howard ordered the column
to move out. With an escort of twenty-five mounted soldiers under Captain Fergus Walker, the sodden wagon train slowly set off.

There were several men among the Poncas who were Omahas and
Yankton Sioux; they'd married Ponca wives and settled down with the
Poncas and raised families. Howard told these men that they were not
considered Poncas by the government and had to take their families and
go back to their own tribes.[47] With women and children wailing at being
separated from their Ponca relatives, these families also departed, some
heading north, some south. They would later follow and rejoin the Poncas
and share in their fate.

Once the miserable Ponca caravan was out of sight beyond the southern horizon with its army escort, Inspector Howard and Agent Lawrence
supervised the military rear guard as it moved through the three Ponca vil-

lages. At Howard's direction every Ponca log house was torn down—236 of them.[48] All the barns and outbuildings were demolished. They knocked down the tribe's grist mill, sawmill, and blacksmith shop, and, since they had been built by the tribe, did the same to the church and schoolhouse. Only one structure was left standing—the government's own agency building.

After Howard set off to join the train of Ponca wagons, the livestock, tools, and personal possessions that the Poncas had brought to the agency were taken away by Agent Lawrence, who was not making the trip south, along with the threshing machines, reapers, and mowers owned by the tribe. The Poncas never saw their possessions again. There is no record of what happened to those possessions, whether Indian Affairs sold them or whether the soldiers sold them and kept the proceeds. On that traumatic day, May 19, 1877, the trials of the Ponca people began in earnest.

Marching south under escort, the Poncas were soon deluged by rain. Day after day they slogged on through a ceaseless downpour that turned their path to thick, clawing mud. Within two days, two Ponca children died from exposure. Showing no sympathy, Howard and the soldiers drove the hundreds of wet, shivering people along mud-clogged byways and across swollen rivers. Standing Bear was in the midst of the throng, trying to protect and provide for his wife Susette and his children—a son, Bear Shield, whose age is variously given as twelve and sixteen, an adult daughter, Prairie Flower, who was married to clan member Shines White and had two very young children of her own, and Standing Bear's infant daughter, Fanny.

The Ponca wagon train was steered away from the Omaha reservation by Howard so that the Omahas would not interfere with the Poncas' removal, but news of the dispossession soon reached Chief Iron Eye. He was angered and saddened by what he heard. He had many relatives and friends among the Poncas, who had regularly intermarried with the Omahas. His mother, Watunna, had been a Ponca. When he was young, Iron Eye had been adopted by the then paramount chief of the Omahas, Big Elk, and had succeeded Big Elk as chief after his death.

Iron Eye's daughter Bright Eyes, who had tried to help the Ponca chiefs earlier in the year by penning the statement and the telegram that Standing Bear took to Iowa and by involving Reverend Hamilton, was determined to again help the Poncas. She had dear relatives among them, including her favorite uncle, White Swan, to whom she was particularly close. Bright Eyes also had many Ponca friends, including Standing Bear's daughter Prairie Flower, who had been her "girlhood companion."[49] The two had apparently gone to school together. Bright Eyes convinced her father that they must ride after the Poncas and see what they could do to help them.

Among his many horses Iron Eye had two ponies that were famous in northern Nebraska for their speed. On these ponies, Iron Eye and Bright Eyes slipped off the reservation without the knowledge of agent Jacob Vore and made an illegal dash south to overtake the Ponca column. At the Loup River they came to the town of Columbus, 120 miles west of the city of Omaha, to find they had arrived ahead of the Ponca wagon train. Before long, the sad Ponca caravan came into sight. They found the Poncas sick and miserable. Among those who had fallen ill was Standing Bear's daughter and Bright Eyes's friend Prairie Flower. Iron Eye found his brother White Swan, and he and Bright Eyes spoke with him about what the government was doing to the Poncas.

From White Swan they heard about the forced removal, and he assured them that no Ponca had signed an agreement to go to Indian Territory. He also told them something that sent a chill down their spines. When some Poncas had expressed a desire to live with the Omahas rather than go to Indian Territory, just as Standing Bear had done, Inspector Howard had told them that was not an option, as the Omahas would soon be going down there too.

When Inspector Howard discovered Iron Eye and Bright Eyes in his column, he ordered them to leave. The Omaha pair only had a chance for heart-wrenching farewells with their relatives and friends before gloomily turning around and going back to their own reservation. As they went north, Captain Walker's military escort followed them, making its way back to its post on the Missouri. From here on, the Poncas, now living on government stores doled out by Howard, were totally dependent on the inspector. After a two-day pause in Columbus, he ordered the Poncas to resume their trek.

As the column continued to trundle south, Standing Bear worried about Prairie Flower's deteriorating health. They had no doctor, no medicines; all Standing Bear and his wife and son-in-law could do was pray for her. Ten days later, on June 6, when the column was outside the town of Milford, Nebraska, just west of the state capital, Lincoln, Prairie Flower died, claimed by pneumonia.

Standing Bear was a Christian. He was one of the score of Poncas who had been converted to Christianity by Episcopalian missionary J. Owen Dorsey six years before. Desperately Standing Bear had prayed to the Great Spirit that his child might be spared. Now the devastated Standing Bear buried Prairie Flower and offered prayers to heaven that the Great Spirit might accept her departed soul. When the Christian ladies of Milford heard that the chief's daughter was dying, they came hurrying out from the town and prayed with Standing Bear and his people. Under their auspices, Standing Bear and his wife interred Prairie Flower in a Christian cemetery at Milford.

That night, as the wails of grieving Poncas filled their camp, a tornado struck out of nowhere, destroying tents, damaging wagons, hurling people into the air, and seriously injuring several tribe members. The next day Inspector Howard still ordered the column to resume its southerly march. Within twenty-four hours a Ponca child died. Soon other adults were also dying. But Howard never permitted the march to pause, apart from allowing the burial of the dead.

When the shambling column reached the Oto reservation on June 14, the Otoes took pity on their Ponca brothers and gave them the few ponies they could spare so that some of the women and children might go on horseback. By the time the bedraggled column reached Manhattan, Kansas, ten days later, Howard was alarmed by growing sickness among his charges and worried how the fatalities might reflect on him. So he employed a white doctor from the town to attend the Poncas. The doctor's attentions were too late for two women of the tribe, who died the next day.

Near Burlington, Kansas, a Ponca male named Buffalo Track suddenly attacked Chief White Eagle, blaming him for the tribe's loss of homeland and the growing list of deaths. Soldiers dragged Buffalo Track off the shaken old chief, and Howard sent the man back to the Omaha reservation in Nebraska under guard to cool off. He later rejoined the tribe down south.

On July 9, fifty days after setting out, the Poncas reached the Indian Territory destination that the Bureau of Indian Affairs had planned for them—the hot, mosquito-ridden reservation of their cousins the Quapaw near the Kaw River. Here the Poncas were reunited with those Poncas who had preceded them. The "half-breeds" and their families were living, weak and dejected, in tents. Without their farming implements they had not been able to work the hard, dry land. Accustomed to three meals a day in the north, they were only being given enough rations for one meal a day by the Quapaw agent, A. G. Boone, a grandson of famous Kentucky pioneer Daniel Boone.

When Standing Bear informed Howard that this land was not suitable for his people and they wanted to go back to the Omaha reservation as the inspector had promised, Howard advised him that the Poncas were now prisoners and would be punished if they attempted to leave the Quapaw reservation. Having done all that Commissioner Smith had required, Inspector Howard then handed responsibility for the Poncas over to Agent Boone and returned to Washington.

Howard had done his job with brutal efficiency, but he was already having doubts about the whole business. Back at his desk, when he penned his official report he told Commissioner Smith that the removal of the Poncas to Indian Territory "will prove a mistake, and that a great mortality will surely follow among the people when they have been here for a time and been poisoned with the malaria of the climate."[50] His superiors ignored him. Howard's prediction proved unhappily accurate. By the end of that year, 158 Ponca men, women, and children had died since the tribe left the Niobrara.

Standing Bear regularly expressed his dissatisfaction with this place to Agent Boone. He also reminded him that the tribe had been promised that once it settled in the Indian Territory its leading men would be taken to Washington to see the Great Father. Standing Bear felt sure that the president did not know how the Poncas had been treated and wanted to tell him of their terrible state, face-to-face.

Boone transmitted the complaints to Washington, and in the summer they came across the desk of Ezra A. Hayt, whom Carl Schurz had just appointed to replace Smith as Indian commissioner. Hayt, a wealthy former dry goods wholesaler from New York City and a onetime member of the board of Indian commissioners, recommended to Schurz that they agree to the Washington excursion—visits to the capital always produced shock and awe among Indian leaders, as they saw for themselves the magnificence and power of the United States in all its glory. Toward the end of the fall, Indian Affairs officials arrived from the East, collected Standing Bear, White Eagle, and other leading men of the tribe, and took them up to Kansas. From there they were conveyed by train to the nation's capital.

In early November, in a large white limestone building on Pennsylvania Avenue named the Executive Mansion, better known as the White House, Standing Bear and White Eagle met President Rutherford B. Hayes. In the cabinet chamber, the bearded, fifty-five-year-old president shook hands with the chiefs and invited them to sit and air their grievances and wishes. Standing Bear reverently, respectfully told the Great Father that his people had been wronged, that they were now in an awfully bad place, and that he hoped he would do something for them. At the president's invitation he told him the story of the forced removal of the Poncas to Indian Territory against their wishes, and of the many deaths that had resulted on the march and since. To Standing Bear, President Hayes seemed astonished by the story of the Poncas' woes. The president told the chiefs that this was the first he had heard of their treatment.

Coming to his feet, indicating that the interview was at an end, he told them he would order an investigation into their situation.[51]

Next the chiefs were taken to the Interior Department, where they conferred with Commissioner Hayt, who bluntly informed Standing Bear and his fellow Ponca chiefs that there was "no way by which their request to be sent back North could be complied with without action of Congress in the matter."[52] Hayt, who was completely bald, was later described as a "bald-headed liar" by Spotted Tail, paramount chief of Brulé Lakota Sioux, after Hayt failed to keep a promise to his people.[53]

Several days later the Poncas were brought back to the White House for a second meeting with President Hayes. Having been briefed by the Interior Department, the Great Father now told the disappointed Ponca chiefs that as their tribe was in Indian Territory they had better stay there. He told them to go back and hunt for better land down there, and he would have the possessions confiscated from them in the north sent to them when they had chosen a new site for a reservation. He assured them that from now on the Poncas would be treated well. Those responsible for their mistreatment were gone, he said, referring to the previous administration, and that was all in the past. The president expressed his confident belief that before long sickness would leave the tribe once the Poncas became accustomed to the new country. Standing Bear replied that he could only obey the president's orders.[54]

The overawed and trusting chiefs went back to Indian Territory to tell their people of their momentous meetings with the Great Father, and of his promise of better times ahead. At first, the president seemed to keep his word. An Indian Affairs inspector soon arrived to take Standing Bear and other chiefs to search for a new Indian Territory reservation site. The best of the locations shown to them was 150 miles away on the west bank of the Arkansas River, around the junction with the Salt Fork. In lieu of going home to the Niobrara, Ponca leaders chose this as their new home.

But Agent Boone received no funds to make the relocation possible—nothing for transport, nothing for extra rations or clothing or for housing once they reached the latest destination. In the spring of 1878, the Poncas were made to walk all the way to the Arkansas River. Until their newly assigned Indian Affairs agent, William H. Whiteman, finally joined them in July, they were left to their own devices and received no rations for months on end. They were in such dire straits that local white settlers collected food for them. Still, the Poncas' spirits lifted a little once they reached their new reservation, for it was more fertile than the Quapaw land. And they looked forward to their possessions confiscated at the Niobrara being sent down to them, as the president had promised.

But during the summer, illness returned to the tribe with a vengeance. Poncas died by the score. Even their horses perished—the tribe had come south with five hundred horses and had acquired another two hundred since, but now only one hundred were still alive.[55] Few Ponca tents were without a fatality. The camp was filled with the moans of the sick and the dying. Some of the sick, lying in their beds, "would ask for another good day to live to get back" to their home country in the north.[56]

Standing Bear's sister succumbed to the sickness and died. Standing Bear himself was ill and became too weak to plow. He felt totally helpless—like a child, he was to say, unable to help even himself, much less help his people.[57] Paramount Chief White Eagle succinctly described how battered the surviving Ponca people felt: "We were as grass that is trodden down."[58]

In October Commissioner Hayt paid a surprise visit to the new Ponca reservation at the Arkansas River. After a cursory inspection he told Interior Secretary Schurz that conditions among the Poncas were "very much improved." Later he noted, "It is true that during the first four months of their residence in the Indian Territory they lost a large number by death, which is inevitable in all cases of removal of Northern Indians to a Southern latitude." But he was certain that the tribe's health would soon improve as they became "acclimated."[59]

The health of the Poncas did not improve. As winter took a grip, one of the many who became ill was Standing Bear's teenage son, Bear Shield. A few years back Standing Bear had lost a son. Now, completely at a loss, with Indian remedies having failed and no white doctor to call on, Standing Bear could only nurse his last son and heir as best he could and pray to the Great Spirit.

Bear Shield had gone to school at the tribe's Niobrara schoolhouse. He could speak English, could read and write, and he had been a great help to his father. Like his father, Bear Shield was a Christian, and to his father's great pride he had often taken aside members of their tribe and read to them from the Holy Scriptures. But as he felt his life slipping away, Bear Shield began to worry about the afterlife. It was a Ponca custom to bury the bones of dead tribe members with those of their ancestors, so that they would not be alone in the afterlife. A Ponca who was not buried with his ancestors was doomed to wander the next world alone. Bear Shield did not want to be alone in the afterlife. In December, with his last breaths, Bear Shield made his sobbing father promise that he would bury his bones among their ancestors beside the Swift Running Water.

His son's death, in his arms, was the last straw for Standing Bear. The Great Father had been wrong. This land was fatal for the Poncas. Their health had not improved. What's more, none of their belongings had been brought down to them from the north as Rutherford B. Hayes had promised. Now Standing Bear, heartbroken over his family tragedies, was also heartbroken at the realization that the almost mystical Great Father had deceived him. Over recent months he'd begun to think of escaping this place. In one scenario that he played out in his mind he would send the women and children on ahead, and he and the warriors would act as a rear guard to fight off pursuit as the Poncas fled to the mountains. But, realizing that most of the warriors were too sick to march, let alone fight, he decided the best chance lay with a small group breaking away. Failure, he told himself, could be no worse than staying where they were.[60]

In the new scheme, the escapees would return to the Niobrara, where Standing Bear would bury his son with their ancestors as he had promised, and where he and his family would resume their former life. Once he reached the old homeland, he would be able to send for other Poncas so that they too could go back home. Sad but determined, Standing Bear began to carefully plan his escape.

✦ *Chapter 3* ✦

THE ESCAPE

I N T H E D I L A P I D A T E D headquarters building at Fort Omaha, General Crook was nodding slowly. Bright Eyes had reached the episode in her tale of Ponca injustice with which he was most familiar— the last stage, when he himself had become involved.

Once Standing Bear had resolved to keep his promise to his dying son and save the lives of at least some of his people, said Bright Eyes, he carefully chose the members of the party he would lead on the escape bid. Agent Whiteman would try to stop him if he knew he was planning to run away, and so Standing Bear told nobody of his plans except those he intended to take along.[61] Standing Bear began with his younger brother Yellow Horse, who was sick with a fever but said that if Standing Bear went back north, then he and his family would go too; his health and that of his family might improve back home in the northern climate. Like Standing Bear, Yellow Horse preferred to die trying to get back home than die here in the Warm Land. Long Runner and Chicken Hunter, both members of Standing Bear's clan, also agreed that they and their families would join the flight north.[62]

Standing Bear also spoke with his good friend Buffalo Chip, chief of the Medicine clan. The middle-aged Buffalo Chip, considered a handsome man with graying hair trailing down his back, said that he would make the journey home with Standing Bear. Three other men also joined the escape bid. One was Buffalo Track, the Ponca from another clan, who had attacked White Eagle on the way south. The other two were Crazy Bear, an

Omaha with a Ponca family, and Cries for War, a Yankton married to a Ponca woman.[63] Both Crazy Bear and Cries for War had followed the tribe south the previous year after being separated from the Poncas by Inspector Howard when he evicted them from the northern Ponca reservation.

There would be a total of twenty-seven escapees; in addition to the eight men, their family members would number six boys and thirteen women and girls. Among the women and children going along were Standing Bear's wife, Susette, his surviving daughter, Fanny, and his infant grandson and granddaughter. Following Prairie Flower's death, Standing Bear and Susette took in her children to raise as their own. Six other members of the party apart from Yellow Horse were quite ill, and all the others were weak from lack of food. But they, like Yellow Horse, hoped that the cooler climate back in their homeland would restore them to the good health they had previously enjoyed.

As Christmas approached, the eight men involved in the scheme discreetly made their preparations. The first priority was transportation; in their condition they would never be able to repeat the epic six-hundred-mile walk home by Standing Bear and seven other chiefs in 1877. All but two of Standing Bear's horses had died, and these remaining underfed steeds could only draw his light, open spring wagon. The other men could provide three covered wagons and teams between them.

The next requirement was provisions. As with the other aspects of their plan, Standing Bear and his fellow plotters knew it was essential not to raise the suspicions of the agent, his white employees, or the Ponca "half-breeds," several of whom spoke English. Standing Bear didn't trust them because the Indian Affairs men tended to favor them. He was now openly at odds with Lone Chief, leader of the "half-breeds," who wanted Standing Bear to stop complaining to the government. So the plotters quietly put aside a little horse feed and a portion of their meager rations for the journey. Standing Bear had $10 in cash; Buffalo Chip had the same—a total of $20 for a trip of several months for twenty-seven people and eight horses. It would have to do.

On New Year's Day, Standing Bear took aside his youngest brother, the giant Big Snake. Confiding the plan to him, he asked Big Snake to take charge of their clan in his absence. If this band succeeded in reaching the Niobrara, Standing Bear told his little brother, then he would send word for others to follow. That night, with Big Snake's help, he loaded a wooden trunk containing the remains of his son Bear Shield onto the spring wagon along with poles and hides for a tipi. The departing families made tearful last-minute farewells and, then, in the cold early hours of the morning of January 2, 1879, the escapees slipped away from the Arkansas River Ponca agency and made for Kansas.

Knowing that they could be arrested for leaving their assigned reservation without a government pass, Standing Bear led his party north via the plains of far western Kansas, well away from white settlements, roads, and soldiers, often changing direction in case they were spotted and their course was passed onto the authorities so the army could intercept them. The farther north they went, the more the winter cold seeped into their bones as they huddled under blankets on their slow-moving wagons or walked to stay warm. Along the way they used their few dollars to buy fodder for the horses from white farmers. After twenty days the money was gone, and so was their food. For two days they ate nothing. Coming to a farm, Standing Bear fetched the farmer to see the sorry state of his little band. The farmer and his boys brought hay and a bag of corn. After the Indian children ravenously devoured the corn, the farmer went away and came back with bread, meat, and coffee. As the band continued up into Nebraska, other dirt-poor white farmers along the way also gave the passing Indians what food they could spare.

Alerted via telegraph by Agent William Whiteman that Standing Bear and a party of Poncas were on the move, Secretary Schurz soon had the army looking for the runaways. Meanwhile, the Kansas press was characterizing them as renegades on the loose, a threat to whites. Despite the hullabaloo, through January and February Standing Bear was able to evade detection all the way up to northeastern Nebraska. Lieutenant John Bourke later wrote that this wretched winter trek was made by Standing Bear's Poncas "molesting nobody, and subsisting upon charity. Not a shot was fired at anyone; not so much as a dog was stolen."[64]

At the end of February, word reached Chief Iron Eye at the Omaha reservation that Standing Bear and his party were drawing near. Without hesitation, Iron Eye, his daughter Bright Eyes, and other members of the Omaha tribe slipped out of Joe's Village at night without alerting Indian Affairs agent Jacob Vore at the village's Omaha agency and hurried south with ponies to meet the Poncas. Linking up with Standing Bear's exhausted party, they took them to their settlement. As the Omaha tribespeople flooded around the Poncas and made them welcome, Iron Eye promised Standing Bear sanctuary. In the summer, he said, once the Poncas regained their strength, the Omahas would help Standing Bear take his son's remains to the Niobrara burial ground and become reestablished on the old reservation. In the meantime, the Omahas had more than enough land—they would give Standing Bear's people land to sow with wheat and corn and vegetables, and loan them all the implements they would need. What's more, said Iron Eye, Standing Bear's people could live with the Omahas for as long as they desired.

On March 4, two days after Secretary Schurz celebrated his fiftieth birthday, he received an unexpected late birthday present. A telegram from Agent Vore at the Omaha agency that day reached Commissioner Hayt saying that "the Poncas [had] just arrived" at his agency and had taken refuge with the Omahas. "Had them arrested; they promise to remain for orders; have no place to confine them. I await instructions."[65]

Schurz responded by having several Indian Affairs officials promptly sent with instructions to interview Standing Bear on the Omaha reservation and convince him to turn around and lead his people back to the Arkansas River settlement. Once these Bureau of Indian Affairs officials arrived, they found Standing Bear determined to continue on to the Niobrara with his son's remains and not to return to Indian Territory. The officials departed, their mission unfulfilled.

When the Indian Affairs men telegraphed Washington that Standing Bear refused to turn back, Secretary Schurz lost what remaining patience he had with the Poncas. This small, insignificant tribe, an annoyance to two administrations for several years, would not be permitted to frustrate the overall re-

settlement of Plains Indians. Once again Schurz contacted Secretary Mc-Crary at the War Department. On March 14, at Schurz's request, McCrary instructed the commanding general of the army, General Sherman, to order the arrest of Standing Bear and the members of the Ponca tribe sheltering with him on the Omaha reservation. Telegrams began to fly. From Washington, General Sherman transmitted the order to divisional commander Lieutenant General Sheridan in Chicago, who on March 17 passed on the order to departmental commander Brigadier General George Crook at Fort Omaha. Faced with a direct order, and irrespective of his personal feelings in the matter, on March 19 Crook in turn ordered Colonel John H. King, commander of the 9th Infantry and post commander of Fort Omaha, to send a detachment to take the Poncas into custody and escort them back to Fort Omaha.[66] The barest minimum number of men necessary was detailed for the job. The next day, First Lieutenant William L. Carpenter set off from Fort Omaha with just a corporal and four enlisted men from the 9th Infantry, using three saddle horses and a military ambulance drawn by four mules.[67]

On the morning of Sunday, March 23, Standing Bear, who had recovered much of his strength during the three weeks he had spent with the Omahas, was working in the fields with several fellow escapees when a panting Omaha runner came with the news that soldiers were at the Omaha agency. The soldiers, he said, wanted to take the Poncas back to Indian Territory. The Poncas must report to the agency in Joe's Village by noon, ready to travel, said the runner, before he hurried off to pass on the same message to the other fugitives.[68] Seized by despair, Standing Bear went to the tipi he had erected for his family and informed his wife of the news. Disconsolate, they folded their tipi, loaded their daughter, grandchildren, and few possessions onto their spring wagon, and slowly made their way to the agency.

It happened that the missionary who had converted Standing Bear to Christianity eight years before, Reverend J. Owen Dorsey, was at the Omaha agency. Dorsey, who had joined the American Ethnology Bureau in Washington as an ethnologist earlier in the year, had started compiling English translations of native American languages for the bureau. He was at the agency updating his records on the Omaha-Ponca language, with the encouragement of Chief Iron Eye and the help of Iron Eye's eldest son, nineteen-year-old Woodworker, also known as Frank La Flesche— Bright Eyes's half brother. When Standing Bear saw Dorsey, he made a beeline for him and pleaded with him, telling him that he and his people could not survive down in the Indian Territory where the Great Father had put them. He begged Dorsey to intervene to let the band stay with the Omahas, to work the land and live peacefully.

Buffalo Chip and several other men also crowded around the clergyman, begging him to help. But Dorsey responded that he could do nothing to prevent the military from carrying out orders to arrest the fugitive Ponca band. He urged the Poncas to go peacefully with the soldiers but promised to write on their behalf to contacts in Washington.[69]

Standing Bear went to Lieutenant Carpenter and asked for a council, and the lieutenant agreed. One of the Ponca men, Long Runner, was so ill in his tipi he couldn't get out of bed, so, as Carpenter's infantrymen stood idly around, seven of the Indians sat down with Carpenter outside the agency building. At the lieutenant's request, they were joined by a white clerk from the agency, twenty-two-year-old W. W. "Willie" Hamilton. Son of Reverend Hamilton, Willie had grown up on the Omaha reservation and spoke the Omaha language fluently. The usual agency interpreter, an Omaha named Charles Morgan, was away, so Willie filled in for him.[70]

Through young Hamilton, Standing Bear gave the lieutenant a review of what led him and his band to escape to the Omahas, and told the officer that he and his companions wished to stay where they were. Lieutenant Carpenter, impressed by Standing Bear's "able speech" and saddened by what he later described as the band's "pitiable condition," told the seven men that he had his orders and they must come with him to Fort Omaha.[71] But when they reached the fort, they could speak with General Crook. He then asked if they would come with him peaceably, and Standing Bear sadly said they would but under protest.

As the men went to hitch up their horses and load their wagons with their folded tipis and cooking utensils, the Omahas generously gave them several additional ponies for the long journey. Lieutenant Carpenter was now informed that one of the Ponca men, Long Runner, refused to go. Taking along interpreter Willie, a soldier, and the agency blacksmith, a burly white man, Carpenter went to Long Runner's tipi. Inside, they found a feverish Long Runner on his bed, wife and young daughter at his side. The lieutenant took out his orders, had the interpreter read them to Long Runner, and then asked the Ponca to come with him. But Long Runner stubbornly refused.

Long Runner tried to sit up, producing a knife. The blacksmith stepped up, took the weakened Ponca's wrist, and forced the knife from his hand. Now Long Runner felt the cold steel of Lieutenant Carpenter's pistol at his temple. The blacksmith and enlisted man bound Long Runner's wrists and bundled him outside.[72]

In another tipi, Lieutenant Carpenter found a moaning Ponca woman who was obviously too ill to be moved, and he decided to leave her in the care of the Omahas and under the observation of the Omaha Indian Affairs agent. But the others had to depart. Standing Bear had given his word that he and his people would go to Fort Omaha, and, respectful of Standing Bear's word and his pride, the level-headed young officer now let the main party travel on ahead without guards. Slowly, dejectedly they left Joe's Village, following the Missouri south, some of them in wagons, some riding the Omaha ponies, some walking. The lieutenant and his soldiers followed along half a mile behind, with Long Runner traveling in the army ambulance, trussed up for the duration of the journey.

As Reverend Dorsey stood with numerous unhappy Omahas watching the Ponca band go, Bright Eyes came up to him. She had been teaching in the school while the drama unfolded outside the agency, and now she told Dorsey they must do something to help the Poncas. He replied that he intended writing to a colleague in Washington who was a friend of Interior Secretary Schurz, who, he was sure, would speak to Secretary Schurz on behalf of the Poncas. But that would take too long, the school mistress reminded him. They must do something now, before the army removed Standing Bear and his party from Nebraska and from General Crook's area of responsibility. General Crook was a good man, she told the minister, someone who would listen to reason. But Dorsey seemed resigned to letting events run their course. After all, not even General Crook could be expected to disobey orders.

Bright Eyes wasn't satisfied with that. She quickly wrote a statement about the mistreatment of the Poncas and gave it to Dorsey, urging him to distribute it to influential friends. He revised the statement in his own words and then sent copies to Episcopal churches in the East under his name and Bright Eyes's name. During the following weeks the statement was read to congregations after the Sunday sermon. But Bright Eyes realized this process was too slow to prevent the removal of Standing Bear's band from Nebraska. Immediate, drastic action was required.

For almost a week after the Poncas were taken away Bright Eyes stewed over their predicament, and then she made up her mind to act personally and decisively. It had to be done discreetly, but it had to be done. Speaking with her father, Chief Iron Eye, she put a proposal to him. Several times before this, she and Iron Eye had done things that were unorthodox and sometimes not strictly legal, but always for the good of their people. Now Bright Eyes reminded her father that he not only knew General Crook personally, he knew him very well indeed, probably better than any other Indian. Bright Eyes was certain the general would listen to Iron Eye—if he went to him to plead for their Ponca brothers and sisters. And Iron Eye had agreed.

On the evening of Friday, March 28, once Bright Eyes finished at the government school for the day, she and her father mounted his two fastest ponies and slipped out of Joe's Village without alerting Agent Vore or anyone else to their plans, and headed south.

Now Iron Eye and Bright Eyes sat before General Crook in his office, exhausted by their journey yet driven by their determination to plead for justice. Bright Eyes made a final plea for the general to prevent the Poncas' return to Indian Territory. She implored him to allow them to go home to the Niobrara River to bury the remains of Standing Bear's son in the traditional Ponca burial grounds and to regain their old way of life in the land of their fathers.

All eyes turned to George Crook.[73]

→ *Chapter 4* ←

THE NEWSPAPER EDITOR

A̲T ONE O'CLOCK in the morning on Sunday, March 30, 1879, a secret meeting took place in the offices of the *Omaha Daily Herald*, one of Omaha's leading daily newspapers. Only a single written account of what took place at that meeting exists. It was related by one of the participants, Thomas Henry Tibbles, in his autobiographical book *Buckskin and Blanket Days*. Another participant, General George Crook, also penned an autobiography, but it breaks off before the events of 1879. The reliability of Tibbles's account in relation to one aspect is open to question. As the Standing Bear story unfolds, it becomes clear that Tibbles had a personal and, in part, honorable reason for claiming that only General Crook and he were present at this meeting.

Thirty-nine-year-old Tibbles, deputy editor of the *Daily Herald*, was filling in as editor in chief while the paper's founder and editor, Dr. George L. Miller, was out of town. Thomas Henry Tibbles—Henry to his friends—had led a colorful life up to this point. Tall, solid, handsome, with tousled black hair and a long face adorned with a mustache and goatee, he looked like a country parson or a tub-thumping politician. He had been the former, and in time he would attempt to become the latter. He grew up barefoot in a basic settler's cabin in Ohio, General Crook's home state, one of nine children born to an outdoorsman father and a deeply religious mother. Tibbles left home at eleven on a quest for the righteous cause that would occupy the rest of his life. Convinced of the evils of slavery, he joined abolitionist John Brown's forces as they fought pro-slav-ery vigilantes for control of Kansas Territory in 1856. After Brown's arrest and execution, Tibbles attended a religious college for three years until the Civil War broke out in 1861. He served in the Union army as a scout and possibly a secret agent, rising to the rank of major by war's end. In later newspaper interviews he spoke little of his wartime adventures ex-cept to mention several battles in which he participated and of narrowly escaping death on one occasion at the hands of Confederate guerrillas led by William Quantrill.

After the war, Tibbles, who claimed to be one of the best pistol shots in the West, worked as a newspaper reporter and frontier guide. He led a posse on the trail of outlaw Jesse James and, after 1871, became a gun-toting circuit preacher for the Episcopal Church in Missouri and then Nebraska. Falling out with the church hierarchy in 1876, he left the min-istry and went to work for the *Omaha Daily Bee* as a journalist, soon mov-ing to the *Herald*, where he was quickly promoted to deputy editor. Hunt-ing and fishing filled much of his spare time (during the Civil War he proved himself to be an expert woodsman and a crack marksman). He also had a good singing voice, putting together church choirs and conducting a choir of *Herald* newsboys. He even penned a hymn or two. But Tibbles's main diversions were community affairs, politics, and worthy causes. Which is where General Crook came in. Literally.

Henry Tibbles later said that just before one o'clock in the morning of the last Sunday in March 1879 he was working late as usual in the edi-torial offices of the *Omaha Daily Herald*, then at the corner of 13th and Douglas Streets. Suddenly the door to the editor's room opened and General Crook walked in and changed his life. Later events suggest that General Crook was not alone, that he had brought two companions with him to talk to Tibbles—the Omaha Indians Iron Eye and his daughter Bright Eyes.[74]

The indications are that Crook brought the pair into town after meet-ing with them at the fort and arranged for them to spend the night at the presbytery of Reverend William Harsha, the Presbyterian minister in

Omaha. Iron Eye had been baptized a Catholic, but he converted to Pres-
byterianism and raised his children as Presbyterians.

It was only four miles from Fort Omaha to downtown Omaha. General
Crook could have made the journey into town during the late afternoon or
evening, but he timed his arrival at the *Herald* offices for the early hours
of Sunday morning so that he and his Indian companions could do so un-
seen. Knowing that his friend Henry Tibbles habitually worked late,
Crook waited until after midnight to hustle Bright Eyes and her father to
the newspaper offices, safe from prying eyes, having shared his plan with
Reverend Harsha.[75]

The newspaper editor was understandably surprised by his friend's un-
heralded late visit. He knew that Standing Bear and his party were under
guard at Fort Omaha, after his city editor had put his head in the editor's
door two hours earlier to tell him that he'd just come back from Fort
Omaha, where he learned the Ponca prisoners had been brought in. Tibbles would have made a note to follow up the story over the coming days,
never imagining that General Crook would soon come calling on him with
two Indians. Tibbles wrote that the general was not a happy man: "I could
see by his face that something had gone very wrong."[76] As General Crook
took a seat across the large editorial table, the newspaperman began by
asking how he could be of help.

"Tibbles," Crook began with force and deep feeling, "during the twenty-
five or thirty years that I've been on the plains in the government service
I've been forced many times by orders from Washington to do most inhuman things in dealings with the Indians. But now I'm ordered to do a more
cruel thing than ever before." The general would then have invited Bright
Eyes to speak on Iron Eye's behalf as she had done before, to explain the
cause of the War Department order in question.

There, sitting at the editorial table in the quietly industrious offices of
the fourteen-year-old *Daily Herald*, a weary Henry Tibbles listened with
increasing interest as, at General Crook's urging, Bright Eyes overcame
her shyness and retold the Ponca tribe's sad story for the newspaper editor. When Bright Eyes finished, Crook again took up the proverbial baton,

explaining that he had been ordered to arrest Standing Bear and the twenty-six Poncas accompanying him, with a view to stopping them from reaching their old home on the Niobrara and returning them under guard to the reservation beside the Arkansas River in the Indian Territory.

"I would resign my commission," the general went on, "if that would prevent the order from being executed. But it would not. Another officer would merely be assigned to fill my place."[77]

Tibbles sympathized with Crook and the Poncas and asked what he could do to help. Which is what the general hoped he would do.

"I've come to ask if you will not take up the matter," said Crook. He showed Tibbles the order he had received from the War Department in Washington via headquarters in Chicago, together with a copy of a communication from Secretary of the Interior Schurz to Secretary of War McCrary. Schurz's communication said, in part, "I respectfully request that the nearest military commander be instructed to detail a sufficient guard to return these Poncas to the agency where they belong."[78] That agency was on the new Ponca reservation in the Indian Territory.

When Tibbles asked Crook if there was nothing he could do to change the minds of the powers that be in Washington, the general responded with exasperation, "It's no use for me to protest. Washington always orders the very opposite of what I recommend." He told Tibbles that the fate of Standing Bear and his people was now in the editor's hands. This was not the first time that Tibbles and Crook had worked covertly together—the previous year Crook had sent Tibbles as his secret envoy to the Brulé, to urge them not to accept a proposal from Washington that the Brulé be relocated, which Crook considered against the interests of Indian and white alike. But Tibbles now protested that in a matter such as this Ponca business he had less power than the general.[79]

To which Crook replied, "You have a great daily newspaper here which you can use."[80] And then George Crook showed why William McKinley and numerous others respected his intellect—the general told Tibbles he had noticed a small loophole in his orders, one that he now urged the newspaperman to exploit. As he pointed out, Secretary Schurz had requested that he be instructed to "detail a sufficient guard to return these Poncas to their agency." Based on that request, the War Department had ordered Crook to arrest Standing Bear and those accompanying him. But that was all.

The general had obeyed Schurz's request and the War Department's order to the letter. He had detailed a guard under Lieutenant Carpenter that had effected the arrest of Standing Bear and his party and now watched over them at Fort Omaha. But, to date, Washington had not ordered Crook to physically remove the Poncas back to their reservation in the Indian Territory. It was a semantic argument, true enough, yet it allowed Crook to delay the forced deportation of Standing Bear and his people. Until someone in Washington woke up and sent a direct order to remove the Poncas to Indian Territory, Crook said, he would simply keep them under guard at Fort Omaha. At the same time, he could not be accused of disobeying orders. Crook's literal interpretation of his orders opened a narrow window of opportunity for someone to take up the Ponca cause.[81]

Tibbles appreciated the subtlety and potential of the general's strategy. The question was, How long would he have before Secretary Schurz closed the loophole? Crook would have told Tibbles that it could be a week, perhaps two, if they were lucky, or just a matter of days, before the Indian Affairs agent at the Arkansas River reservation, William Whiteman, telegraphed Washington to ask why the army was not returning the Standing Bear party to the reservation as he had been led to expect, setting off alarm bells in Commissioner Hayt's office and then Secretary Schurz's office.

Crook had come to know Henry Tibbles well during his years in Nebraska. They shared outdoors pursuits, an interest in the Indian peoples, and a liberal temperament. When Tibbles was reluctant to become the champion of the campaign that Crook was advocating, the general appealed to his friend's righteous zeal.

"You're perfectly acquainted with all the crimes of the Indian Ring at Washington," Crook said. "I ask you to go into the fight against those who are robbing these helpless people. You can win. I'm sure of it! The American people, if they knew half the truth, would send every member of the Indian Ring to prison."[82]

"General," Tibbles answered, "if I once went into such a fight as that, I should never give up till I won or died. It would require at least five years and would cost thousands of dollars."[83]

Tibbles described this conversation some years later with the benefit of hindsight in an attempt to enlarge his original motive. Crook and Bright Eyes were asking for a one-off press campaign for this little band of Poncas, just like the other one-off crusading editorial campaigns that Tibbles had embarked on in the past for various causes. Neither Crook nor Tibbles could have imagined on that day in March the huge Pandora's box that the campaign for Standing Bear ultimately opened.

Tibbles also protested that publicly taking up the cause of an Indian would make him very unpopular in some quarters, could even threaten his newspaper career. This was a very real possibility that would have been apparent to both men at the time. "You're asking a great deal of me," he told Crook.[84]

According to Tibbles, the general replied, "I know I am. But no matter what we do, all that any of us can get out of this world is what we eat, drink, and wear, and a place to shelter us. If we can do something for which good men will remember us when we're gone, that's the best legacy we can leave. I promise you that if you'll take up this work, I'll stand by you."[85]

There was another factor that had the capacity to influence the attitudes of both men to this case—the Soldier Lodge. All the Plains Indians had secret warrior societies. Among the Omaha, the Ponca, and the tribes related to them the Soldier Lodge was the most sacred and the most secret of all. It was a great honor for a tribesman to be invited to become a member, but he had to pass an initiation ceremony to gain membership and the high respect of other Indians that went with it.

Soldier Lodge initiation traditionally took place during the tribe's summer buffalo hunt. Portable lodges, or tipis, were set up in a circle around the central holy lodge and the three-day Sun Dance religious ceremony was conducted. Each initiate had four slits cut in the flesh of his chest, two on each breast. Two slivers of wood were forced between the slits. Leather thongs tied to the pieces of wood trailed away to the top of a tall wooden pole at the center of the dance circle, the sacred pole. This, it was believed, put the dancers in touch with Wakanda, the Great Spirit. The initiate then danced around the pole to a monotonous drumbeat until the pieces of wood ripped from his skin, which could take a number of hours. The longer the better, for that meant the initiate spent more time in touch with Wakanda. As Henry Tibbles revealed in his autobiography, over the years two white men were invited by the Omaha tribe to submit to Soldier Lodge initiation, and both passed the test. Until Tibbles revealed the secret in his life story, which was not published until long after his death, no other white was ever aware of the pair's initiation. Tibbles identified himself as one of these two white initiates; the other, he wrote, was General Crook.[86]

Apparently Chief Iron Eye went to Crook at Fort Omaha hoping that their links through the Soldier Lodge brotherhood would induce the general to help him and the Ponca people. And now Crook expected his fellow initiate Tibbles to acknowledge the unique honor the Omaha had bestowed on the pair, and the trust that had been placed in them by the tribe, by helping the cousins of the Omaha—as the Omaha had themselves helped the Ponca people.

The presence of the chief of the Omahas at the meeting between Tibbles and Crook would have highlighted the obligation that the Omaha tribe felt its two white brothers were under—especially when Bright Eyes told them that if the government would not permit the Poncas to return to the Niobrara, then it should let them live with the Omaha tribe. Anything would be better than a return to the deadly Warm Land. Iron Eye had already told Standing Bear that the Omaha people would happily give up some of the land on their reservation to their Ponca cousins.

The meeting at the newspaper office lasted several long, emotion-packed hours. When Tibbles, General Crook, Iron Eye, and Bright Eyes walked out of the offices of the *Omaha Daily Herald* together that Sunday morning, the first rays of dawn were streaking the eastern sky. It was 4:30 A.M., half an hour after the paper's other editorial staff had left for the day. By this time, Henry Tibbles had decided to take up Standing Bear's cause.

→ ←

As his past made clear, Henry Tibbles was a serial crusader. He joined the Standing Bear coalition for all the right reasons. He was a good man, and he saw the injustices done to Standing Bear and his people for the crimes they were. But, for all that, he simply could not help himself when a budding crusade came knocking at his door. Tibbles was addicted to just causes, and to challenges. And he was never happier than when his current crusade pitted him against dangerous opposition.

He had begun young, dodging bullets and vigilantes' nooses as a sixteen-year-old abolitionist in Kansas. After the Civil War, during his circuit preaching days in Missouri, his gospel tent was regularly shot up by drunks and atheists. When he moved to Nebraska, he claimed that he didn't possess an item of clothing without at least one bullet hole in it. But he wouldn't have missed a minute of it.

It wasn't as if he hadn't had considerable success as a crusader in the recent past. Assigned by the church to southern Nebraska's more civilized and sedate Republican Valley in 1873, he set about ministering to the needs of the dirt-poor settlers of the region. Within a year, he had a new cause. A severe drought parched Nebraska in 1874. In the Republican Valley, the few crops that didn't fail were blighted by a grasshopper plague. Wheat-growing settlers living in sod houses with high hopes and very little else began to struggle. Some packed up and left. Others were too poor to go anywhere; they stayed and starved, and a number died. Yet the problem was denied by local politicians, land speculators, and merchants in the far-flung rural communities on the recently opened prairies. "Boosters" these people were called—their wealth depended on "boosting" the prospects of their areas to attract a steady stream of new immigrants who would spend money with them. It wasn't good for business to admit that new settlers living in famine-hit counties were having a tough time.

It was only when the U.S. Army identified the need for urgent drought relief in thirty-six Nebraska counties that people in authority began to take notice and the government began to muster emergency supplies for the affected areas. Nonetheless, as the winter of 1874–1875 loomed, Henry Tibbles was convinced that the slow relief effort would yield too little too late. And he took it on himself to do something about the problem.

Deciding to go east to make a public appeal for funds to help the starving farmers of southern Nebraska, Pastor Tibbles sought and received the endorsement of the Nebraska Aid Society. Then he set off for Illinois and the booming city of Chicago, center of the wheat trade. Hoping that wheat traders would spare a thought for struggling wheat farmers, the first thing Tibbles did when he arrived in the city was address the Chicago Board of Trade. Its members promptly donated $3,500 and set up a Nebraska Relief and Aid Committee.

But the very next day the Chicago press ran a report from Omaha denying a famine crisis in Nebraska and claiming that T. H. Tibbles was a fraud. Soon some eighty local papers throughout Nebraska were repeating the story. Tibbles moved quickly to salvage his reputation and his crusade, providing the Chicago committee with documentary proof from the U.S. Army that the army quartermaster was handling the distribution of relief funds and supplies in the Republican Valley. The Chicago farmers aid committee stuck by Tibbles, as did another that was set up in Milwaukee after he visited there. The crusade and the fund-raising meetings continued. But stories that he was a con man who was pocketing the relief money followed him and would be revived after he took up the fight for the Poncas.

Finding that the bad press was discouraging famine relief donors, Tibbles hurried back to Nebraska and recruited another Protestant minister to the crusade, Reverend G. W. Frost. The pair then set off on a new fund-raising foray in the East. This second time around Tibbles also took along a written endorsement from Brigadier General Edward Ord, General

Crook's predecessor as commander of the U.S. Army Department of the Platte, a document confirming the plight of thousands of destitute Nebraska farmers. In Detroit, Buffalo, Utica, Troy, and finally New York City, Tibbles and his platform partner, Frost, spoke at public meeting after public meeting. Together they succeeded in raising $80,000 for the farmers in thirty days.

The Nebraska drought relief crusade taught Tibbles a lot, most importantly, the need to hope for the best while preparing for the worst when advocating a cause that had influential enemies. And at every step of the way he had to be seen as having nothing to gain personally from his efforts on behalf of those less fortunate than himself.

That Sunday morning in March 1879, walking the quiet streets of Omaha from the *Daily Herald* office to his nearby home in the golden light of the new day, Henry Tibbles was deep in thought about how he should approach this latest challenge.

Chapter 5

THE CHIEF'S INTERVIEW

AFTER CATCHING A couple of hours sleep, Henry Tibbles rose on the morning of Sunday, March 30, and quickly ate breakfast, gushing a distilled version of the story of the Poncas' plight to his devoutly Methodist English-born wife Amelia, who had soldiered through many a crusade at his side since their wedding in 1861. He then set off for Fort Omaha on foot, taking along his reporter's notebook and walking fast, with expectations of a fascinating day ahead. As he passed through Omaha, with the locals heading off to church all around him, he knew that Iron Eye and Bright Eyes were on their way back to the Omaha reservation.

At their secret early-morning meeting, General Crook had told Tibbles that he planned to conduct a formal interview with Standing Bear and his fellow Ponca chief, Buffalo Chip. Crook was under no obligation to do so, but Lieutenant Carpenter had promised the two Ponca chiefs an opportunity to speak with the general, and George Crook always kept his word, to Indians as well as everyone else. Because Sunday was officially a day of rest, the interview had to take place the next day, and the general set down 10:00 A.M. Monday as the time for the meeting. But Henry Tibbles couldn't wait until Monday. He went out to the fort on his one day off determined to see the Poncas' situation with his own eyes, hear their story from their own lips, and, most importantly, obtain verbatim quotes before he sat down at his desk at the *Omaha Daily Herald* to write the article that would launch a campaign on their behalf.

When Tibbles reached the fort after a brisk forty-five-minute walk, General Crook granted him access to the prisoners under detention in their three temporary lodges on the parade ground. Tibbles found most of the Poncas in their shelters, many suffering from the malarial fever they had contracted in the Indian Territory. In one shelter, he wrote, he came across a sick Ponca child moaning piteously. In another, a Ponca woman wailed "heart-breakingly" as if mourning for a dead loved one.[87] According to the commander of their guard, Lieutenant Carpenter, six members of the fugitive band were considered too ill to travel at the moment.[88]

Tibbles then located Standing Bear. The newspaper editor was a regular visitor to the Omaha reservation but had little if anything to do with the reclusive Poncas up in the Dakota Territory, and it's unclear whether he and Standing Bear had ever had dealings before. What he found was an imposing man of above-average height, with thick black shoulder-length hair parted in the middle, a square jaw, long, straight nose, large mouth, pronounced cheekbones, and sad dark eyes. His strong features were striking rather than handsome.

In the center of his forehead Standing Bear bore a round tattoo the size of a dime—the "honor mark." While the designs varied, most Poncas and Omahas of both sexes had similar small honor marks on their foreheads. There were exceptions. Bright Eyes, for example, did not carry an honor mark because her father Iron Eye had chosen not to tattoo any of his children so that they might assimilate more easily into white society. Two conflicting years are given for Standing Bear's birth, 1829 and 1834, meaning he was forty-five or fifty at this time.

To his disappointment, Tibbles found the chief unwilling to talk to him. Informed that General Crook would allow him to make a statement at a formal hearing next day, Standing Bear told Tibbles through an interpreter that he did not think it proper to grant the editor an interview for his newspaper prior to that. Determined to get the chief talking, Tibbles tried out some secret Soldier Lodge signs on him. When Standing Bear realized that Tibbles was a Soldier Lodge initiate, he immediately called a gathering of his little band. In one of the three temporary lodges, sitting cross-legged in a circle with the women and children seated behind them, listening to all that was said, the Ponca men smoked an Indian pipe that was shaped like a large tomahawk, passing it to Tibbles in turn, and talked long into the afternoon while the reporter made copious notes.

As translator, Tibbles used Charles P. Morgan, a full-blood Indian of the Iowa tribe who worked as a clerk for Agent Vore at the Omaha agency.[89] Morgan once served as official Indian Affairs interpreter at the Ponca Agency in the Dakota Territory, until Agent Lawrence replaced him with Charlie Le Claire. He was not considered the most accurate of translators and was in fact responsible for the faulty translation which Inspector Kemble had insisted gave him authority to move the Poncas to Indian Territory.[90] But Morgan was the only translator then available at Fort Omaha. He had been away from the reservation at the time of Standing Bear's arrest, apparently collecting supplies for Agent Vore in Omaha, and General Crook had asked him to stay on awhile to act as interpreter when he met with Standing Bear's band.

In deference to his seniority in age and his status as head of the Medicine clan, Standing Bear allowed Buffalo Chip to speak first. Using graceful gestures, the medicine man told Tibbles how the Poncas made the land their best friend, farming it to provide for their families. The land had never lied to them, he said; it had never made promises that it did not fulfill. The Poncas had learned to plow and sow the fields, had built houses of wood, had raised horses, cattle, pigs. Their families had always possessed good clothes and always had enough to eat. They were happy and healthy. Now all that had changed; Buffalo Chip and his people had been deprived of all they possessed. Now he was a prisoner. For what? He had done no wrong. If they went back to Indian Territory, he said, they would not be able to farm; they would fall sick and die. It would be better if the soldiers lined them all up and shot them, he said; better for them, better for the government.[91]

An awful silence fell over the gathering. Tibbles noticed that a Ponca woman sitting behind the circle of men was silently weeping as she rocked a baby in her arms. Beside the newspaperman, Morgan the interpreter turned to Tibbles and said, "This is awful. These men are my friends. They are of my blood."[92]

Buffalo Chip spoke a little longer, asking that Indians be allowed to farm their lands, be given tools to farm and laws to protect them. If that were to happen, he said, the Indian would "soon be like a white man."[93]

Then Standing Bear spoke slowly, deliberately, and at length, giving Tibbles a detailed history of all that had happened to the Poncas since the treaty of 1868 had taken their land from them, through the Sioux problems of 1875 and the subsequent trials of 1877, from the trip with Inspector Kemble to Indian Territory and the chiefs' walk home to the tribe's tragic forced march with Inspector Howard that had taken them to misery and death in the Indian Territory. Standing Bear spoke sadly of his promise to his dying son and pointed to a wooden trunk in the corner. It contained Bear Shield's remains, waiting to be interred among the bones of his ancestors on the Niobrara.

Now Standing Bear's wife, Susette, spoke up. Around Standing Bear's age, tall and thoughtful looking, she said, "My mother is buried there," referring to the Ponca burial grounds on the Niobrara, "my grandmother and another child. My boy was a good boy, and we tried to do what he wanted us to do." As tears chased one another in quick succession down her cheeks, she asked Tibbles to speak with General Crook and ask him: if the Poncas must go back to the Indian Territory, then to at least let them bury Bear Shield on the Niobrara before they went.

Tibbles promised to talk with General Crook. He couldn't tell her that Crook had come to him in confidence only hours before and, being in no position to help them officially, had asked Tibbles to help Standing Bear and his people.

As Susette continued to cry, she said apologetically, "My eyes are full of tears all the time. And ever since I came to this place there is an ache here." She put her hand over her heart. "If we must go back these little children will soon die too." She cast her hand around the infants in the shelter.[94]

No one spoke. A pall of gloom settled over the gathering. This was too much for Tibbles. Choked with emotion, he got up and went outside. After walking around the parade ground and composing himself, he returned to the council circle. Tibbles now entered into a long dialogue with Standing Bear, posing questions and discussing what Indians wanted for themselves. The sun was almost setting when Tibbles jammed his notebook into his pocket and said farewell to Standing Bear and his people and set off for town.

By this time he had worked out the tactics for his campaign on behalf of the Poncas. He and General Crook agreed that writing an editorial on behalf of the Poncas would not be enough. Tibbles had a newspaperman's instincts, and he knew that he had to make a news event out of the Poncas' plight. And he knew how to achieve that—he would recruit the soldiers of heaven to the cause. Universally known by the clergymen of Omaha for his dedicated pastoral work, Tibbles intended to make the rounds of the city's Protestant churches that evening while they were packed for their Sunday services and address their congregations.

He hoped to catch a ride back into Omaha with a passing carriage, but every vehicle that went by was going in the opposite direction. Afraid that he'd be too late to reach some of the churches before their services ended, he broke into a trot and ran the last two and a half miles into town. Starting with Reverend William Harsha, who had already shown support for the Ponca cause and whose Presbyterian Church maintained a church and school on the Omaha reservation, Tibbles made pleas to the ministers, who then let him make speeches to their congregations.

Tibbles claimed that he was no public speaker, but the intensity of his delivery and the urgency of his message combined to stir the righteous indignation of the God-fearing folk of Omaha. By the time he finished he'd wrung an agreement from the ministers of the city's Presbyterian, Baptist, Episcopalian, and Congregationalist churches that come Monday morning they would send a telegraph message to Interior Secretary Schurz in Washington begging him "to let the sick, weary Poncas stay on the Omaha reservation"[95] and to follow it up with a detailed letter.

At eleven o'clock that night Tibbles arrived back at his Omaha home, worn out and hungry but elated. Seventeen and a half years before, when Henry Tibbles had proposed to English girl Amelia Owen, she could never have imagined what sort of life they would lead as husband and wife. Whether she married with her parents' permission is unknown. But she was the granddaughter of a wealthy pottery factory owner in England, and a genteel, cultured life would have been expected for her. The young American minister she married was neither genteel nor cultured, and neither was the life Amelia led as Mrs. Henry Tibbles. With remarkable grace Amelia shared her husband's postwar career, from a primitive and precarious existence toting a gospel tent and their two infant daughters around wild frontier settlements in Tibbles's preaching days, to his night owl life as a newspaper editor. It was only when they settled in Omaha and Henry built a church and a parsonage that they had a house to call home, and even then it belonged to the church.

When Tibbles arrived home after his hectic day, Amelia served him a wholesome cooked supper, his first meal since breakfast, heard his excited account of the productive meeting with Standing Bear, then watched him start work on his Ponca material for the *Herald*, all apparently without a word of complaint. With his daughters Eda (11) and May (9) fast asleep, the crusader would have looked in on them and then sat down at the desk in his parlor and spread his pages and pages of shorthand notes in front of him.

By the time he had finished transcribing and organizing his notes and thought to look at his fob watch it was 5:20 in the morning, and the sun was up. Dragging himself to his bed, he fell into it. He was asleep as soon as his head hit the pillow.

➜ ⬅

For the second night in succession Henry Tibbles had managed to grab the bare minimum of sleep—little more than ninety minutes. Adrenaline was keeping him going. Rising at 7:00 A.M., he borrowed a carriage, and, with notebook at the ready, he was at General Crook's office by 10:00 A.M. Monday, when Standing Bear's interview was to take place. In the end, it was closer to noon by the time proceedings got under way; Tibbles would have been grateful for the additional two hours in bed.

The hearing before the general had no legal standing. This was not an appeal hearing in the legal sense. Considered wards of the state, Standing Bear and his Poncas had no legal rights of any kind. But to Crook there was no justice in that, just as there was no justice in Washington's determination to send Standing Bear and his people back to the alien land of the Indian Territory. Throughout the Standing Bear affair, George Crook was driven by a personal moral principle that had influenced his attitude to and dealings with native American peoples over the past several years. Three years later he put it into a standing order to the officers and men serving under him: "One of the fundamental principles of the military character is justice to all—Indians as well as white men."[96]

While he now strove to deliver a large measure of justice to the Poncas through his behind-the-scenes activity with Henry Tibbles, General Crook saw no justice in locking twenty-six Ponca men, women, and children in the unhealthy post guardhouse. Besides, he knew from experience that Indians did not cope well with close confinement. As his aide John Bourke later said, "The American Indian, born free as the eagle, would not tolerate restraint."[97] That was why Crook had condemned the guardhouse and allowed the Poncas to rig up shelters on the parade. He was also conscious of Indian sensitivities in another respect. The Indian system of justice permitted both the accused and all elders of a tribe to speak to an accusation. Crook was allowing the Ponca chief the courtesy of speaking for himself as would be the case in an Indian council.

The hearing took place in General Crook's office before the general and several of his officers, his ADC Lieutenant Bourke, Colonel William B. Royall, Assistant Adjutant General R. Williams, and Lieutenant Carpenter. Henry Tibbles was present in his capacity as a representative of the press with Crook's permission to report on what took place. Once the officers were assembled, Standing Bear, Buffalo Chip, and the six other men of the fugitive band were brought in, accompanied by Morgan the interpreter.

John Bourke noted in his diary that the long-haired Buffalo Chip and six of the others were dressed in shabby European shirts, jackets, and vests, with Indian leggings, and each wore a green Mexican blanket around his shoulders. But Standing Bear came in his official regalia, which included a buckskin smock that reached almost to the floor. Over this he wore a very wide belt of beads at the waist and a necklace of bear claws, both of which represented powerful medicine to Plains tribes. His long black hair hung in two braids, one at either side of his bronze face. He wore two eagle feathers in his hair. One was upright, another sloped down his shoulder.

To Standing Bear, his most important prop was the blanket of vivid red trimmed with blue stripes, which he wore around his shoulders. This was his council blanket, worn whenever he sat in council with fellow elders to discuss important business. To Standing Bear his red blanket was as important an official accoutrement as a wig was to an English judge or an academic gown to a graduating college student. According to Henry Tibbles, this garb was "the only proper attire whenever he was to speak officially for his people."[98]

Standing Bear and his companions squatted in a semicircle on the floor in front of General Crook's desk, with Standing Bear looking, in Henry Tibbles's words, calm yet sorrowful.[99] There was no need for a military guard; the prisoners had given the army no reason to suspect they would be troublesome. According to John Bourke, Lieutenant Carpenter, who had guarded the prisoners since their arrest, told him that Standing Bear and his people acted with "perfect sobriety and good behavior" throughout their time in custody.[100] In a later statement to the *Herald*, Carpenter commended the "civilized" demeanor of the Ponca band— men, women, and children.[101]

Across the floor from the Poncas, sitting on a chair with the gathered military officers, Henry Tibbles readied his notebook and pencil. Beside him, Lieutenant Bourke was also preparing to take notes for his diary.

Bourke was such a habitual note taker that the Apaches named him Paper Medicine Man during his service in Arizona under Crook. The Sioux had given him the name Ink Man.

General Crook began the proceedings by calling on Standing Bear to give an account in his own words of the removal of the Ponca tribe from its reservation in the Dakota Territory. Standing Bear slowly came to his feet and addressed the general personally, telling much the same sad Ponca story he had told Tibbles the previous day. He spoke in the halting Ponca tongue, pausing every so often for Morgan the interpreter to relate his words in English, then resuming. When he finished he resumed his position on the floor.

"It's a downright shame!" exclaimed an officer beside Henry Tibbles, probably Lieutenant Bourke.[102] Standing Bear then asked General Crook for permission to address the other officers, which Crook readily gave.

Again Standing Bear came to his feet, this time turning to face the officers and newspaperman. Addressing them as "my friends and brothers," Standing Bear told the officers that he wanted to go back to his old home in the north, he wanted to save himself and his tribe. He beseeched God to send a good spirit to guide the officers and move them to take pity on him and help him save the women and children. Finally he said, "My brothers, a power I cannot resist crowds me down to the ground. I need help." With that, Standing Bear resumed his seat, saying, "I have done," pulling his red blanket around his shoulders as if he had suddenly grown cold—a sign among his people that he had finished speaking. Once again he faced General Crook with a solemn face.

The general now invited Buffalo Chip to speak, and with Morgan again interpreting, he made a short speech that focused on the reasons why the fugitives should not be sent back to the Indian Territory, why they should be allowed to stay in the north and provide for their families through their farming.[103]

When Buffalo Chip finished, General Crook said to the officers, "I have heard all this story before. It's just as they say." He was referring to the detailed account given to him by Bright Eyes two days before. But to preserve her anonymity and that of her father in the behind-the-scenes activities on behalf of the Poncas he could not tell Royall, Williams, or Carpenter where he had heard it. Then, as if to cover his tracks, he added, "It has long since been reported to Washington."[104]

After *Daily Herald* readers encountered this latter comment in Henry Tibbles's subsequent newspaper account of the interview, many expressed surprise to Tibbles that officials in Washington could know of the mistreatment of the Poncas and still decline to help them.

The general then turned to Standing Bear and through the interpreter told him, "It is a very bad case, but I can do nothing myself. I have received an order from Washington and I must obey it."[105]

One of the senior officers, Royall or Williams, leaned forward and whispered to Tibbles, "Such orders as these always come through the influence of civilians." He was referring to the Interior secretary. "The Army is in no way responsible for this."[106]

"They have all the facts in Washington," General Crook said again, "and it would do no good for me to intercede." Of course, he had already interceded covertly. This comment was for public consumption or, more precisely, for his superiors in Chicago and Washington. "I might send a telegram, but it is likely to do more harm than good." Looking over to Lieutenant Carpenter, he announced that the Poncas could stay a few more days at the fort to allow their horses to gain strength.[107]

Standing Bear now asked if he could speak one more time, and the general told him to go right ahead. Again the chief came to his feet. He told Crook that he knew the general had an order to send him and his people back to Indian Territory, and Standing Bear acknowledged that it must be obeyed. He asked just one thing. As he had lost all his property over the past several years, he asked that the Great Father provide money for provisions for the journey, and money to pay for the burial of members of the band who must surely die on the way back down to Indian Territory.

The general replied that all the army could do was provide rations to the Poncas for the trip south. "It is a very disagreeable duty to send you down there," he said, coming to his feet, "but I must obey orders."[108]

While this very interview was part of a ploy to keep the Poncas from being sent back to Indian Territory, he must be seen to be playing this whole affair by the book. And a soldier always obeys orders.

General Crook then adjourned proceedings and ordered Lieutenant Carpenter to return his prisoners to their quarters. The Poncas came to their feet and trooped out. The officers returned to duty. The interpreter returned to the Omaha reservation. And Henry Tibbles hurried back to Omaha to finalize his story for next day's edition.

→ ←

Back in his *Herald* office by 3:00 P.M., Henry Tibbles sat down to write an extended news article about the Standing Bear case. The end product would dominate several pages of the paper. His article reported, word for word, much of Standing Bear's and Buffalo Chip's interviews with General Crook, Tibbles's interview with the pair the previous day, and a supporting interview with interpreter Charles Morgan. It finished with the text of the telegram sent by Omaha church leaders that day petitioning Interior secretary Schurz on behalf of Standing Bear and his band.

As the Ponca text headed for the print shop and Tibbles turned to his normal editorial work for the day, the latest in communications technology was employed to send the news story throughout the United States: the telegraph transmitted the story to newspapers in cities nationwide. There was a technical term for a multiple telegraph transmission—a message was sent out "broadcast." It was a term that would later be appropriated by the radio industry and then the television industry. Henry Tibbles would live to experience one but not the other.

Tibbles's labors meant that he didn't arrive home until close to 3:30 A.M., totally exhausted. Amelia awoke as he lay down beside her in their bed. Telling her that the Ponca story had gone out to the eastern papers, he remarked that this latest campaign, with just his pen for a weapon, required as much physical endurance as his youthful adventures as an abolitionist, when his weapons had been a gun and a sword. Amelia consoled him with the reminder that as taxing as his work to free the Poncas was, "the whole country would know about it in the morning."[109] He knew she was right. As he closed his eyes, a glow of contentment settled over him. He knew that he had written a story too good for other editors to ignore. He knew that he had set the fire. The question was, How would it be received by a nation bent on westward expansion at the expense of the Indian peoples? Would the fire rage or would it flicker and then die?

→ *Chapter 6* ←

THE FIRE IS LIT

O N APRIL FOOL'S Day 1879, the small army of newsboys ranging the streets of Omaha with the new day's edition of the *Omaha
Daily Herald* were touting sales with lines like "Criminal Cruelty—The
History of the Ponca prisoners now at the barracks," and "A tale of cruelty
that was never surpassed—read all about it!"[110]

The newspaper sellers were soon doing a roaring trade, with the edition
being snapped up by an intrigued populace. Soon all of Omaha was reading T. H. Tibbles's Standing Bear news story. As Tibbles had anticipated,
that same Tuesday, as Nebraskans were reading his material in the *Herald,*
the Standing Bear story broke around the entire country. The vast majority of the editors who had received the story by Tibbles ran it, adding their
own editorial comments.

Throughout the day, those press articles came ticking into the Omaha
telegraph office, and the transcribed messages were piling up at the *Daily
Herald.* The first in were from the *Chicago Tribune* and *Missouri Republican.* Both were for the Poncas "and denounced the cruelties practiced
upon them."[111] New York papers soon followed—the *Herald,* the *Tribune,*
and the *Daily Sun*—in what became a tide of national coverage over the
next few days. Tibbles and his staff devoured each new report with growing elation. Some editorial writers were negative, but as Tibbles was able
to report to General Crook and the church leaders of Omaha, "Newspapers everywhere came out strongly pro-Indian."[112]

Tibbles waited expectantly throughout the day to hear that the newspaper coverage had spurred a positive response from Secretary Schurz in Washington. By day's end, to his disappointment, the churchmen all advised that no reply had been received from the secretary of the Interior. That night, while fulfilling his double duties as acting editor and chief subeditor of the *Herald*, he plotted his next move in the Standing Bear affair. Henry Tibbles the crusader had only begun to fight.

Tibbles's nocturnal fourth estate lifestyle meant that six days a week it was his habit to sleep until noon, before starting work at 1:00 P.M. for a fifteen-hour shift at the *Herald*. To give himself the time to devote to the Standing Bear case, he decided that he would get by on a few hours sleep a night until the case was won. It seems that during the morning of April 2 he went out to Fort Omaha to consult with General Crook, and he and the general agreed that if pressure from the clergy had no effect on Carl Schurz, then they had to find another way to prevent the secretary from having Standing Bear and his Poncas deported back to Indian Territory. Crook remarked that a white man in Standing Bear's situation could have the legality of his arrest tested before a judge.[113] Surely there had to be a legal remedy to Standing Bear's problem, even though he was an Indian. Both men agreed that what they needed first and foremost was a good lawyer to advise them and, preferably, represent Standing Bear and his Poncas.

Omaha had plenty of attorneys who were looking for new business—R. R. Gaylord, John D. Howe, McBride and Bevins, T. W. T. Richards, John M. Macfarland, and Warren Switzer among them.[114] But none wanted the Poncas for clients. For fear of offending the legal fraternity of Omaha, Tibbles didn't write in detail about how every lawyer he approached in the city turned him down when he sought representation for Standing Bear and his people. The typical excuse from these lawyers would have been that they could not afford to act for the Poncas without a fee. But there was a more potent reason. As Tibbles had told George Crook when he first approached him, anyone who took the side of an Indian and thus took on the government could be marking himself for disfavor, discrimination, and perhaps even destruction.

It must have seemed to Henry Tibbles that no lawyer in Omaha had his scruples or his courage. There was also the fact that the Ponca cause seemed doomed to failure. As more than one attorney would have politely but firmly reminded Tibbles, the Poncas were Indians and as such had no rights under the law; and they would have told him that in their opinion the Poncas legally couldn't even hire a lawyer, no matter how just their cause might be, without BIA approval.

As days passed with no response from Washington and with law office doors hitting him on the way out, Tibbles became even more determined. If no lawyer would offer him a solution, he would find it himself! He began spending his mornings in the Omaha Public Library, poring over law books. Far from enlightening him, the legal jargon only clogged his mind. The problem seemed insoluble.

There was a lawyer in the town who had all the qualifications to handle the case on behalf of the Poncas. And Tibbles had an entrée to him—both had gone to Mount Union College in Ohio, although Tibbles had left by the time the lawyer began attending. A prominent member of the Omaha Episcopal Church congregation, the Honorable John Lee Webster was a former politician and constitutional lawyer. Webster had practiced law in his hometown of New Philadelphia, Pennsylvania, for a year after graduating from law school at the top of his class. He had come west more than a decade ago during Nebraska's frontier days seeking to make a legal career but found himself attracted to the opportunities offered by territorial politics. After a stint as mayor of Omaha he served in the Nebraska legislature. Four years back he had been president of the Nebraska Constitutional Convention of 1875, which formulated the new state's constitution. Tibbles considered Webster "a man whose opinions commanded respect in the courts and outside."[115] But Webster had a large practice[116] and wasn't looking for new clients.[117] Would this prominent, expensive attorney even give Tibbles a hearing? There was only one way to find out.

→ *Chapter 7* ←

THE LAWYERS

O N WEDNESDAY EVENING in that first week in April, the day after the Ponca story hit the Omaha streets in his paper, Henry Tibbles paid lawyer John L. Webster a visit at his Omaha home. The round-faced Webster was in his thirties. He sported a neat handlebar mustache and combed his hair over on top to hide his spreading baldness. Like just about everyone else in Omaha, he would have read the previous day's *Herald*, so he could guess why Tibbles had come calling. Offering Tibbles a seat, he asked what was on the editor's mind.

Tibbles proceeded to tell him the complete Standing Bear story. He "laid the case before him," backing up his verbal presentation with documentary evidence, as was his habit.[118] Tibbles later wrote that Bright Eyes bombarded him throughout April with almost daily letters from the Omaha reservation containing information about the case. Some information she already possessed, some she diligently gathered from people on her reservation and from letters she received from her Ponca kin stranded down in the Indian Territory. Tibbles would have had the first of those letters in hand at the time of his meeting with Webster. This information from Bright Eyes would have included statements she gathered from members of the Omaha and Ponca tribes relating to the appalling treatment dealt out to the Poncas by government representatives. First and foremost among these statements would have been one from her father Iron Eye, chief of the Omahas, a statement formalizing his offer to make a home on the Omaha reservation for Standing Bear and his fugitive band.

Bright Eyes would also have committed a statement of her own to paper and sent it down to Tibbles with the others. Among the matters to which she could personally testify was the innocent character of Prairie Flower, Standing Bear's daughter, who had died on the forced march of 1877. Prairie Flower had been around Bright Eyes's age when she died. Bright Eyes described her as "my girl companion," and the two evidently grew up together and were close.[119]

When he finished his presentation, Tibbles eagerly asked Webster if he would represent the Poncas—and without a fee at that. Webster would have sighed deeply. The matter of a fee was neither here nor there to him. He was genuinely moved by the Poncas' story. But as he would have pointed out to Tibbles, this was a case without precedent, and, on the face of it, a case without any hope of success because Standing Bear was an Indian and therefore in the eyes of the law a ward of the state. And wards of the state could not enter into contracts or be represented in a U.S. court of law.

Naturally Tibbles was disappointed by this response, assuming that Webster was as spineless as the rest of the local legal fraternity, but as he rose to leave, Webster told him to hold his horses. He asked the newspaperman to give him a night to consider the Standing Bear case. He would, he said, take "the matter under advisement" and suggested that Tibbles call back to see him next morning.[120] It's also likely that Webster, being a constitutional lawyer, suggested that in the meantime Tibbles go back to his law books and take a look at the Fourteenth Amendment. Tibbles later took credit for employing the Fourteenth Amendment in the Standing Bear case, but it is more probable that Webster, whom Tibbles described as brilliant, recognized its potential and directed the newspaperman's attention to it.[121]

With his hopes raised for the first time since he embarked on the Ponca crusade, Tibbles left for his office. There, on a high shelf, he located a copy of the Constitution, opened it toward the end, and ran his finger down the page until he came to Article 14, the so-called reconstruction amendment, and read section 1.

> All persons born or naturalized in the United States, and subject to the jurisdiction thereof, are citizens of the United States and of the State wherein they reside. No State shall make or enforce any law which shall abridge the privileges or immunities of citizens of the United States, nor shall any State deprive any person of life, liberty, or property without due process of law, nor deny to any person within its jurisdiction the equal protection of the laws.

It is likely that even after reading it, Tibbles was unclear about how John Webster proposed to apply the Fourteenth Amendment to the Standing Bear case. The amendment spoke of "citizens," yet Indians were not citizens of the United States and had no rights as far as U.S. law was concerned. Section 2 expressly excluded non–tax paying Indians from the calculation of population size in the allocation of seats in the House of Representatives. And the number of Indians who had assimilated into white society and paid tax, like Ely Parker, a Seneca chief who had become President Grant's commissioner of Indian Affairs, was miniscule. It was probably a confused Thomas Henry Tibbles who returned to John Webster's house the next day.

Webster now informed a delighted Tibbles that after considering the facts, he was convinced that the Standing Bear case was a matter concerning "the natural rights of men." The attorney went on, "You have raised a constitutional question of vast importance," adding, "The principles to which you are appealing underlie all personal liberty."[122] Despite this, Webster had his doubts about how successful the proposed case might be. "I am not satisfied that a writ would hold, on account of the peculiar relation of Indians to the Government."[123]

Tibbles's heart must have sunk. Webster loved history and music. He had an encyclopedic mind and no detail escaped him, but he was not a magician. Tibbles would have given him credit for being pragmatic enough to know when not to flog a dead horse.

But then Webster said, "It seems to me there ought to be a power somewhere to stop this inhuman cruelty. And if it doesn't reside in the courts, where shall we find it?" He would have smiled and leaned forward as he went on, "Mr. Tibbles, my services are at your disposal. But on account of the magnitude of the questions involved I would like to have assistance."[124] Webster firmly believed that an advocate would need the ability to charm a bird from a bough in order to convince a judge of the applicability of the Fourteenth Amendment argument and set a legal precedent. "If the Honorable A. J. Poppleton will assist me, I will go right ahead and draw up the papers."[125]

Tibbles's eyes must have popped out of his head on hearing this. Andrew Jackson Poppleton was an institution in Nebraska. Tibbles knew that "he was considered without a peer in the legal profession in the state" and that he had an awesome reputation as a public speaker and debater.[126]

With a note from Webster to Poppleton explaining the case and how Webster proposed to approach it, Tibbles hurried away to track down the second lawyer, thinking of the pros and cons of Poppleton agreeing to take on the case as Webster's courtroom partner. The pros were many. In his youth, Poppleton left Michigan to find fame and fortune in gold-rich California. In 1854 he came to Omaha and discovered a new town with opportunities for a twenty-four-year-old attorney. There he terminated his journey and set up as Omaha's first lawyer. In an era when cardsharps and frontiersmen walked the city's streets alongside immigrants and fortune hunters, he struck gold of a different kind. He was soon elected to the Nebraska legislature as a Democrat, serving as Speaker for a time, and became Omaha's second mayor, all before he was thirty. First president of the Nebraska Bar Association, president of the Omaha Board of Trade, major shareholder of a bank, director of the Omaha Public Library, where Tibbles had been spending so much time lately, and now, at age forty-eight, chief attorney for the Union Pacific Railroad, A. J. Poppleton was wealthy and influential, a man to be reckoned with in this part of the world.

Described as "a most eloquent and fascinating speaker," Poppleton was a passionate debater in his political heyday, with the ability to make things warm for his opponents.[127] He developed the ability to catch the Speaker's eye and always be recognized first during debates in the legislature. When it came to advocating a cause, Andrew J. Poppleton displayed all the oratorical skills and all the tricks to win the day. But there was one problem, which caused Tibbles to doubt whether Poppleton had what it took to win over a judge in what was shaping up as one of the most famous cases in U.S. legal history—Poppleton hadn't appeared in court for a private client since beginning work for the Union Pacific sixteen years before, in 1863.

With its headquarters in Omaha, the Union Pacific Railroad was a catalyst for the city's spectacular growth and was one of the region's major employers. Because he knew Poppleton as a commercial lawyer, Tibbles probably did not think of approaching him. But, as Webster would have pointed out, Tibbles's fellow Episcopalian and Webster's colleague was accredited to the Omaha bar and could appear in court on behalf of litigants.

Poppleton's offices were then located in Hearndon House. A four-story brick building on the corner of Omaha's 9th and Farnam Streets, it opened in 1857 as the Hearndon House Hotel and was promoted as the most luxurious hotel west of Chicago. With the philosophy that a grand enterprise deserved a grand edifice, the Union Pacific Railroad took over the hotel and turned it into its head office several years later.

Poppleton's staff informed Tibbles that Poppleton had just returned from attending to Union Pacific legal business in St. Louis and was too busy to see him. Painfully aware that every minute was crucial in this affair, let alone every day, Tibbles stressed the urgent nature of his business and implored Poppleton's people to place the note from John Webster before their boss at once, along with the written material about the Standing

Bear case that he turned over to them. He left only after promising to return first thing next morning for an answer.

Tibbles then put in his usual fifteen hours labor at the *Herald* that
Thursday afternoon and evening. After four hours of sleep, he appeared,
bleary-eyed, at Poppleton's rooms on Friday, April 4, and was relieved to
be ushered straight into the great man's office.

The Webster connection did the trick. Despite their different political leanings—while Poppleton was a Democrat through and through,
Webster was a Republican—the two men liked and respected each
other. There in Andrew Poppleton's plush Hearndon House office, sitting on a soft leather chair before a grand marble fireplace, Tibbles put
the case for Standing Bear, appealing to Poppleton's creed that all men
were equal in the eyes of God. A solidly built man with a shiny bald
head, a full beard, and a pronounced paunch, Poppleton sat with as-
sessing eyes, taking it all in.

As Tibbles gushed his tale, he referred to his editorials and newspaper
articles on behalf of Standing Bear and the Poncas, and he would have
produced Bright Eyes's statements. Tibbles later wrote that he also made
a point of telling Poppleton of General Crook's covert but supportive part
in the enterprise.[128]

The most telling moment must have come when Tibbles raised Webster's suggestion of basing an argument on Standing Bear's behalf around
the Fourteenth Amendment. No general in his right mind goes into battle
without ammunition, and here was the ammunition the Standing Bear
case needed. As Webster would have told Tibbles, the Fourteenth Amendment, then only eleven years old, had rarely been tested in court.

The pitiable plight of the Poncas and the opportunity to test the U.S.
Constitution in court combined to win Poppleton's interest. "I believe you
have a good case," Poppleton told Tibbles. "I think we can make the writ
hold." He agreed with Webster that the ward of the state issue had to be
overcome, but on principle he felt that it should be contested. "A ward
cannot make a contract, but it doesn't follow that from that the guardian
[in this case the U.S. government] can imprison, starve or practice inhu-

man cruelty upon the ward." He held out his hand to the editor. "I will undertake this case, and you can inform Mr. Webster that I will give it my close attention and my best efforts." And, he added, like Webster, he would appear for the Poncas without a fee.[129]

Tibbles gratefully, triumphantly shook Poppleton's hand on it. Now Standing Bear had a legal team. And a potentially formidable legal team at that. Webster would have to do all the preliminary work; the bulk of Poppleton's time was committed to his railroad employer. As Poppleton began to think about dusting off his courtroom skills, Tibbles hurried back to see John Webster.

Much now needed to be done in a short time. Webster, thrilled that Poppleton was on board, brought out the petition he had drafted overnight, and together he and Tibbles took a carriage out to Fort Omaha to visit General Crook. The general saw them at once. Webster advised Crook of the course he proposed to follow—he and Poppleton would apply to a judge to issue a writ of habeas corpus against General Crook, as the commander of the military district ordered by Washington to arrest Standing Bear. The writ would require the general to appear before a district court judge and show cause why the Ponca chief and his companions should not be released and allowed to go free.

The issuing of a writ of habeas corpus was an ancient legal process inherited from Great Britain. As a basic tenet of British law, habeas corpus had been in force in North America during British colonial days and was retained by American lawmakers after the United States achieved its independence. In full it was *habeas corpus ad subjiciendum*, a question in Latin: Have you the body to answer? Directed at a person detaining another, it commanded him to produce the body of the prisoner before a judge or court and to submit to whatever that judge or court might decree.

The intent of habeas corpus was to prevent a person from being imprisoned indefinitely without being charged. In practice, it required a law officer to either charge a prisoner with a crime or immediately set him free. Poppleton and Webster were convinced that Standing Bear and his tribespeople had committed no crime and had to be released. The secretary of the Interior was clearly of the opinion that these Poncas had committed a crime by leaving the reservation in Indian Territory without the government's permission and by entering the Omaha reservation without the government's permission, making their arrest lawful.

There was also the question of whether Indians could litigate in a U.S. court of law. Webster, the constitutional expert, had discovered an answer to that, unearthing an 1870 report by the Senate Judiciary Committee which deemed that the Fourteenth Amendment of the Constitution did apply to Indians who had dissolved their relationship with their tribes. As General Crook was informed by Webster, for the purposes of a habeas corpus petition, Webster and Poppleton would contend that in leaving the bulk of the tribe at the Indian Territory reservation and traveling to the Omaha reservation and commencing to farm there, Standing Bear and his companions had severed relations with the Ponca tribe and were therefore entitled to the protection of the law under the provisions of the Fourteenth Amendment.

For these reasons the two lawyers felt that, given their day in court before an impartial judge, they could successfully argue for the issuing of a writ of habeas corpus for Standing Bear and his fellow applicants and force the government to release them.

But how would George Crook react to this? The lawyers were proposing that the general take the part of the bad guy. If he agreed to cooperate, he would be hauled into court by Standing Bear, who would demand his freedom before a judge on the basis that Crook had no legal right to arrest him in the first place or to continue to detain him. The attorneys didn't know the imposing, stern-faced general very well, and they must have worried how he would react to their proposal. After all, how many generals would agree to become a willing accomplice in their own trial in a federal court, for the sake of a bunch of Indians? As John Bourke wrote, those who were not well acquainted with General Crook found him "aloof, stern, even gloomy."[130]

If they had known him better, Poppleton and Webster would have known that George Crook was totally without ego. A man of honor, he could be counted on to do the right thing, no matter how his actions painted him. Those close to him, such as his aide John Bourke, knew that under the taciturn exterior he was "sunny and genial."[131] They also knew that he was not afraid to do the unexpected. As he had proven with his initial approach to Tibbles on Standing Bear's behalf, George Crook did things that other men would not even dream of doing.

Crook listened to the strategy that Webster proposed with the expressionless face of an expert poker player, which he happened to be. His officers often found his ability to listen patiently without a flicker of emotion or a word of comment disconcerting. But as he appreciated both the implications and the potential of the plan, Crook's blue eyes began to sparkle, and finally a smile tugged at the corners of his mouth. The idea tickled Crook enormously. He urged Webster to proceed on the proposed course—the attorneys must take him to court, and without delay.

A potential flaw in the strategy, as Webster and Poppleton well knew, was the matter of finding a friendly judge who would agree to issue the writ. The Standing Bear habeas corpus writ would be the first of its kind issued in the name of an American Indian, and not every judge would have the initiative or the courage to set a precedent by taking the case on. In fact, most judges could be counted on to steer away from precedent or controversy. The consensus among the quartet was that their ideal candidate, in fact their only realistic candidate, would be Judge Elmer S. Dundy. Both Crook and Tibbles knew the judge well. Dundy was an avid woodsman and Tibbles counted him among his friends, having hunted and fished with him on a number of occasions. Crook had also hunted with him. To Tibbles's mind, no judge was more learned or more liberal minded. The others agreed: Elmer S. Dundy it must be.

While Tibbles remained at the fort, Webster rushed back into Omaha and sent a telegram to Judge Dundy's chambers at Lincoln, the state capital, to determine the earliest possible time that he and Poppleton could appear before the judge to present the petition on behalf of Standing Bear and his band. At the same time, he sent an Omaha notary public, Homer Stull, galloping out to the fort with the final draft of the petition, which was in the name of Standing Bear and the twenty-five Poncas under arrest with him, including the women and children.

Tibbles had in the meantime explained to a stunned Standing Bear and his followers that the two white lawyers had taken their case. When Stull arrived with the petition, Tibbles had it read to them and then had Standing Bear and the seven other men of his band sign it with their marks. Tibbles and Lieutenant Carpenter, commander of the Poncas' guard detail, then signed the document as witnesses.

When Tibbles arrived back in town with the signed petition, he found Webster looking worried. Judge Dundy's clerk had wired back from Lincoln to say that the judge had set off into the wilds on a bear hunt, and no one was sure when he would be back. Webster had sent a series of telegrams to various towns along the judge's possible route hoping to track him down, but for good measure Tibbles arranged for several mounted men to go off in search of the bear-hunting judge.

Two days passed over the weekend without word of Dundy. Tibbles later said that General Crook, who was dreading the momentary arrival of orders from Washington to remove the Poncas to Indian Territory, "was the most anxious person I ever saw to have a writ served on him."[132]

To the relief of Crook and his colleagues Judge Dundy returned to civilization on Sunday night, having been located by one of Tibbles's messengers. From his Lincoln residence the judge sent word he would hear Standing Bear's habeas corpus petition during a session of the district court at Lincoln the following Tuesday.

Another anxious thirty-six hours lay ahead—enough time for Washington to order General Crook to remove the Standing Bear party to Indian Territory, an order that Crook could not and would not disobey. All it would take was a telegram clicking down the line from the War Department via General Sheridan's headquarters in Chicago. And that would be the end of the matter.

Chapter 8

THE JUDGE

.

JUDGE ELMER SCIPIO Dundy's middle name came from Scipio Africanus, the Roman general who defeated Carthaginian general Hannibal to end the Second Punic War in the third century B.C. It suited him admirably—Judge Dundy was similarly unafraid of taking on formidable odds if he thought the cause was just.

Physically, the forty-nine-year-old Dundy was a trim, slight figure. Almost completely bald, he had a closely trimmed gray mustache and beard, high cheekbones, a sloping brow, and small but intense eyes. Initially a lawyer and subsequently a member of the Nebraska territorial legislature for two terms, Dundy became Nebraska's first district court judge when it gained statehood in 1867. He'd been a territorial and then a federal judge for the past fifteen years. Dundy had a crusty, austere manner and was a little self-important and patronizing (as some judges can be) and had the habit of using the royal "we" when on the bench. He scared the daylights out of some people, none the least being his seventeen-year-old son, Elmer Scipio Dundy Jr. (or Skip), who had grown up with a severe nervous stutter.

Judge Dundy had four main interests in life—good hunting, good horses, good literature, and the administration of justice. But hunting was his passion. He counted among his colorful friends and hunting partners the legendary Buffalo Bill Cody. The chief scout for the 5th Cavalry, Cody gained his nickname as a buffalo hunter for the Kansas Pacific Railroad by delivering 4,280 dead bison in eight months to feed the railroad construction workers. He was made famous by dime novelists Ned Buntline and Prentiss Ingraham, and for the past seven years had been appearing in hugely successful (if largely fictional) stage plays about his adventures written by Buntline.

When Buffalo Bill came to dinner at Dundy's Lincoln home, young Skip Dundy would listen wide-eyed to his tales of adventure and his musings about the commercial possibilities of a Wild West troupe that would tour the entire country. Four years later, Cody launched his Buffalo Bill's Wild West and Congress of Rough Riders of the World, and the Wild West show was born. Young Skip Dundy eventually also became a showman. With a partner, Frederick Thompson, he developed Coney Island's Luna Park and Manhattan's Hippodrome Theater.

On Monday, April 7, 1879, Judge Dundy would have had the pending petition from Omaha attorneys John L. Webster and Andrew J. Poppleton on his mind. Dundy was aware of the nature of the submission that Webster and Poppleton intended making to him, and it's likely that he had already decided his attitude to their petition. That same Monday, Webster and Poppleton took the train down to Lincoln prior to presenting their petition to the judge on behalf of Standing Bear and their other Ponca clients the next day.

The following morning, Judge Dundy presided over the district court session in the state capital. There, on April 8, attorneys Poppleton and Webster presented the detailed written petition prepared by Webster on behalf of their twenty-six clients and signed by the eight men of Standing Bear's party. Once the clerk verified the petition and the judge read it, Dundy issued the writ of habeas corpus on behalf of Standing Bear and the other members of the Ponca tribe in custody with him—who, in legal jargon, were now considered his "co-relators." Now the fox was set among the chickens.

A relieved General Crook was served with the writ later that same day, as Webster and Poppleton returned to Omaha. The serving of the writ effectively blocked any further action by the secretary of the Interior, directly or through the War Department, until the district court either validated or dismissed the habeas corpus action. General Crook was restrained from acting on any further orders from Washington regarding the Poncas until the writ had been confirmed or dismissed. It would have been with disguised pleasure that Crook promptly advised General Sheridan in Chicago that he had been served with the writ.

The shocked, outraged reaction in official Washington circles can only be imagined. Secretary Schurz had previously ignored pleas on behalf of the Poncas from the clergy of Omaha and a subsequent pro-Ponca petition from the people of Niobrara and the leading citizens of Yankton. He had agreed to a meeting to discuss the Poncas with a former employee of the Bureau of Indian Affairs, Alfred B. Meacham, the friend of Reverend Dorsey to whom Dorsey had written on behalf of the Poncas. The Washington-based Meacham was also editor of *The Council Fire*, a monthly journal on the subject of the American Indian. Meacham reported back to Dorsey that in their meeting, held in early April, Schurz expressed sympathy for the Poncas but declared that his hands were tied in the matter. Commissioner Hayt was at the same meeting and did most of the talking, telling Meacham that "there was no use talking about the Poncas going North" and insisting that Standing Bear and his fellow escapees must return to Indian Territory.[133] The reason that Schurz and Hayt had discussed the Poncas with Meacham when they didn't even acknowledge other approaches on their behalf would soon become apparent—before long *The Council Fire* would support the government line on the Poncas.

The unprecedented legal maneuver and the issuing of a writ on behalf of Standing Bear by a district court judge would have seemed laughable to Hayt and Schurz had it not seriously challenged their Indian policy. And they didn't intend to let that challenge stand.

Given ten days to answer the writ of April 8, the government acted quickly. On April 10, the Associated Press reported out of Washington: "The United States district attorney has been directed to appear for the United States and endeavor to have the writ dismissed. [The commissioner of Indian Affairs] takes the ground that under the law, and according to repeated decisions of the Supreme Court, the Indians stand as wards of the government, and are under the same relations to the government as minors to their parents or guardians." In a pointed comment aimed at Judge Dundy, castigating him for even entertaining the petition by Webster and Poppleton, Commissioner Hayt had told the Associated Press, "No attorney has the right or can appear for an Indian, until authorized to do so by the Indian Department."

Also on April 10, Commissioner Hayt released to the press copies of a long letter he had sent Secretary Schurz relating to the Ponca case. In that letter, reproduced in part or in full by many newspapers across the country, Hayt firmly stated the government's position—that the Poncas had been lawfully moved from their old reservation to Indian Territory as required by Congress, and there were no legal grounds for their return to Dakota Territory. According to Hayt, any blame for the Poncas' situation had to be laid at the feet of the Ulysses S. Grant administration and Congress. His department, he said, had merely followed orders.[134]

Referring to the Poncas' relocation place, he noted that he had visited the Poncas in the Indian Territory the previous October, and "there is probably no finer location for an Indian settlement in the Indian Territory, and in all respects it is far superior to their old location in Dakota, from which, in previous years, they had themselves asked the department to remove them."[135] The latter reference was to the Poncas' request in 1876 to be relocated to the Omaha reservation to escape Sioux attacks. Hayt knew that the Poncas hadn't asked to be removed to the Indian Territory, a place they had never even heard of in 1876. But, like his inspector Edward Kemble, he was happy to misconstrue that request to suit his purposes.

Judge Dundy would have read that letter in the press, together with the Associated Press article containing Hayt's barbed comment aimed specifically at him. As he became further acquainted with the Ponca case through the month of April, he would have appreciated that Hayt had emphatically drawn a line in the sand, signaling the Interior Department's intended tactics in and out of court. In his letter to Schurz, Hayt said, "If the reservation system is to be maintained, discontented and restless or mischievous Indians cannot be permitted to leave their reservations at will and go where they please."[136] The Interior Department, or more specifically Carl Schurz and his underling Hayt, feared that if they acceded to the request of one insignificant Indian tribe for a return to its original homeland, even if that request had a legitimate basis, all the relocated tribes would clamor for the same treatment. But it was not Judge Dundy's task to consider other tribes. He could only and would only consider the case that was brought before him, the case of Standing Bear and his Poncas.

While the Indian commissioner was conducting his publicity campaign, the district attorney's office in Lincoln, acting on behalf of General Crook and the U.S. government, worked quickly to counter the petition for the writ of habeas corpus, sending General Crook a detailed return of writ that set out the general's authority to arrest the Ponca band. On April 11, Crook swore before a notary public that the return was true and correct and forwarded it to the DA's office together with copies of all orders received and issued by him in relation to the arrest of the Poncas. The DA subsequently lodged the return with the clerk of the district court by the due date.

Judge Dundy then required all parties to appear before him in the U.S. district court in Omaha on Wednesday, April 30, to present legal argument for and against the execution of the writ. If the judge found that Standing Bear and his people had been arrested contrary to federal law, he would order the prisoners released. If, on the other hand, the judge was convinced that the original arrest had been legal, then he would dismiss the writ and the government would be free to remove the prisoners to Indian Territory as Secretary Schurz had requested.

The battle lines had been drawn. Now the fate of the Standing Bear case was in the hands of the legal combatants.

→ *Chapter 9* ←

THE DISTRICT ATTORNEY

I N T H E L A S T days of April, Genio Madison Lambertson, U.S. attorney for the district of Nebraska, came up from Lincoln, where he was based, to represent General Crook and the government of the United States in district court and contest the writ issued on behalf of Standing Bear and his band.

The Indiana-born Lambertson had settled in Lincoln in the summer of 1874 with a new law degree and high hopes for a successful legal career, starting with a local law firm that soon made him a partner. Ambitious and energetic, he left Lamb, Billingsby & Lambertson in December 1878 to become district attorney. When he arrived in Omaha to discuss the Standing Bear case with General Crook in late April 1879, he was several weeks short of his twenty-ninth birthday and had been DA for just five months. This was his biggest case to date.

Lambertson would have previously corresponded with General Crook about the case, but now he traveled to Fort Omaha to formally interview the general, verify the facts of the case as he understood them, and inform Crook of how he intended to approach the hearing in court. The intelligent, determined, self-confident young district attorney (who was nonetheless so self-conscious about his unusual first name that he signed and introduced himself as G. M. Lambertson) was as certain as a man could be of having the writ thrown out. With no case like it in the annals of U.S. legal history, and with the seemingly indisputable fact that Indians had no rights under U.S. law, Lambertson would have assured General

Crook when they met in his Fort Omaha office that the case was laughable and the general had nothing to worry about.

Lambertson was of the view, as was the government he represented, that Judge Dundy had been wrong in law to issue the writ on behalf of an Indian. Once the district attorney presented his argument to that effect, the court would have to find in the general's favor and dismiss the writ. With the writ thrown out, Lambertson would have told Crook, the general could move Standing Bear and his Poncas back to Indian Territory without any further hindrance.

Little did twenty-eight-year-old Lambertson know that the blank-faced brigadier general sitting across the desk from him in civilian clothes not only had actively encouraged the other side to take him to court but wanted to lose the case. But Crook was not about to let Lambertson in on the secret.

Lieutenant John G. Bourke would have escorted the district attorney from General Crook's office once the interview ended. Bourke later wrote that on one occasion he overheard Sioux war chief Crazy Horse, considered by many the cleverest Indian tactician of the nineteenth century, pay General Crook a remarkable compliment. "He [Crazy Horse] had a great admiration for Crook, and the feeling was reciprocated. Once he said of Crook that he was more to be feared by the Sioux than all other white men."[137]

Crazy Horse did not refer so much to General Crook's unflinching courage or his famously dogged determination as to his wiles. Now young Genio Lambertson was a pawn in wily General Crook's plan to see the Poncas receive justice. At least Crazy Horse and the Sioux had known which side the general was on.

When the DA settled into his Omaha hotel on Tuesday, April 29, he would have been ignorant of the fact that it was a month to the day since Bright Eyes made her plea to General Crook on behalf of the Poncas and set this whole affair in motion. As he made final preparations for the opening of the case the next day and probably dashed off a confident note to his fiancée, Jane Gundry, at her Mineral Point, Wisconsin, home (they were to marry the following spring), Lambertson had no idea what he was letting himself in for.

✣ PART TWO: THE COURT CASE ✣

They have had some friends who have done them justice, yet as a part of all systems of justice whenever it is meted to the poor Indian, it comes invariably too late, or is administered at an ineffectual distance, and that too when his enemies are continually about him, and effectually applying the means of his destruction.

George Catlin,
American frontier writer and artist,
1841, thirty-eight years before
the Standing Bear case

→ *Chapter 10* ←

THE TESTIMONY

OMAHA WAS A bustling city by the spring of 1879. Within another decade it would boast a population of around 150,000, a far cry from the handful of pioneers who twenty-five years ago had established a log cabin township beside the Missouri as a supply station for emigrants heading west. Westward expansion quickly turned Omaha from a wild frontier town that attracted hard-drinking gamblers and hard-living pioneers to a rich city: a railroad terminus and home to massive warehouses that stockpiled goods brought up the Missouri by paddle wheeler, a city that attracted cultivated, liberal-minded emigrants from the eastern states and Europe. Omaha had a university, its wooden churches were being replaced by cathedrals of brick and stone, and its cultural life and institutions were beginning to gain stature.

It inspired a certain pride in the people of Omaha that the court case set to open on Wednesday, April 30, 1879, in the federal courthouse above the post office in downtown Omaha was attracting national attention and putting Omaha on the map, even if few realized the potential that the case had to shake the very foundations of U.S. Indian policy. Not even the instigators of the case anticipated the eventual repercussions. John G. Bourke wrote that "the case of the Poncas was, beyond question, the most important one occurring within General Crook's jurisdiction after the pacification of the Sioux."[138] But none of the Ponca crusaders fully realized what a floodgate they were tampering with.

As it turned out, the case had a false start. Held up in Lincoln, Judge Dundy wired District Attorney Lambertson on the morning of April 30 that he did not expect to arrive in Omaha until that afternoon and asked him to pass on his apologies to attorneys Webster and Poppleton. In the end, the judge reached Omaha in the early evening. Calling the lawyers for both sides together for an informal meeting that night, Dundy discussed with them the procedure he intended to follow the next day.

At 10:00 A.M. on Thursday, May 1, a warm, close day, the courtroom was packed for the opening of *Standing Bear et al. v. Crook*. Henry Tibbles reported that the public gallery was filled with "clergy, finely dressed men and women, and deeply interested lawyers."[139] Bishops were numbered among the clergy present, alongside doctors and retired judges. Apart from Tibbles there were several Omaha and out-of-town reporters, who described the proceedings for their own readers and for scores of other newspapers around the country. Henry Tibbles was the best placed of them all, sitting up front close by lawyers Andrew Poppleton and John Webster with a fresh notebook at the ready to jot down in journalist's shorthand all that took place during the hearing. Tibbles had done a fine job of publicizing the Standing Bear case; national press interest had swelled in the weeks and days leading up to the hearing. In the words of John Bourke, "By the time that Judge Dundy's court was convened the attention of the people of the United States was to some extent converged upon the trial."[140]

In Omaha the *Daily Herald*, in a brief article beneath an advertisement for Royal baking powder on April 30, urged "the large number of ladies and gentlemen who have expressed a desire to attend" the Ponca hearing to do so, as everyone was welcome. On May 1, as those large numbers of ladies and gentlemen converged on the courtroom, the paper noted that the government had not given anything away about how it would defend the matter, although, the *Herald* suggested, whatever the outcome in the district court the case was likely to end up in the Supreme Court.

The owner of the *Herald*, Dr. George L. Miller, was back in town and back in the editor's chair, allowing Tibbles to resume his deputy editor's duties and freeing him up to spend most of his time on the Ponca story. Since his return, Dr. Miller had endorsed Tibbles's actions in the Standing Bear case and had taken a similar pro-Ponca stand editorially. The *Herald* was an unabashed pro-Democrat journal and was known for swinging its editorial weight behind liberal causes, which helps explain why Miller employed Henry Tibbles in the first place. Surprisingly, to some, the *Herald's* arch rival and Tibbles's former employer, the *Omaha Daily Bee*, had taken a bipartisan approach, with editor Edward Rosewater also editorializing in favor of Standing Bear. Tibbles and his fourth estate colleagues had done all they could. Now it was up to the lawyers.

All heads turned when General George Crook entered the courtroom, accompanied by his aide, Lieutenant Bourke, and the army's judge advocate for the Military Department of the Platte, Colonel Horace B. Burnham. Knowing how much General Crook disliked wearing a uniform of any kind, Tibbles would have smiled at the sight of all three officers in full dress uniform. The general's dress blues were adorned with two rows of brass buttons down the front and wide embroidered epaulets from which much gold braid dangled. Over his right shoulder he wore a sash, and at his side he carried a sheathed sword. As he took a seat at one of the two tables at the front of the courtroom, he placed his hat and gloves in front of him. Crook was giving every impression that he was the diligent general officer come to represent his government in this matter and contest the issuing of the writ.

Beside the general, District Attorney Genio Lambertson reached over and shook his hand. Lambertson would have been brimming with confidence. Despite the tide of press and public sympathy running with the Poncas, the facts in the case had not changed, and neither had the law. Lambertson was certain that the writ would be dismissed once he presented his legal argument. This high-profile case, and Lambertson's expected victory in it, would be good for his career, as he would have written Jane, his fiancée in Wisconsin, hoping to impress her and his future father-in-law, Joseph Gundry. He had good reason to be confident in his abilities. Although no one in the courtroom could know it then, G. M.

Lambertson would go on to build an impressive list of court victories during eight years as district attorney and several terms as Lincoln's city attorney.

A side door opened, and this time it was Standing Bear's turn to make an entrance. Standing Bear's legal team and General Crook had agreed, for a variety of reasons, practical and theatrical, that just five of the twenty-six Poncas named in the habeas corpus petition would attend the hearing. Escorted by Lieutenant Carpenter, Standing Bear was accompanied by his brother Yellow Horse, Medicine clan chief Buffalo Chip, and Standing Bear's statuesque wife Susette (she was inches taller than Standing Bear), who carried their baby grandson, Prairie Flower's child.

As always, the Ponca men wore the only European clothes they owned, "hopelessly tattered" clothes, as Tibbles described them.[141] Standing Bear appeared in his council attire of buckskin smock, beaded belt, claw necklace, and red blanket. Calm and proud, he took a seat where Lieutenant Carpenter politely indicated, in the corner behind Poppleton and Webster, who shook hands with him. Yellow Horse sat down next to his brother. Buffalo Chip was seated next in line, and finally Susette, nursing her grandson. Lieutenant Carpenter also took a seat. The three most senior Ponca men were there to testify if required. At the lawyers' request, Standing Bear's wife and grandchild were there to show the gallery a softer side of the fierce Plains Indian they had heard and read so much about. The ploy worked. Picking up the story from one of the reporters present, the St. Louis Republican noted in its coverage of the case that day the presence of "Standing Bear's handsome wife Susette."[142]

Unable to communicate with Webster and Poppleton because he did not understand English, Standing Bear could only nod gravely to the attorneys when they greeted him. His fate, and the fate of his people, was now in the hands of these two white men. He would sit through the hearing impassively, hiding the fact that he had little confidence in these unfamiliar proceedings producing an outcome that would benefit his people. In all his dealings with the whites over the years, the red man came off second best. Once, when he was younger, fifteen Poncas on their way to visit relatives on the Omaha reservation were attacked in their camp by drunken 7th Cavalry soldiers who killed three of the women and a girl.[143] When missionaries tried to win justice for the Poncas, they were told that white man's law did not apply to Indians. Then there was the case of two Yankton Sioux who killed a Ponca in an argument. When missionaries tried to have the Yanktons charged with the Ponca's murder, again the Poncas were told that white man's law did not apply to them. Now Standing Bear was in a white man's court, and despite the sympathy and kindness of his lawyers, nothing the bemused Ponca chief had seen to date gave him reason to expect justice in his case.

Expressing the view of all the Poncas in custody, Standing Bear's friend and fellow clan chief Buffalo Chip had said to General Crook on March 31, "I have been told since the great war that all men were free men, and that no man can be made a prisoner unless he does wrong. I have done no wrong, and yet I am here a prisoner."[144]

While in custody at Fort Omaha, Standing Bear may have seen troopers of the 9th Cavalry Regiment pass through, since the unit served in the Platte Department during this time. While the officers of the 9th Cavalry were white, the enlisted men of the regiment were black. Standing Bear might have asked whether black people were allowed by the U.S. government to choose where they buried their children. And he would have been informed that Americans had to fight a bloody civil war before black people were granted the kinds of rights that Standing Bear and his people were asking for. As kind as some whites had been to him, Standing Bear could not have imagined the entire American nation going to war on his account.

Two other Indians were present in the gallery, although Henry Tibbles didn't mention them—Bright Eyes and her father, Iron Eye. With a large vested interest in the case, they had come down from the Omaha reservation for the hearing, with General Crook's blessing. As one of the catalysts of the campaign in defense of the rights of the Poncas, Bright Eyes would not have missed being there. While she attended the court case, her younger sister, eighteen-year-old Rosalie, filled in for her at the Omaha reservation school. Rosalie had recently been appointed assistant teacher at the school.

For weeks Bright Eyes had written almost daily from the Omaha reservation to Henry Tibbles at the *Herald* office. According to Tibbles, "she had followed every word about our Ponca struggle in my *Herald* articles and editorials" and "had written me a lot of valuable facts from her own knowledge or from letters she received from her Ponca kinsfolk in the territory."[145]

There was an interpreter present, but not to keep the Poncas informed of what was being said in court. There was no provision in U.S. law for providing translation services to an Indian litigant because no tribal Indian had previously been accepted as a litigant. Standing Bear had to sit through the entire hearing without understanding a word that was said for or against him. The interpreter was there solely to translate when Standing Bear was called to the stand to testify. A new interpreter had been engaged for the court case, as neither Henry Tibbles nor Bright Eyes had great confidence in Charles Morgan's translation skills. For one thing, Morgan had incorrectly translated the name of one of the Poncas when the habeas corpus writ was drawn up. The new interpreter was Willie Hamilton, son of the Presbyterian minister at the Omaha reservation.

This was the scene—a colorful blend of military uniforms, Indian attire, and the well-dressed elite citizenry of Omaha—when the door to the judge's room opened, and a U.S. marshal cleared his throat and then called, "All rise!"

Everyone in the room came to their feet, with John Webster probably tugging at Standing Bear's sleeve to bring him to the upright position. Beside him, the other Poncas (who, like their leader, had never before been in a white man's court) followed suit with uncertainty.

Gray-bearded Judge Elmer S. Dundy then entered the court and strode to the bench. Whether it was hunting with Buffalo Bill or presiding over a case in his court, Judge Dundy had a reputation for cautiousness. As the judge took his seat on the bench, his poker face betrayed no emotion.

Now the marshal called, "Hear ye! Hear ye! The Honorable United States District Court is now in session, His Honor Judge Dundy presiding. Be seated."

The people in the crowded courtroom silently resumed their seats, with the Poncas raggedly and confusedly following the example of those around them. From his bench, Judge Dundy took in the sight of Standing Bear and his colleagues—this was the first time he ever laid eyes on any of them. Then he looked across to the respondent in the case, the characteristically blank-faced George Crook.

It is apparent that during the three weeks leading up to this hearing Henry Tibbles had discreetly but thoroughly briefed his friend the judge on the background to the case. As the newspaperman later admitted, he had no scruples about going to see the judge privately during the hearing itself, so a quiet chat leading up to it was not out of the question. One way or another, by the time he took his seat in court on May 11, Judge Dundy knew precisely where George Crook's sympathies lay. Several weeks later, the judge, who described General Crook as a "brave and distinguished officer," said that Crook "has no sort of sympathy in the business in which he is forced by his position to bear a part so conspicuous."[146]

Calling the court to order, the judge required the attorneys at the bar to identify themselves. The learned and distinguished Andrew J. Poppleton announced his name and informed the judge that he and his distinguished colleague John L. Webster were representing the "relators" in the matter of Standing Bear versus George Crook. He was followed by young District Attorney Lambertson, who advised that he was present in the capacity of U.S. attorney in this matter to represent the respondent, Brigadier General Crook, and the U.S. government.

Opening the papers in front of him, the judge then began.

On the 8th of April, 1879, the relators, Standing Bear and 25 others, during the session of the court held at that time at Lincoln, presented their petition, duly verified, praying for the allowance of a writ of habeas corpus and their final discharge from custody thereunder. The petition alleges that the relators are Indians who have formerly belonged to the Ponca tribe of Indians, now located in the Indian Territory, that they had some time previously withdrawn from the tribe, and completely severed their tribal relations therewith, and had adopted the general habits of the whites, and were endeavoring to maintain themselves by their own exertions, and without aid or assistance from the general government.

This would have surprised most spectators. The content of the petition lodged with the court was known to the lawyers on both sides and to Crook and Tibbles, but had not been made public. For the first time the world was hearing the Poppleton/Webster argument, a novel and controversial one—that Standing Bear and his companions had consciously and permanently separated from their tribe and were therefore not reservation Indians and no longer subject to the laws relating to reservation Indians and should be treated like any other person under the laws of the United States. "The petition also alleges that while they were thus engaged and without being guilty of violating any of the laws of the United States, they were arrested and restrained of their liberty by order of the respondent, George Crook."[147]

The judge explained the government's contention that Standing Bear and his companions had fled or escaped from a reservation set aside for their tribe in the Indian Territory without the permission of the government. Then, at the request of the secretary of the Interior, the general of the army issued an order requiring Brigadier General Crook to arrest and return the band to their tribe in the Indian Territory. Pursuant to that order, the general caused Standing Bear and his Poncas to be arrested on the Omaha reservation, and they were now in the general's custody for the purpose of being returned to Indian Territory. What the court now had to determine was whether the relators had been lawfully arrested and detained in custody.

Andrew Poppleton and Genio Lambertson then argued over legal points, Poppleton saying the government had to prove that it had the jurisdiction to hold Standing Bear and the others, Lambertson claiming the facts of the case were so self-evident he proposed to either make a motion to quash or file a demurrer. As they argued, Lambertson said that he particularly wanted to contest the claim that Standing Bear and his Poncas had severed their tribal relations. Poppleton said the government should have stated that in its return. Debate now raged over what the central issues of the case really were, and it was agreed that the government's return was insufficient to cover all the writ's propositions. So Judge Dundy agreed to allow the district attorney to formally add a denial of the severed relations claim to the return in due course.

All this legal talk went over the heads of 99 percent of the people in the courtroom, and the attention of many a spectator would have lapsed for a time. But now the real action began. John Webster came to his feet to launch the case for Standing Bear. Because he represented the petitioners and had to make the case for the petition to be granted and the writ exercised, a case for which he was primarily responsible, he was to speak first. When planning their courtroom strategy, he and Andrew Poppleton had previously decided that Webster would present their evidence and a preliminary summation while Poppleton would use his famed eloquence to deliver the final argument on behalf of their clients. Webster began by calling as a witness for the relators Willie Hamilton, the white clerk and interpreter from the Omaha Agency store.

When the twenty-two-year-old Hamilton took the stand, Webster established via his questions that the young man had lived on the Omaha reservation for twelve years, had worked in the agency store for the past six, and was fluent in the language spoken by the Omahas and Poncas. Hamilton testified that he had seen Standing Bear and his band arrive at the Omaha reservation, sick and with few possessions, and had witnessed some of the band who were well enough to do so commence farming on land given to them by the Omahas. For the benefit of the court he identified Standing Bear and each of his four Ponca companions.

When Lambertson cross-examined Hamilton, the young man's knowledge of the Poncas proved imprecise at best—for one thing, he didn't even know exactly how many of them had arrived at the Omaha reservation.

More importantly for the government case, Lambertson got Hamilton to agree that not all the Ponca men had commenced farming on the Omaha reservation and that the band had received a handout of government blankets from Agent Vore and clothing from white supporters in Omaha—all of which indicated they were not entirely self-sufficient individuals as their lawyers claimed but rather members of a mendicant Indian tribe.

In redirect, Webster tried to repair some of the damage, only for Hamilton to volunteer that Standing Bear's band had also received rations from Agent Vore on one occasion, information that would have pleased the DA. But at least Webster was able to solicit from Hamilton the fact that the Omahas had offered to sell land to the Poncas, who were not a part of their tribe, so that the Poncas could become citizens, as they were trying to be.

When Webster finished with the witness, Lambertson had more questions for him. Did the Poncas obey the Omahas? Hamilton replied that they took advice from them, they didn't obey them, but he agreed they followed the same customs as the Omahas.

Lambertson then asked if the Omahas had a chief. Willie Hamilton knew that the case for Standing Bear relied greatly on establishing that the members of his band were now individuals, not members of a tribe. And he recognized that Lambertson had been angling to get him to say that Standing Bear's Poncas had been incorporated into the Omaha tribe. To counter this, Hamilton tried to suggest that the Omahas were themselves no longer a tribe by replying that the Omahas no longer had chiefs. Technically this was true, or was becoming true. Indian Affairs had recently begun discouraging the Omahas from appointing clan chiefs, and Iron Eye would be the last recognized paramount chief of the Omahas. But there was no doubting that while he was alive Iron Eye led his people, or that the Omaha tribe had elders whose opinions were respected by its 1,000 or so members.

Lambertson then got Hamilton to agree that as recently as the last summer the Omahas recognized a chief and head men. John Webster quickly chimed in, asking, "They live like white men, then?"

"They try to," Hamilton replied, before being excused.

In the gallery, Bright Eyes would have been whispering to her father beside her in Omaha or perhaps in French, telling him that their friend Willie had done more harm than good to Standing Bear's case.

Webster now called his next witness, Lieutenant William Carpenter, the officer directly responsible for the arrest and detention of Standing Bear's Poncas. After removing his cap and taking an oath to tell the truth, so help him God, the lieutenant took the stand and testified to the circumstances of the arrest. Webster then tried to have Carpenter testify to the band's attempt to farm and behave like citizens on the Omaha reservation. Although Webster rephrased his questions several times, the lieutenant was prevented from answering as a result of the sustained objections of the DA because Carpenter had not personally witnessed their activities on the Omaha reservation.

In his cross-examination Lambertson attempted to have Carpenter state how many chiefs the Poncas had, but Judge Dundy would not allow that line of questioning. Carpenter was discharged without being of value to either side, and the judge adjourned the court for lunch.

At 2:00 P.M. the hearing resumed, with the most important witness of all, Standing Bear himself, being called to give evidence, as a buzz of anticipation went around the courtroom. As Standing Bear took the stand, Willie Hamilton stepped up to act as his interpreter. After both took the oath, John Webster came to his feet to commence questioning his witness. But before he could open his mouth Genio Lambertson jumped up and lodged an objection. "Does this court think an Indian is a competent witness?" Lambertson asked the judge.

Elmer Dundy scowled down at the young DA. "They are competent for every purpose in both civil and criminal courts," he sourly advised. "The law makes no distinction on account of race, color, or previous condition." By "previous condition" he meant previously a member of an Indian tribe. Dundy was signaling to a chastened Genio Lambertson that he had already accepted the premise that Standing Bear and his corelators were no longer members of an Indian tribe. He instructed Webster to proceed.

Webster began by asking questions, via Hamilton, about the life Standing Bear and his people lived on the Niobrara before they were sent to Indian Territory. In his answers Standing Bear told of how he and his family had worked hard and lived well from their farming efforts. His children were going to school and everything was going nicely. He said that he tried to be like a white man—a civilized white man, John Webster suggested.

Overcoming the DA's objections, Webster had Standing Bear narrate the conditions the Poncas faced after their removal to the Indian Territory. In detail, Standing Bear told of the bad country and poor farming conditions in the Indian Territory, of the sickness and death of 158 of his people. Then Standing Bear said, "I thought to myself, God wants me to live, and I think if I come back to my old reservation he will let me live. I got back as far as the Omahas, and they brought me down here." His eyes were on the silent, transfixed spectators. "I see you all here today. What have I done?" He came to his feet, his voice growing louder. "I am brought here, but what have I done? I don't know. It seems to me as if I have no place on earth. I want a place where I can work and support my family, and when done with life, die peaceably!"

"Tell the witness not to get excited," Judge Dundy cautioned from the bench, "but to take things coolly." When the interpreter passed on the instruction, Standing Bear sank back onto his chair. John Webster continued with his questions, which focused first on the poor farming conditions in the Indian Territory, the lack of a school for the Ponca children, and then on the reasons for Standing Bear's flight north and what he and his companions meant to achieve when they reached their old reservation. Webster then posed questions that allowed Standing Bear to say that he and his companions intended never to return to the tribe in the Indian Territory—establishing that they had permanently severed their relations with the tribe. In response to his attorney's questions, Standing Bear also said that he no longer considered himself a chief of his tribe; he felt as poor as the rest of them. Webster had no more questions for his key witness.

All in all, Standing Bear's supporters felt he had handled himself very well. But now it was Lambertson's turn to question him, with Willie Hamilton again acting as intermediary. Lambertson used his opening questions to establish that in the Indian Territory Standing Bear was a leader of part of the Ponca tribe and that members of his own clan escaped north with him. When he asked how many members of other clans escaped with Standing Bear, John Webster jumped up and objected to the question as immaterial. "I just wanted to see if he could count," Lambertson retorted facetiously.

The judge ruled against the DA on this and several similar questions before Lambertson asked pointedly if Standing Bear had been a chief of the Ponca tribe in the Indian Territory. "I don't count myself a chief," Standing Bear guardedly replied. He was fully conscious of the briefing he had received from his lawyers prior to the hearing that for his case to be successful he must not say that he was a chief of the Ponca tribe but was merely an individual Indian trying to live like a citizen.

Lambertson didn't persist with that line of questioning but moved on. He succeeded in having Standing Bear admit that two of the wagons used in the escape from the Indian Territory had been provided by the government—but at the old Dakota Territory reservation, Standing Bear added. The DA then asked if Standing Bear had informed Agent Whiteman of his intent to take care of himself without government aid when he left Indian Territory.

Standing Bear answered that he had several times told the agent of his desire to go back north. "I wanted to go on my own land, land that I had never sold. That's where I wanted to go. My son asked me when he was dying to take him back and bury him there, and I have his bones in a box with me now. I want to live there the rest of my life and be buried there."

A wave of sympathy for the Ponca swept the gallery. Henry Tibbles would have been elated that Standing Bear went to the emotional core of his case.

Genio Lambertson would have cursed silently. He quickly threw Standing Bear a barbed question. "Do you intend living in the same manner you did before?"

John Webster knew this was a trick question—Standing Bear had previously lived as a part of an Indian tribe on a reservation, subject to U.S. government support. If he answered in the affirmative, he would destroy his claim that he had disassociated himself from life as a tribal Indian. Webster objected, but the judge ruled that the witness could answer the question.

Standing Bear was no fool. He recognized the district attorney's intent and answered, "I might go there and go to work." He said the Omahas wanted him to stay on their reservation and raise a crop in the summer before he continued back to the Niobrara, as he would have a hard time of it without food or farm implements.

Lambertson then had Standing Bear concede that he and the other members of his band received rations on one occasion from the government agent at the Omaha reservation, with Willie the interpreter adding that he personally weighed out the rations for the Poncas.

Several more questions from the district attorney were disallowed by the judge, after which Lambertson said that he had no more questions to put to the witness and resumed his seat. Once the judge excused Standing Bear from the witness stand, John Webster advised the court that the attorneys for the relators had no further witnesses to present.

When the judge called on the DA to present the case for the government, Lambertson surprised everyone in the courtroom by announcing that he did not intend to call any witnesses but would rely on the facts in the case, which he would discuss in summation. But before he handed the floor back to the other side, Lambertson proposed to file the addition to the return that the judge had approved of that morning and he had prepared during the lunch break.

The young DA now read aloud the additional paragraph, which stated the government's contention that Standing Bear and his fellow complainants "are members of the said tribe of Ponca Indians" and that they had not "dissolved, but still retain their tribal relations with" the tribe and still paid allegiance to its chief, and were not "pursuing the habits and vocations of civilized life."

To the astonishment of everyone in the room, General Crook now spoke up and voiced a strong objection. With uncharacteristic fervor he declared that he would not have this assertion entered into the return, which bore his signature, as he didn't agree with it. When Judge Dundy told the general that he was not permitted to address the court, Crook instructed the army judge advocate, Colonel Burnham, who was seated at his side, to object on his behalf, which Burnham did.

"General," Judge Dundy then responded, "you are not signing this amended return as General Crook but as a brigadier general of the army, and for the government."

Still the general protested, via Colonel Burnham, that, contrary to the district attorney's assertion, he firmly believed that Standing Bear and his Poncas had severed relations with their tribe and were attempting to live a civilized life, so he therefore could not have the assertion included on a document that bore his signature. For the first time, the stunned district attorney, the surprised audience, and, via the reporters present, the rest of the country were made aware of Crook's true feelings in the Ponca case.

Again the judge explained that the amendment was a mere formality, and, with the attorneys for both sides agreeing to the inclusion, and General Crook still shaking his head unhappily, Dundy instructed the clerk of the court, Watson Smith, to include the additional paragraph in the return on file.

With that drama dealt with, and with the district attorney coming to terms with the fact that his client was rooting for the other side, Judge Dundy turned back to John Webster and called on him to proceed with his argument on behalf of the relators. It was now late in the afternoon. Caught unprepared by Lambertson's failure to call any witnesses, Webster and Poppleton were reluctant to go ahead with their summations, knowing that they would have to break off part way through when the judge adjourned for the day, so they entered a motion for an adjournment. But Dundy impatiently dismissed their petition and told them to get on with it.

Slowly, unhappily, Webster came to his feet. The sun had been beating in through the naked courtroom windows all day, and the ventilation was poor. It was stifling in the courtroom. As Webster cast his eyes around the room, he saw perspiration dripping from men in the gallery; ladies in their bonnets, gloves, and high-necked dresses fanned themselves to gain some relief. The attorney began to address the court, stumbled through several sentences, then stopped in midsentence and loosened his tie. Apologizing to the judge, he claimed that he was too unwell to continue and sagged back down onto his chair, accompanied by a gasp from the gallery.

Judge Dundy scowled down from the bench, taking in Webster's pale face and labored breathing, and with a sigh, announced, "Court adjourned until ten o'clock tomorrow morning." He came to his feet.[148]

"All rise!" bellowed the marshal.

→ *Chapter 11* ←

THE ARGUMENTS

O THER THAN STANDING Bear's testimony, the Poncas did not understood a word spoken on the first day of the hearing. They returned under guard to Fort Omaha late Thursday uncertain about what had taken place in the courtroom and far from optimistic about their chances of being granted their freedom.

Knowing this, Henry Tibbles followed the prisoners out to the fort before he went back to his office to write up an account of the hearing for his editor at the *Herald* and expectant editors around the country. That night, through an interpreter, identity unknown, Tibbles tried to fill the Poncas in on the day's legal proceedings. Despite his best efforts, the complexities of the arguments went over their heads.

Standing Bear was not happy with the way things were going. When he testified he was not able to make the points he wanted. The process of answering questions put to him was too limiting as far as he was concerned. For one thing, he wanted to brand Commissioner Hayt a liar. In the second week of April, Tibbles had read him Hayt's open letter to Secretary Schurz saying that Indians must be made to give up their nomadic ways and become farmers. But, Standing Bear pointed out, Commissioner Hayt knew very well that the Poncas were farmers, not nomads. In that letter Hayt also said that when he visited the Poncas in the Indian Territory, he recognized Standing Bear as a troublemaker who was the only chief to show what he considered a bad spirit. In response, Standing Bear gave

Tibbles a character reference Hayt had written for him in December, two months after Hayt's October visit, in which the commissioner said that Standing Bear's "influence has been to preserve peace and harmony between the Ponca Indians and the United States, and as such is entitled to the confidence of all persons whom he may meet."[149] But the lawyers did not present this reference in court, and they and Tibbles counseled Standing Bear not to say anything bad about Hayt.

Standing Bear, accustomed to speaking for himself in council, was frustrated by the white man's way of doing justice, where strangers spoke on his behalf and he could only say what others wanted him to say. The attorneys had told him they'd given the judge written statements dictated by Standing Bear and his co-relators, but that hardly seemed enough to him. Tibbles wrote that the chief asked him many searching questions about what the attorneys were saying, before he finally commented to the newspaperman, "No man can talk for another as well as he can for himself."[150]

Next morning, Friday, May 2, before the court convened for the second day, Tibbles went to see his friend Judge Dundy in his chambers and asked him to allow Standing Bear to make a statement to the court on his own behalf. Dundy smiled and responded, "Was Standing Bear ever admitted to the Bar?"[151]

If only attorneys recognized by the court could speak at the hearing, it seemed that Standing Bear's request would be denied. But that morning the judge and Tibbles made a secret agreement. Tibbles was able to discreetly inform Standing Bear, General Crook, Poppleton, and Webster that the chief would indeed be given the chance to personally plead his case. He told them it would be in a way that was unorthodox but perfectly legal and above board. They would have to wait to see how this was accomplished.

➔ ◆

Court resumed at 10:00 A.M. on May 2 to a packed courtroom. John Webster, though professing to be feeling very unwell, prepared to launch into his argument. At Judge Dundy's invitation, Webster took the floor to begin summing up the case for Standing Bear and his corelators.

Webster's summation lasted until noon, when the judge adjourned for lunch. Resuming at 1:30, Webster spoke for another hour. He addressed several main points. With detailed supporting quotes from a variety of sources, he argued that the Omaha tribe's legal title to their land was recognized in their treaties with the U.S. government. Consequently the Omahas had every right to invite friends such as Standing Bear and his band to share their land. He went on to assert that Indian tribes could not be moved "at the whim and pleasure" of the commissioner of Indian Affairs, for they had been recognized by treaties endorsed by Congress as independent nations, even quoting Thomas Jefferson in support of his argument.

He pointed out that the treaties signed by the Ponca tribe expressly required the tribe's consent before it was relocated from its Dakota Territory reservation. Despite the efforts made by Inspector Kemble in 1877 to represent a request for temporary relocation to the Omaha reservation as giving permission for the tribe's removal to the Indian Territory, the Poncas had never consented to go to Indian Territory, making their removal by the government a breach of those treaties and therefore unlawful.

"They are called barbarian tribes, but these Omahas and Poncas are not savages nor wanderers," he went on to say. "They cultivate the soil, live in houses and support themselves." It was the whites who were the savages, he contended, going on to give examples of cruelties inflicted on Indian tribes by whites over the years.

But could an Indian present himself in court to redress an injustice done to him by the U.S. government? Webster cited a number of authoritative legal opinions supporting his argument that an Indian who had severed his tribal relationship and sought to live as a citizen was entitled to be protected by U.S. law.

Webster then elaborated the sad tale of the injustices done to the Poncas over the past two decades, up to and including the death of Standing Bear's son Bear Shield, before turning to the issue of the power of the Indian commissioner to use the U.S. Army to enforce his orders. He pointed out what the statutes did and did not allow, and stressed that the law only gave the army power "to hold persons who had committed crimes for five days, and then hand them over to the civil authorities."

Webster next dealt with the appalling conditions the Poncas had endured in the Indian Territory, including the fact that one in four of them had died during and after their forced removal from their own land, a higher mortality rate, he said, than Union army prisoners suffered in the worst Confederate prisons during the Civil War. Standing Bear and the other prisoners before the bar, said the attorney, fled the potential prison of Indian Territory to save their wives and children "and now ask the protection of this court."

"A man belongs to himself," Webster declared, employing the words of black rights activist Frederick Douglass, and would remain so "until you storm the citadel of heaven and wrest from the bosom of God man's title deed to himself!" With that, he sat down, his words making a favorable impression on the spectators.

Judge Dundy now invited the district attorney to make the case for the government, and Genio Lambertson came to his feet. Shaken the previous day by the revelation about General Crook's true loyalties in the case, the young district attorney had been given a night to get over it and prepare to strut his stuff on this second day of the hearing. Now he was as ready as he ever would be to step into the spotlight and dispose of his learned opponents' propositions.

Lambertson began with a syrupy tribute to Poppleton and Webster, "for their generosity in coming to the assistance of these poor people, prisoners and friendless in a strange land." He indicated Standing Bear and his four fellow Poncas.

Lambertson then turned to the evidence. He was confident of having the case thrown out without the judge even giving thought to the submissions of Webster and Poppleton in their writ of April 8 about the right of expatriation or the provisions of the Fourteenth Amendment to the Constitution. But he considered himself a thorough individual and would cover all the bases before he was finished.

Without fear of offending the judge, the young DA questioned the jurisdiction of the court to issue the writ or even hear and determine the case put by the petitioners. Lambertson was of the opinion that Judge Dundy had erred in law in agreeing to consider a petition from an Indian, a noncitizen, and told the court so. It's not recorded, but Judge Dundy may have broached a smile at this point—before he invited Lambertson to "support his theory" with legal argument.

Lambertson proceeded to argue that Standing Bear and his colleagues had no legal recourse to habeas corpus. To him, whatever the precise wording of the act, the intent of the legislators who created habeas corpus and passed it into American law was clear, as was evident from subsequent practice—no application for a writ by an American Indian, a noncitizen, had ever been entertained by a federal court. To prove his submission, he embarked on a detailed discussion of how and why the writ of habeas corpus had been created in the first place and used over time, beginning with the origin of the writ and how it had been applied in Great Britain.

The crux of the twenty-eight-year-old district attorney's lengthy argument on this point was that in Britain the act of habeas corpus had limited the right to this writ to the *free subjects* of the kingdom. By extension, this meant that only American citizens were entitled by law to be granted a writ of habeas corpus in a federal court, and so it had always been interpreted in the United States. Accordingly, the DA respectfully submitted that no grounds existed for His Honor to create a precedent and grant a writ to a noncitizen. Like it or not, he said, Congress had deemed that Indians were not U.S. citizens. And so, Indians had no more rights in a court of law than beasts of the field.

As strongly as he felt that he had shown that the Poncas had no grounds for their writ and that the judge must find in his client's favor in that regard and dismiss the application, Lambertson was obliged to also answer the relators' assertion that the government had illegally arrested and detained them for the purpose of returning them to Indian Territory.

He contended that the treaties of 1858, 1859, and 1865 (extracts from which he read aloud to the court), treaties that the Ponca tribe had signed, very clearly stated that members of the tribe could not leave their reservation without government permission. He submitted that, no matter what Standing Bear may have told Agent Whiteman, the members of the tribe who departed the reservation in the Indian Territory were still Ponca Indians by virtue of their ancestry and place of birth; they could not cease to be Ponca Indians simply because they said they were no longer Ponca Indians. And they certainly hadn't claimed to have left their Indian Territory reservation with government permission. They were therefore to be considered escapees in the eyes of the law.

In addition, the treaties that the Omaha tribe had signed with the U.S. government prohibited any person who was not a member of the Omaha tribe from entering their reservation. Those treaties obliged the U.S. government to arrest and remove any person who was on the reservation without government permission. As Standing Bear and the other relators had been found on the Omaha reservation by General Crook's troops, a fact that no one denied or disputed, and as neither General Crook nor any other person in authority had given the Poncas permission to enter the Omaha reservation, Lambertson contended that General Crook had both the right and the obligation to arrest and remove them.

As to the reasons and circumstances of the Ponca tribe's removal to Indian Territory, Lambertson did not believe that it was necessary to discuss them. They didn't have a bearing on the right of the U.S. Army to arrest and detain Standing Bear and his companions for being illegally on the Omaha reservation. But prior to beginning his summation (either before 10:00 A.M. or during the lunch interval), the district attorney was informed by Judge Dundy that he intended to give Standing Bear the opportunity to make a statement at the close of the hearing. Knowing that what he said in defense of the government was destined to be considered in the national court of public opinion as well as in the district court, Lambertson decided to counter what he expected Standing Bear to say in his upcoming statement by reading the court a letter from former Indian Affairs commissioner John Quincy Smith. In that letter Smith explained the reasons for removing the Poncas to Indian Territory and the legal basis for that removal—the acts of Congress that required and authorized the removal and allocated funds for it to take place.

As to John Webster's contention that the removal of the Poncas to Indian Territory had been unlawful because the tribe had not given its consent, Lambertson pointed out that in 1871 Congress had determined that no more treaties would be entered into between the U.S. government and Indian tribes. The laws passed by Congress since that time requiring and allowing for the Poncas' removal to Indian Territory had superseded the earlier treaties, he said, just as all new laws superseded old laws on the same subject, making it unnecessary for consent to be sought or given.

In summation, Lambertson declared that the federal laws which applied to Indians clearly and unequivocally gave the government the legal right to order its military forces to arrest any Indian who escaped from his reservation and return him to it. In the same way, General Crook could legally use his troops to remove any outside person, Indian or white, who was on a reservation without his permission. For their part, the relators did not claim to have such permission. Consequently the order issued by General W. T. Sherman commanding Brigadier General Crook to arrest and detain Standing Bear and his Poncas was lawful. Therefore, on these grounds too the writ of habeas corpus must be dismissed.

As Lambertson resumed his seat after three long and sometimes eloquent hours, there would have been a feeling in the body of the court that his credible, cogent argument might win the day. But Henry Tibbles was not impressed. While he devoted several pages in the *Daily Herald* to the arguments made by Standing Bear's lawyers, he dismissed Lambertson's address with a nineteen-line synopsis.[152]

Judge Dundy, who had a busy court schedule in the days ahead and had allocated only two days to the hearing, wanted to wrap it up this same day. So he announced that he would adjourn the session until after supper that evening, at which time he would hear final arguments. An evening session was not considered unusual. This was a time when professional people such as doctors typically kept office hours of 8:00 A.M. to 1:00 P.M., 2:00 to 6:00 P.M., and 7:00 to 8:00 P.M., six days a week.

Many an observer who trooped down the stairs from the courtroom and headed for city restaurants and nearby private dining rooms would have felt swayed toward the district attorney's view that Standing Bear and his Poncas did not have the right to appear in court or sue for a grant of habeas corpus.

When court resumed at 7:30 P.M., again with a crowded gallery, Andrew Poppleton rose to deliver the final address on behalf of Standing Bear and his band. It had been sixteen years since Poppleton had last stood up in a courtroom to argue on behalf of a private client. Sixteen years of handling contracts for land acquisition and construction works involving millions of dollars for the Union Pacific Railroad. But the years had not dulled the public speaking skills that had won him the admiration of voters who sent him to the legislature and later hung Omaha's mayoral chain around his neck. The proverbial rust dissolved, and the courtroom warrior went to war.

"May it please the court," he began. "I suppose it would be impossible for counsel under any circumstances to approach a case of this character without a feeling of oppression at its magnitude and the consequences involved in it."

Poppleton's argument extended well into the night, the spectators hanging on his every word. Many had come specifically to witness Poppleton in action for the first time in years, such was his past reputation as a podium speaker. He had a rich voice, and he used evocative words, dramatic pauses, theatrical gestures. It has been said that many a courtroom lawyer is a frustrated stage actor. The courtroom, like the floor of an elected assembly, was Andrew Poppleton's stage.

In the course of his address he quoted from numerous treaties, laws, and legal opinions, invoked the Greeks and ancient Romans, even read from the latest edition of an encyclopedia. But the early part of his address was like an appetizer before the main course, with Poppleton frequently making reference to himself and his feelings about the case. In this opening he made a point of saying how surprised he'd been by the defense offered by the "gentleman" representing the government, a defense that characterized the Poncas as savages who were entitled to no rights whatsoever.

He moved on. "May it please Your Honor, it is said that it must be 'presumed' that these Indians were lawfully in the Indian Territory. I take issue with that proposition." Poppleton then went into a lengthy discussion of the treaties signed by the U.S. government with Indian tribes, and the treaties signed by the Poncas in particular, and their interpretation by various legal authorities, and also of Congress's subsequent appropriation bills for the removal of the Poncas. He made three key points. One, that no new reservation was set aside by Congress for the Poncas in the Indian Territory—they had been sent south to share the reservation of the Quapaw people. Two, Lambertson had failed to remind the court that while Congress had decided in 1871 that it would no longer enter into treaties with Indian tribes, it had stated that this measure in no way affected the rights granted to Indians in treaties agreed prior to that date. And three, the appropriation bills repeated the stipulation set out in the treaties that any removal must be with the written consent of the Ponca tribe.

He also pointed out that while Lambertson had made much of the fact that the government had given the Poncas wagons, stock, and farming equipment, this had in fact been in exchange for tens of thousands of acres of the Poncas' Dakota Territory land that the tribe had ceded to the United States in the 1860s.

Poppleton then focused on the right of Standing Bear and his companions to apply for a writ of habeas corpus. He did not believe, he said, that U.S. courts would agree to the proposition that these people were nothing more than wild beasts. They were human beings, and as such had as much right to the protection of the courts as anyone else. He asked the court to consider the language used by the U.S. Constitution and the relevant statutes. None expressly forbade Indians from seeking the protection of habeas corpus. Unless a law could be found that excluded the relators as *persons* from the benefits of habeas corpus, he contended it must cover them. In the past, he said, the courts had recognized that children and even the insane had a right to the protection of habeas corpus, whether U.S. citizens or not. It had even been found to apply to slaves.

At this point Genio Lambertson interjected with a derisory comment about a famous case decided against a black slave appellant by the Supreme Court in 1857. Poppleton frowned at the young district attorney and dismissed the example cited by Lambertson as irrelevant and out of date.

The district attorney had used the example of habeas corpus as it had originally applied in Great Britain to "freemen" to suggest that in the United States it could only, by extension, be applied to "citizens." Poppleton disagreed and read from numerous reference works to show that nowhere was a petitioner for relief under the habeas corpus act required to be a citizen. Opening the new *American Cyclopedia* to an article on habeas corpus, he remarked that it was as good an authority as the letter from John Quincy Smith tendered by his opponent.

Again Genio Lambertson interjected. "I put that letter in as an offset to the speech that Standing Bear is going to make."

Again a frown crossed Poppleton's face. "That is about the only way that Standing Bear has been answered (before today)—by a letter from the Interior Department," he shot back, before reading aloud the *Cyclopedia*'s description of the history and interpretation of habeas corpus.

He went on to quote from numerous books describing the petition of habeas corpus, none of which stipulated that petitioners had to be citizens. Yet the district attorney contended that Indians must be citizens for habeas corpus to apply to them. Poppleton suggested that the only way the court could find against his clients' petition would be to find that they were not human beings. But who had not been touched by Standing Bear's heart-rending description of his son's death in his arms, and of Standing Bear's promise to him that he would bury his bones in their home soil? No one could tell him that these were not human beings, Poppleton dramatically declared.

Poppleton reminded the court that in his argument the district attorney said he had not been able to find a single instance where an Indian had been permitted to sue for a writ of habeas corpus. Because such a thing was without precedent, Lambertson had said, the writ must not be allowed to stand. "If there is no precedent for the issuing of a writ on behalf of an Indian," said Poppleton, "then I say in God's name it's high time to make one!" He turned to the judge. "If I sat where Your Honor does I should consider it a pleasant duty to establish a precedent on behalf of these poor Indians!"

Poppleton then returned to a condemnation of the government for characterizing the Poncas as savages—because Indians had not achieved in two hundred years the same degree of civilization that whites had achieved in two thousand. Was this really the way the government proposed to treat all Indians who, like Standing Bear, attempted to step away from their tribal ways and lead a civilized life and provide for themselves, just like whites? As for the government resting its entire defense on the proposition that Indians had no rights in any court, "I say that is a monstrous proposition, and I shall continue to say so until I have seen better authority than has been produced here."[153]

Checking the courtroom clock and realizing that he had been talking for over two hours, and feeling exhaustion creeping over him, the attorney wrapped up and expressed the hope that the court would find in his clients' favor and open the way to a whole new era for all Indian peoples.

→ *Chapter 12* ←

THE CHIEF'S PLEA

WHEN BOTH SIDES had presented their case, Judge Dundy announced that he would give due consideration to their submissions and hand down his decision at a future date. The crowded courtroom was now completely silent. Most spectators had already formed their opinion about which way the judge should find, and there would have been disappointment that a verdict was not delivered on the spot to end the suffering of Standing Bear and his people.

But the session was not completely at an end. Now occurred what Tibbles described as "an interesting bit of routine."[154] After Andrew Poppleton resumed his seat at the end of his address, the U.S. marshal got up and walked across to the bench. Tibbles says that what followed was heard by only a handful of people nearest the bench, including himself. Judge Dundy leaned down to the marshal and murmured, "Court is adjourned."

The marshal, facing forward, meaning that few in the gallery could even see his lips move, whispered, "Hear ye. Hear ye. The Honorable District Court of the United States is now adjourned."[155]

Judge Dundy then looked over to the patient clan chief of the Poncas and said that he could now speak. A ripple of excitement ran through the crowd. Tibbles and Crook had made sure that, in Tibbles's words, "an excellent interpreter" was ready and waiting. This was not the far from excellent interpreter Willie Hamilton, who had apparently been sent back to the Omaha reservation after completing his translation of Standing Bear's testimony the previous day. This time the interpreter was Bright Eyes.[156] Tibbles did not name her, as he attempted to obscure his personal contact with her during this period. Publicity and the cover blurb for *Plowed Under* (1881), Reverend Harsha's book to which Bright Eyes would contribute a foreword, said that she "testified" at the Dundy hearing. She didn't testify in the accepted sense; this reference relates to her role as translator of Standing Bear's closing address. What's more, the fact that she performed this role at the court hearing is part of Omaha and Ponca tribe tradition to this day, and has been included in several books about her family.

Standing Bear had no problem with his words being translated by a woman. At that time a number of men, white as well as Indian, would not have agreed to a female spokesperson. Before long, Bright Eyes was translating for him in other forums. What's more, Standing Bear knew and trusted Bright Eyes, had watched her grow up with his daughter Prairie Flower.

In the courtroom, now that the judge had played out his little charade with the marshal, which was primarily for Standing Bear's benefit, to give him the impression that he was addressing the court while it was still in session, Bright Eyes rose and went to Standing Bear and informed him that he could now plead his case. Slowly, Standing Bear came to his feet and moved to sit in front of the judge. Tibbles, who had been expecting this turn of events, wrote that neither Standing Bear nor the unwitting crowd in the gallery "dreamed that the court session was officially over," although the lawyers for both sides had been forewarned by the judge that he would allow Standing Bear to speak after the close of the hearing.[157]

According to Henry Tibbles, all eyes were fixed on "the sad, mild, yet strong face of Standing Bear, who sat in front of the judge."[158] Standing Bear half faced the bench and half faced the audience. The *St. Louis Republican*, which was represented by a journalist in court that day, reported, "It was strange to see the red man in all his gorgeous attire defending himself and his followers before a court of justice."[159]

Standing Bear had no real time to prepare his address, since Tibbles told him that same day, via Bright Eyes, that the judge would allow him to speak in the evening. Tibbles would have told him to keep it brief and to the point. Apart from that, the Ponca chief was on his own.

Holding his red blanket around his shoulders with one hand, Standing Bear came to his feet and then stretched out the other red-brown hand in front of him and held it there. For fully a minute he did not utter a sound, and the members of the audience, with their eyes fixed on him, began to grow tense and uneasy, as if they feared he could not go on. At last, to the relief of his many supporters, he looked up to Judge Dundy on the bench and began to speak, slowly, softly, with Bright Eyes repeating his words in a "sweet, girlish, and expressive voice."[160]

"I see a great many of you here," Standing Bear began. He paused, waiting for Bright Eyes to translate. Henry Tibbles wrote that the chief made his entire speech in this manner, with sentence by sentence translation, displaying an expert natural sense of timing and drama, for the stop-start delivery only added to the increasing emotional tension of the occasion. Now Standing Bear smiled sadly. "I think a great many are my friends." He asked the audience where they thought he came from. From the water? From the woods? Or from where? No, God made him, just as he made all of them, and God put him on his land. But a man he did not know came and ordered him to leave his land. Standing Bear objected. He looked around for a friend to help him, but there was none. "Now I have found someone," he said, casting his sad eyes in the direction of his attorneys and waiting for the translation, "and it makes me glad."[161]

He said that 158 of his people died in the foreign land down south. He did not want to die there. He came away to save his wife, his children, his friends. He wanted to go home, to live and be buried in the land of his fathers. He never tried to hurt a white man. Once, when out hunting, he found an American soldier on the prairie, almost frozen. He took him home, made him warm, and fed him until he could go away. Another time he found a white man who was lost and hungry. This man too he took home and fed, and he set him on the road to his own people. Had he been a savage, he would have killed these men and taken their scalps.[162]

The *St. Louis Republican*, noting that "Standing Bear is a man of rare ability for an Indian," commented that "his oration was marked by its intense feeling and eloquence."[163] Now came the most eloquent and intensely felt passage of all. Slowly, Standing Bear again raised his hand to the perpendicular and held it there.

"That hand is not the color of yours." He paused, allowing Bright Eyes to render his words in English, then resumed. "But if I pierce it, I shall feel pain." Again he waited for the translation. "If you pierce your hand, you also feel pain," the Ponca chief went on. "The blood that will flow from mine will be of the same color as yours. I am a man. The same God made us both."[164]

This came from a man who had never heard of William Shakespeare, never read or witnessed a performance of *The Merchant of Venice*. Yet his speech, with its eerie echoes of Shakespeare's victimized moneylender Shylock, was, we are led to believe, all of his own creation, without any contribution from his white friends.

Now Standing Bear turned his gaze to a window and the spring Nebraska sky beyond. His tone, says Henry Tibbles, grew tense. "I seem to stand on the bank of a river. My wife and little girl are beside me. In front, the river is wide and impassable, and behind there are perpendicular cliffs. No man of my race ever stood there before. There is no tradition to guide me.

"A flood has begun to rise around us. I look despairingly at the great cliffs. I see a steep, stony way leading upward. I grasp the hand of my child. My wife follows. I lead the way up the sharp rocks, while the waters still rise behind us. Finally, I see a rift in the rocks, I feel the prairie breeze strike my cheek.

"I turn to my wife and child with a shout that we are saved! We will return to the Swift Running Water that pours down between the green islands. There are the graves of my fathers. There again we will pitch our tipi and build our fires.

"But a man bars the passage! He is a thousand times more powerful than I. Behind him, I see soldiers as numerous as leaves on the trees. They will obey that man's orders. I too must obey his orders. If he says that I cannot pass, I cannot. The long struggle will have been in vain. My wife and child and I must return, and sink beneath the flood. We are weak, and faint, and sick. I cannot fight."

He paused, bowing his head. Women in the audience were crying. Slowly he raised his head again and turned to look at Judge Dundy. The look on his face, Henry Tibbles wrote, was one of "pathos and suffering." Standing Bear looked Elmer S. Dundy steadily in the eye, then declared in a low, intense voice, "You are that man!"[165]

For a moment, the courtroom seemed to catch its breath. Henry Tibbles saw tears in Judge Dundy's eyes. Glancing over to George Crook, he saw that the general sat leaning forward, covering his eyes with his hand. Not a soul spoke. The only sound was the sobbing of several female audience members. Then, glassy-eyed, the judge looked at the marshal and nodded.

Breaking the spell, the marshal called, at normal volume, "All rise!"

As the entire court came to its feet, a sudden roar erupted from the gallery. Some people cheered, others yelled—with exultation. The audience came crushing forward. General Crook strode the few paces to Standing Bear and, smiling, shook his hand. In moments Standing Bear was surrounded by scores of well-wishers, all wanting to shake the surprised chief by the hand, clap him on the back, and congratulate him. Wiping his eyes, Judge Dundy quietly slipped from the courtroom.

Standing Bear, surprised by the warmth of the people of Omaha, had no idea what his speech had achieved. At first, by the public reaction, he may have thought he had won his case. It would take Bright Eyes to tell him that Judge Dundy had gone away to think about the matters raised in the submissions by the lawyers, before he announced his decision one way or another.

Now came the waiting for the announcement of that decision.

Chapter 13

THE JUDGE'S VERDICT

NO ONE KNEW how long Judge Dundy would deliberate over his decision in the Standing Bear case. In the meantime, Standing Bear and his band remained under guard at Fort Omaha, although their newfound national celebrity meant they had a constant stream of visitors. Most were church people who came to offer their moral support.

After the drama of the hearing, when the days had seemed to fly by, time dragged through the weekend and into the first full week of May as the members of Standing Bear's defense team tried to get on with their lives and think about anything but the case. General Crook concentrated on military affairs, Andrew Poppleton returned his attention to railroad business, John Webster went back to his practice, and Henry Tibbles went about the business of newspaper reporting and editing, regularly making the trek out to Fort Omaha to see Standing Bear and keep up his spirits.

Back on the Omaha reservation, Bright Eyes returned to the government school and tried to focus on teaching her students their lessons, assuring her tribespeople that if they had faith their Ponca kinfolk would receive justice from the white judge. Her confidence in the U.S. judicial system was not shared by many of her people. As the days passed, her heart must have stopped every time a horseman arrived at the Omaha settlement in case it was a messenger bearing news about the judge's decision. But still no word came.

Midway through the second week of May, news came at last. Attorneys Webster and Poppleton were advised that Judge Dundy would hand down his judgment at a session of the district court on the following Monday, May 12. The word flashed around Omaha, and around the country.

Henry Tibbles was among a throng of reporters who converged on the second-floor courtroom on May 12 along with interested locals. Standing Bear and his wife were there, so too were Bright Eyes and General Crook, all hoping for justice for the Poncas at last. Poppleton, Webster, and Lambertson came to their feet with their clients as Elmer Dundy entered the court and then, with guarded apprehension, resumed their seats.

Judge Dundy had spent the last twelve days poring over copies of acts of Congress, Indian treaties, and other relevant legal and government documents, and then writing a detailed judgment that ran to many pages. He now began to read that judgment aloud. "During the fifteen years in which I have been engaged in administering the laws of my country, I have never been called upon to hear or decide a case that appealed so strongly to my sympathy as the one now under consideration."

It is not unusual for a judge to make a personal comment when handing down a judgment. This comment would have caused young Genio Lambertson to shift uncomfortably in his seat at what was, to him, an inauspicious opening.

The judge had more to say in the same vein. "On the one side, we have a few of the remnants of a once numerous and powerful, but now weak, insignificant, unlettered and generally despised race. On the other, we have the representatives of one of the most powerful, most enlightened, and most Christianized nations of modern times.

"On the one side, we have the representatives of this wasted race coming into this national tribunal of ours, asking for justice and liberty to enable them to adopt our boasted civilization, and to pursue the arts of peace, which have made us great and happy as a nation. On the other side, we have this magnificent, if not magnanimous government resisting this application with the determination of sending these people back to the country which is to them less desirable than perpetual imprisonment in their own native land." There was no doubting that the judge had fully comprehended the despair that the Ponca people had come to feel.

"But I think it is creditable to the heart and mind of the brave and distinguished officer who is made responsible herein, [Crook], to say that he has no sort of sympathy in the business in which he is forced by his position to bear a part so conspicuous.

"So far as I am individually concerned, I think it not improper to say that, if the strongest possible sympathy could give the relators title to freedom, they would have been restored to liberty the moment the arguments on their behalf had been closed. No examination or further thought would then have been necessary."

The district attorney would have been glowering at the judge by this time.

"But in a country where liberty is regulated by law," Dundy went on, "something more satisfactory and enduring than mere sympathy must furnish and constitute the rule and basis of judicial action. It follows that this case must be examined and decided on principles of law, and that unless the relators are entitled to their discharge under the Constitution or laws of the United States, or some treaty made pursuant thereto, they must be remanded to the custody of the officer who caused their arrest, to be returned to the Indian Territory, which they left without the consent of the Government."

Lambertson would have been feeling a whole lot better by this point. It almost sounded now as if the judge was making an excuse in advance for the verdict he was going to hand down—while Dundy sympathized with the Poncas, the law was the law and he had to rule in favor of the government. At Standing Bear's table, Poppleton and Webster would have begun to worry that their case might be lost.

The judge turned the page and then began again. "The District Attorney very earnestly questions the jurisdiction of the court to issue the writ, and to hear and determine the case made herein, and has supported his theory with an argument of great ingenuity and much ability. But, nevertheless, I am of the opinion that his premises are erroneous, and his conclusions, therefore, must be wrong and unjust." The judge would have glanced at Lambertson, before continuing, "The great respect I entertain for that officer, and the very able manner in which his views were presented, make it necessary for me to give somewhat at length the reasons which lead me to this conclusion."

Dundy was talking about Lambertson's submission that the original intent in Britain had been that habeas corpus should only apply to free citizens. The judge said that while he had not made a detailed examination of English laws, they seemed to him to be inferior to American law, for the U.S. Congress legislated on behalf of all mankind who came within its jurisdiction, not just the favored few.

"I cannot doubt," he went on, "that Congress intended to give to *every person* who might be unlawfully restrained of liberty under color of Authority of the United States the right to the writ and a discharge thereon. I conclude then, that so far as the issuing of the writ is concerned, it was properly issued, and that the relators are within the jurisdiction conferred by the habeas corpus act."

Round 1 to Standing Bear. Judge Dundy ruled that Standing Bear was a human being and was therefore legally entitled to sue for a writ of habeas corpus. This was a momentous, groundbreaking decision. In the eyes of the law, Standing Bear was a person!

But Standing Bear's victory on this point would count for nothing if the judge subsequently found that the Poncas had been on the Omaha reservation illegally and that their arrest had been lawful. In that case, the judge would dismiss their application and return them to the army's custody. The smarting Lambertson would have been glad that he had put some effort into defending the arrest of the Poncas on the Omaha reservation, even though he had never expected the judge's deliberations to extend that far.

Judge Dundy next turned to the matter of the right of Standing Bear and his fellow Poncas to separate themselves from their tribe and live and support themselves independently like any white person. In their written petition, the relators claimed that they had done the former and had been attempting to do the latter at the time of their arrest; the district attorney, for the government, submitted that Indians did not have this right of expatriation from their tribe and a separate life as citizens. The judge now proclaimed that he had not found a law preventing Indians from doing this. And an Indian, like a foreigner traveling in the United States or a foreigner who separated from his former nation and came to the United States as a migrant, who had separated from his tribe and the laws governing that tribe and was living as an individual in the United States, even if not a citizen of the United States, had an inalienable right to the protection of U.S. law.

"A question of much greater importance remains for consideration," Judge Dundy continued, "which, when determined, will be decisive to this whole controversy. This relates to the right of the Government to arrest and hold the relators for a time, for the purpose of being returned to a point in the Indian Territory from which it is alleged the Indians escaped. I am not vain enough to think that I can do full justice to a question like the one under consideration. But, as the matter furnishes so much valuable material for discussion, and so much food for reflection, I have tried to present it as viewed from my own standpoint, without reference to consequences or criticisms, which, though not specially invited, will be sure to follow." Dundy would prove to be so right on that score.

Again the judge elaborated, going into a detailed discussion of the matters arising from this point before moving on to conclude that "General Crook had the rightful authority to remove the relators from the reservation, and must stand justified in removing them therefrom." But that was not all. "When the troops are thus employed they must exercise the authority in the manner provided by [section 2149 of] the revised statutes. This law makes it the duty of the troops to convey the parties arrested by the nearest convenient and safe route, *to the civil authority of the territory or judicial district in which persons shall be found, to be proceeded against in due course of law.*"

This revelation would have stunned the courtroom. John L. Webster, in his verbal submission, had stated that the army could only hold a prisoner for five days before handing him over to the civil authorities, but he hadn't elaborated. What the judge was saying was that General Crook had been right to obey the order from Washington to arrest the Poncas; Standing Bear and his band did not have government permission to be on the Omaha reservation, and as far as the law was concerned they were trespassing. *But* the orders to General Crook from General Sherman had been faulty. As the judge now pointed out, the law required that anyone caught on a reservation without permission must be arrested and immediately handed over to the nearest civil law officer and brought before a judge. General Crook had been ordered to arrest the Poncas for removal back to the Indian Territory, but he had not been ordered to hand them over to the civil authorities to be proceeded against in a court of law, as he should have been.

Either someone in Washington had screwed up badly, or someone in authority at the highest level in Washington had deliberately and arrogantly ignored the requirements of the laws governing such actions. Judge Dundy felt the latter had been the case. "This course was not pursued in this case. Neither was it intended to observe the laws in that regard, for General Crook's orders, emanating from higher authority, expressly required him to apprehend the relators and remove them by force to the Indian Territory, from which it is alleged they escaped. But in what General Crook has done in these premises no fault can be imputed to him. He was simply obeying the orders of his superior officers. But the orders, as we think, lack the necessary authority of law, and are, therefore, not binding on the relators."

Put plainly, in the judge's opinion the orders to General Crook had not complied with the law and therefore could not be enforced. Judge Dundy then ruled:

1. That an *Indian* is a PERSON within the meaning of the laws of the United States, and has, therefore, the right to sue out a writ of *habeas corpus* in a federal court, or before a federal judge, in all cases

where he may be confined or in custody under color of authority of the United States, or where he is restrained of liberty in violation of the Constitution or laws of the United States.

2. That General George Crook, the respondent, being commander of the Military Department of the Platte, has the custody of the relators, under color of the authority of the United States, and in violation of the laws thereof.

3. That no rightful authority exists for removing by force any of the relators to the Indian Territory, as the respondent has been directed to do.

4. That the Indians possess the inherent right of expatriation, as well as the more fortunate white race, and have the inalienable right to *life, liberty, and the pursuit of happiness*, so long as they obey the laws and do not trespass on forbidden ground. And,

5. Being restrained of liberty under color of authority of the United States and in violation of the laws thereof, the relators must be discharged from custody, and it is so ordered.[166]

Translated from the legalese, the judge found that an Indian was a person and could apply for a writ of habeas corpus, that the orders to General Crook from Washington to arrest and *detain Standing Bear and his party for removal back to Indian Territory* were in contravention of the law, and they must be released.

Judge Dundy brought down his gavel. With the rap of wood on wood, the case of Standing Bear versus George Crook was concluded, and Standing Bear was a free man. The response from the gallery was spontaneous and deafening, a shout unlike any sound normally heard in a courtroom. The *St. Louis Republican* wrote of the reaction of Standing Bear and his wife, Susette, "At the close of the reading they received their liberty and congratulations of friends with feelings of great joy."[167]

Amid the excited crowd, the numbed Genio Lambertson attempted to grasp the enormity of the decision that had gone against him. There would be people in Nebraska, in Washington, and throughout the country who would want his scalp after this, demanding to know how he could have bungled such an apparently simple case, and how he could have permitted such a precedent to be set. Lambertson would turn twenty-nine in five days time, and this was definitely not the way he had planned to celebrate his birthday.

But to Standing Bear's joyous supporters, it appeared that Judge Dundy's groundbreaking decision was the dawning of a new era in American history. It seemed no accident that the Ponca tribe's name translated as Those Who Lead.

→ *Chapter 14* ←

THE INTERIOR SECRETARY'S RESPONSE

T HE NEWS FLASHED around the country—Standing Bear had won! The short version of the Dundy judgment, containing the five points of his determination, would have been telegraphed at once to Washington—to the War Department, the Interior Department, and the Bureau of Indian Affairs. The complete written judgment, with the judge's detailed reasoning for his decisions, would follow a little later.

As the *Omaha Herald* and countless other papers across the country reported the judge's decision on May 13, nothing but silence came out of Washington. On the next day, Wednesday, May 14, Secretary of War George W. McCrary in Washington issued an order: "General Crook was to immediately release Standing Bear and those in custody with him and to locate them on Federal Government land near to but separate from the Omaha Indian reservation."[168] The order was to take effect on Monday, May 19.

Judge Dundy's determination made the release order mandatory. But allocating land to Standing Bear's party was not, and it showed a certain magnanimity on the part of Secretary of War McCrary. Perhaps he had not been a wholehearted supporter of the hard line taken in the Standing Bear case by his colleague Secretary of the Interior Carl Schurz. Perhaps it was a parting gesture—McCrary resigned his post several months later and was replaced by Alexander Ramsey.

Leading lights in the Interior Department were not so generous. That same afternoon of May 14, Commissioner for Indian Affairs Ezra A. Hayt issued a public statement in Washington. The "perfectly bald" fifty-six-year-old Hayt ("lacking even those three hairs which cartoonists like to implant on all bald heads") was described by Henry Tibbles as "unimposing" and "insincere."[169] Hayt, Spotted Tail's "bald-headed liar," had no admirers in the pro-Indian camp. Lieutenant John Bourke noted in his diary on February 5, 1880, "it would be impossible to find 'a more thorough rascal'" than Commissioner Hayt.[170]

The unpopular Hayt, who had been in his post since 1877, was a man of fixed ideas about the American Indian and the firm way the U.S. government should deal with him. His Standing Bear statement of May 14 was published around the country. In it he announced that "the District Attorney at Omaha has been instructed to take the necessary steps to carry the question to higher courts. . . . The decision of Judge Dundy at Omaha in the Standing Bear *habeas corpus* case in which he virtually declares Indians citizens with the right to go where they please, regardless of treaty stipulations, is regarded by the Government as a heavy blow to the present Indian system, that, if sustained, will prove extremely dangerous alike to whites and Indians."[171]

Newspapers considered supportive of the Indian Ring were immediately outraged by the Dundy decision. The *Chicago Times* of May 14, for example, branded the verdict "sentimental idiocy." Others took a good hard look at the decision and as editorial writers began to postulate over its ramifications, the Indian Affairs line began to take hold. The national mood of sympathy for the Poncas weakened in some quarters, as people who initially took a charitable view of a small band of mistreated Native Americans began to fear the broader implications and repercussions of the case when applied to all Indians.

In a typical reflection of Commissioner Hayt's attitude, the editor of Minnesota's *St. Paul Pioneer Press* wrote on May 18, "If the decision of Judge Dundy, of the U.S. Court of Omaha, to the effect that Indians have the legal rights of citizens, is sustained, the Indian policy of the government will undergo a revolution. Any comprehensive and rational Indian policy contemplates the ultimate civilization of the savages." But the "comprehensive and rational Indian policy" advocated by the St. Paul editor did not envisage an immediate grant of equality to all Indians that the Dundy rulings seemed to them to imply.

Many Americans were all for "civilizing" the Indians, but they saw this as a gradual process of assimilation, with Indians earning their rights as they moved away from tribal customs and culture and into the white man's world. These people were certainly not ready for the overnight equality that Dundy's many critics warned would now follow. A sensible observer like Lieutenant John Bourke, who was in court for the Standing Bear judgment, could see that as a result of the Dundy decision "the path to citizenship was opened for the Indian."[172] Bourke rightfully perceived this path to be a long one. But, fed and led by the likes of Commissioner Hayt, some fearful Americans saw the path leading right to their door, and sometime soon.

Particularly in the frontier states, the local press fanned fears of savage Indians immediately being granted citizenship and let off their reservations en masse. The *Daily Commonwealth* of Topeka, Kansas, whose editor now looked anxiously to his state's southern horizon, took a common line when it declared following the Dundy verdict, "Under this decision, there is nothing to prohibit the Cheyennes, the Poncas, the Nez Perces and other tribes now held by force in Indian Territory from immediately taking up their line of march for the North."[173]

The reaction in Washington was typified by that of General Sherman, the man whom Judge Dundy found had issued the illegal order that resulted in both the Poncas' arrest and their discharge. Writing to his boss, Secretary of War McCrary, a week after the Dundy decision became public, Sherman expressed his incensed disapproval of that decision. He declared that the Poncas, who had been "fed and maintained by the Indian Bureau," were now "paupers turned loose on the community." He facetiously suggested that since Dundy had seen fit to set them free, he should personally foot the bill for their future care.[174]

By contrast, in the Standing Bear camp all was heady joy and celebration. In an editorial aside on May 15, the *Omaha Daily Herald* chortled,

"Mr. Hayt says he is a victim of political persecution. Suppose this persecution should land him in the penitentiary, what then, Mr. Hayt?" Standing Bear himself was at first astounded by the court decision.

On May 12, feeling elated by the day's events, Tibbles parted from Standing Bear as the five Poncas were taken back to the fort by Lieutenant Carpenter. He headed for his desk at the *Herald* to write up the Ponca victory for next day's paper and for papers throughout the country waiting on the outcome of the Standing Bear hearing.

Little did Tibbles know that another unexpected drama would soon play out in the Standing Bear affair, a drama involving him personally. Tibbles said that before Poppleton and Webster took their leave of Standing Bear in the courtroom, they passed on a warning to him. "If you set foot now on any Indian reservation, you can be arrested as an intruder."[175] Since, in the eyes of the law, Standing Bear had severed his connections with the Ponca tribe, this included the Ponca reservation in the Indian Territory and the old Ponca reservation in Dakota Territory. Unless they obtained government permission, Standing Bear and his refugee band could never again visit their Ponca relatives in the Indian Territory. Their Pyrrhic victory even excluded them from the Omaha reservation.

The Interior Department decided to exploit this consequence of the Dundy judgment to its advantage. On Tuesday, May 13, the day after Judge Dundy's judgment was handed down, apparently under instructions from Indian Affairs Commissioner Hayt, who in turn would have been acting on orders from Interior Secretary Schurz, several government lawyers arrived at Fort Omaha to see Standing Bear. Whether District Attorney Lambertson was one of them is unclear, but it is likely. General Crook could not prevent the lawyers from talking to Standing Bear. He was a free man now, even if technically he remained a prisoner until May 19. The government attorneys sat down with him in private. Only later did the general learn what transpired at this meeting.

Through an Indian Affairs interpreter, the government attorneys informed Standing Bear that he could now go back to his old home "perfectly safely."[176] There was definite underhanded intent in this advice.

The 1868 act of Congress that erroneously allocated the Ponca reservation to the Sioux had never been corrected. Officially the old Ponca reservation beside the Niobrara was a Sioux reservation, and if Standing Bear or any of his people set foot in their homeland north of the Niobrara they would be considered trespassers and subject to arrest and trial.

After the government attorneys left Fort Omaha, Standing Bear seems to have asked at the fort whether it was truly safe to go home and was told it was not. The guard placed on the Poncas had been deliberately loose, and now that Standing Bear would soon be a free man, it had been relaxed even more. Which, as it turned out, was not a good thing. Since the previous December, Standing Bear had been nursing a "notion"—he must keep his promise to Bear Shield and take his son's remains home to the old tribal burial grounds. The government attorneys had given weight to that notion. In the early hours of the next morning, believing what he wanted to believe, Standing Bear slipped out of the fort and set off to walk home to the Niobrara.

John Bourke indicates that Standing Bear headed home with the bones of his son hanging in a sack around his neck.[177] Up to that time, Standing Bear had kept Bear Shield's remains in the larger of two wooden trunks he had brought up from Indian Territory. The Ponca and Omaha Indians shared the same traditional burial practice. The bodies of the dead were left in trees or on raised platforms of rock, earth, and branches, and exposed to the elements, together with tribal religious artifacts. Once the flesh rotted away, the bones were removed and buried among the bones of relatives in a sacred riverside burial ground. In this way, it was believed, the deceased could mix with their ancestors in the afterlife. This was why Bear Shield had wrung the promise from his father on his deathbed—that Standing Bear would inter his bones among their ancestors on the Niobrara—so terrified was the youth of being alone in the afterlife.

The night of May 13, a message was relayed to Henry Tibbles in Omaha from General Crook at the fort, telling him that Standing Bear had disappeared. Tibbles could guess where his friend was heading and feared for him. If found on the Niobrara reservation by government representatives,

Standing Bear would be arrested and dragged into court. If he resisted, he could be shot by a trigger-happy soldier. If he was arrested, his cause, and that of his people, would suffer significant damage, since Commissioner Hayt and Secretary Schurz were looking for an opportunity to discredit him.

Tibbles suspected that Schurz was hoping for just this sort of rash reaction from Standing Bear when he sent the government lawyers to see him at the fort. For all he knew, Indian Affairs officials were lying in wait for Standing Bear at the Niobrara. Tibbles didn't have to think twice about what to do—he set off after the chief, determined to bring him back before he was caught on the old Ponca reservation.

Standing Bear had at least an eighteen-hour start on Tibbles by the time the pursuit began that night. The newspaperman apparently borrowed a buggy and set off north, driving like a maniac, for the Omaha reservation. He knew Iron Eye kept two fast ponies at his house in Joe's Village, the house that housed him, his two wives, and his numerous children, including Bright Eyes. Tibbles reached Joe's Village in the middle of the night after driving all day and told the chief about Standing Bear's flight. Iron Eye unhesitatingly loaned the ponies to his friend.

Tibbles also needed a good interpreter who could help him talk Standing Bear into turning around and coming back. It would have to be someone the chief knew and respected. Tibbles says he took "a young Indian" with him for that purpose.[178] That rules out Willie Hamilton, a white, and Iowa Charles Morgan, who was apparently a mature man, as well as a middle-aged Omaha who sometimes served as an interpreter, Henry Fontanelle, son of a famous Omaha chief of the 1850s. The "young Indian" may have been Iron Eye's son Frank La Flesche. He spoke excellent English and had a good mind. After his sister described the performance of Andrew Poppleton and Andrew Webster in court on behalf of his people, and in the wake of the unexpected legal victory, Frank La Flesche set his sights on becoming a lawyer one day. But if Frank was the interpreter used by Tibbles on this occasion it's strange that Tibbles chose not to name him.

The fact that Tibbles didn't reveal this person's identity makes it likely that interpreter was in fact Bright Eyes. Standing Bear liked and trusted the twenty-four-year-old school mistress. Besides, she had translated for him in court, and he knew that she had been acting in his best interests ever since she went to General Crook to initiate his defense. If anyone could talk Standing Bear out of his notion, it would be Bright Eyes. What's more, at Tibbles's instigation, Bright Eyes and her father would carry out another sensitive mission involving the Poncas within the next few weeks. As with previous episodes, Tibbles failed to identify Bright Eyes as the interpreter at his side in this Standing Bear chase for reasons that became clear later.

Iron Eye would have had concerns about his daughter riding off into the night with a white man, but he trusted no one more than he trusted his "brother" and fellow Soldier Lodge member Henry Tibbles. The urgent and imperative nature of the mission would have convinced the chief of the Omahas to let Bright Eyes go along. The pair set off toward the Niobrara together on Iron Eye's horses at four o'clock in the morning.

Tibbles says he had traveled 120 miles in eighteen hours by the time he and his Indian companion caught up with Standing Bear in the night. The Ponca chief was warming himself at a campfire, waiting by the bank of the fast-flowing Niobrara for the dawn to show him a safe crossing place. It must have taken some doing, convincing Standing Bear to turn around when he was so close to his destination, so near to interring his son's bones with those of his ancestors. But Tibbles and his companion eventually made him realize the danger of being found on the old reservation by government representatives. They would have pointed out that those representatives may have been lying in wait at the ruined Ponca settlement north of the river, where Standing Bear's house had previously stood, a place that Standing Bear would have been drawn to once he crossed the river.

Tibbles and his companion escorted Standing Bear back south, first to Joe's Village. At the Omaha settlement, Tibbles and Standing Bear rested briefly and spoke with Iron Eye and Bright Eyes about their strategy in the fight to bring all the Poncas home from Indian Territory. Tibbles and

Standing Bear then transferred to the newspaperman's buggy and continued on to Fort Omaha. It would have been when Tibbles brought the miserable chief back to the fort that Lieutenant Bourke saw Standing Bear and noted the bag of bones around his neck as he dejectedly dismounted from the vehicle. It would have been an image that lodged in Bourke's mind for the rest of his days.

With the broken-hearted Standing Bear confined to the fort under a closer watch until the following week, when he was due for release, General Crook, Tibbles, and Webster met to discuss the fate of his little band. They agreed that a committee of concerned citizens should be formed to support the Poncas in their endeavors to start a new life. Now that Standing Bear's group had been legally declared separate and individual from their tribe, and Standing Bear had given the understanding that he and his people could support themselves, the government was under no obligation to provide them with protection, food, shelter, livestock, seed, tools, or education, as provided by past treaties between the Ponca tribe and previous U.S. administrations.

Tibbles made the rounds of his church connections, and before long the Omaha Ponca Relief Committee was formed. Chaired by Robert Clarkson, Episcopal bishop of Nebraska, the committee's founding members included James O'Connor, Congregational bishop of Nebraska, Reverend William Harsha of the Presbyterian Church, and Judge James W. Savage. O'Connor and Savage were later replaced by Leavitt Burnham, W. M. Yates, and P. L. Perine. The committee treasurer was Congregational minister Alvin F. Sherrill. While the committee deliberated on the most constructive ways to help the Poncas, General Crook looked at maps of Nebraska as he considered the best place to settle Standing Bear and his little band.

On Sunday, May 18, one day before Standing Bear's official release date, Henry Tibbles went to the fort to say good-bye to the Poncas, and Standing Bear took him out to a low hill outside the fort behind General Crook's residence. Over the past six weeks Standing Bear had sometimes gone to this wildflower-dotted hill for contemplation.

There on the hill, Standing Bear said, "When I was brought here a prisoner, my heart was broken. I was in despair. I had no friend in all the big world. Then you came. I told you the story of my wrongs. From that time until now you have not ceased to work for me." On his worst days, he said, he came out here to the hill and looked toward the city of Omaha, knowing that there was a man in that city who was working to save him. And now he was saved.[179]

Taking Tibbles back to the fort, he led him into his shelter. Opening a trunk, he took out his tomahawk, a war bonnet, and beaded leggings. The leggings he presented to Tibbles. "If you ever want a home, come to me or my tribe," he said. "While there is one Ponca alive you will never be without a friend. Mr. Poppleton and Mr. Webster are my friends. You are my brother."[180]

He asked Tibbles to give his tomahawk and bonnet to Webster and Poppleton, but Tibbles suggested that it would be more meaningful if he did it himself. So Tibbles took Standing Bear into Omaha to pay his respects to the two lawyers and present his gifts. At the Webster house Standing Bear shook hands with the Webster ladies and then stood before John L. Webster himself.

"Hitherto," he said through an unidentified interpreter, "when we have been wronged, we went to war to assert our rights." He looked sternly at Webster. "We had no law to punish those who did wrong to us, so we took our tomahawks and went to kill. If they had guns and would kill us first, it was the fate of war. But you have found a better way. You have gone into the court for us, and I find that our wrongs can be righted there. Now I have no more use for the tomahawk. I want to lay it down forever." The chief then stooped and placed the tomahawk on the ground at his feet, before straightening and folding his arms. "I lay it down, I have no more use for it," he said. "I can now seek the ways of peace."[181]

In accepting the chief's tomahawk, Webster declared, "I shall continue to fight your battles as long as it is necessary to give you the protection of the laws."[182]

Tibbles and Standing Bear moved on to Andrew Poppleton's house. "For many years we have been chased about as a dog chases a wild beast," Standing Bear told Poppleton. "God sent you to help me. I thank you for what you have done."[183] He held out his gift. A traditional Plains Indian feather headdress, it reached almost to the ground when worn, which was only on the most sacred ceremonial occasions. Standing Bear said that this was his clan's most ancient relic, and Tibbles estimated it to be at least three hundred years old. Standing Bear, referring to the bonnet as a "holy thing," had told Tibbles he'd previously refused large sums for it. It was all he had to give, he said, as he handed the headdress over with tears in his eyes.[184]

Both Poppleton and Webster would treasure their gifts from Standing Bear, the most valuable possessions of a man who had lost virtually everything except his freedom. Had it not been for the attorneys, Standing Bear would not have had his day in court, and Henry Tibbles deserved every word of praise he received. Yet, in reality, the man who deserved the most thanks from Standing Bear was Judge Elmer Dundy. In their submissions to the district court, Webster and Poppleton had missed the one point of law which resulted in Standing Bear's release. Webster had brushed over it in his address, but it had taken Dundy to explore the statute fully and realize the army should have been ordered to hand the Poncas over to the civil authorities. A less thorough judge, or a judge less inclined to the Indians' cause, may not have gone to such lengths.

More than that, Judge Dundy was concerned about what would happen to Standing Bear following his release. Webster and Poppleton had used the claim of expatriation in their initial petition merely to ensure the Poncas qualified for protection under the Fourteenth Amendment. They had not explored the issue of expatriation in their addresses, but Dundy had when considering his judgment. In conferring the right of expatriation on Standing Bear and his companions, the judge guaranteed them the right to live wherever they chose. But it was illegal to give gifts to judges, so an embarrassing incident was probably avoided when Standing Bear failed to realize his debt to the judge in his case.

Meanwhile, though the government may have failed in a bid to trick Standing Bear and arrest him a second time, it was not going to stop there in its efforts to counter the district court judgment. A smarting Genio Lambertson appealed to the Supreme Court, as he had been instructed. The *Daily Herald* had heard from unidentified contacts in the government that two judges, Miller and Dillon, had been instructed to set aside an early date to hear the government's appeal.[185] It was duly brought before Associate Justice Samuel F. Miller of the Supreme Court on June 5.

But, to Lambertson's embarrassment, the judge refused to hear the government's grounds for appeal because "the Indians who had petitioned for the writ of *habeas corpus* were not present, having been released by the order of Judge Dundy," and District Attorney Lambertson had not taken steps to require "security for their appearance" at a subsequent appeal.[186] Genio Lambertson had screwed up.

The district attorney applied for a continuance and went away to prepare his case all over again—a setback and delay the Interior Department hadn't reckoned on. With their fresh appeal unlikely to be heard for another six months or more, Secretary Schurz and Commissioner Hayt would have to devise a new strategy to counter the Standing Bear decision and prevent the feared "revolution" in U.S. Indian policy.

Chapter 15

THE SECRET MISSION

T HE SECRETARY OF war had instructed General Crook to install Standing Bear and his little band on government land. The Poncas wanted to go home to their land on the northern bank of the Niobrara, but technically that was part of the Great Sioux reservation. Following the Dundy determination, if Standing Bear or any of his twenty-five fellow relators were found on an Indian reservation, *any* Indian reservation, they could be arrested, removed, brought before a judge, and possibly imprisoned.

After carefully studying maps of Nebraska and Dakota Territory, Crook discovered another loophole through which he could slip Standing Bear. Several fertile islands that split the Niobrara River into five fast-flowing channels just before it hit the Missouri did not fall within the boundaries of the Sioux reservation when they were extended in error in 1868 to include Ponca lands. The surveyors had used the river as the southern boundary of the new Great Sioux reservation. The Poncas, however, considered these islands part of their ancestral homeland.

On May 19, General Crook loaded Standing Bear and his band into their wagons and had them escorted north to the largest of the islands. This lush green island was, in Tibbles's words, "a safe distance outside the Omaha reservation boundaries."[187] It was also separated from the Sioux reservation by the river, which the general warned Standing Bear and his party not to cross. At least this way Standing Bear and his Poncas would be on home ground.

But Crook knew that Standing Bear's Poncas longed to live and die north of the Niobrara, where their ancestors were buried and where their most productive cornfields lay. To make the hearts of the Poncas ache even more, Yankton Sioux had been encouraged by the government to settle on the Ponca land north of the Niobrara, to legitimize previous government errors. The determined general set his sights on the Poncas' desire for complete repatriation to their homeland before he was done. A Wyoming newspaper reporter had written of Crook, after accompanying him on his 1876 campaigns against the Sioux and the Cheyenne, "He has a dogged, stubborn pertinacity. When he once takes hold he never lets go."[188] Regaining title to the Poncas' Niobrara land now topped Crook's agenda, and he worked behind the scenes with Henry Tibbles, John L. Webster, and the Omaha Ponca Relief Committee to see that objective achieved.

The white settlement of Niobrara was located just two miles from the island where Standing Bear and his followers set up their tents, and Tibbles says that as soon as they had arrived at the site of their new home Standing Bear put his entire band—men, women, and children—to work chopping wood, which they bartered with the townsfolk for provisions. They had to use sign language to complete the exchange because not a single member of the Ponca band spoke more than a few words of English. The people of Niobrara, who had spoken up on behalf of the Poncas in the past, welcomed the return of Standing Bear's band and were pleased to help them.

The complex legal maneuvering involving the Poncas and their land went over Standing Bear's head, but he understood that U.S. law had been made to work for him and his people. When he asked why the court decision did not apply to his Ponca kinfolk in the Indian Territory, why they could not also return to the Niobrara and be reunited with Standing Bear's band, it was explained to him that it would require a separate application to the court, and a second successful judgment. Standing Bear reasoned that if the law could work for him, it must also be made to work for the rest of his people, so he urged Henry Tibbles to help the Poncas one more time.

Tibbles later claimed that he himself had set his sights higher. With the precedent established, he says, he failed to see why the Standing Bear case could not be "the first step in freeing all Indians everywhere from the selfish and arbitrary domination of the Indian Ring and of Washington officialdom."[189] But for the moment, with most of the Ponca tribe still stranded in the Indian Territory, the focus had to be on them.

Tibbles says that he, General Crook, and John Webster talked long and hard about what move to make next. If they went through the courts, Webster indicated, they would need to officially make clients of Chief White Eagle and the rest of the Ponca tribe in Indian Territory. With that in mind, when Tibbles was taking Standing Bear back to Fort Omaha, stopping off at Joe's Village along the way, he had discussed with Bright Eyes and her father the possibility of the pair going down to Indian Territory to secure the rest of the Ponca tribe's authority to act on their behalf before a judge. Father and daughter had agreed to make the journey, but certain obstacles had to be removed first.

The true purpose of the trip would be kept confidential, to prevent Indian Affairs officials from interfering with it; there was no way that Secretary Schurz would want the Indian Territory Poncas roped into this affair. Officially, the journey to the Arkansas River would be made on the excuse that Iron Eye and Bright Eyes were visiting Iron Eye's brother, White Swan, and his family. The trip would be authorized in writing by General Crook and funded by the Omaha committee—the Omaha Ponca Committee as it had become known. Crook quickly agreed to his part, and the committee gave its full blessing to the mission and provided the necessary funds once Tibbles presented the plan to the members.

Tibbles took credit for coming up with the idea for this secret mission, but it may have originated with Bright Eyes, and Tibbles was trying to protect her. She had no qualms about going behind the backs of people in authority, as she demonstrated by going off her reservation to obtain her teaching certificate, by drafting the 1877 presidential telegram and press statement for the Ponca chiefs and bringing in Reverend Hamilton, by making the illegal dash to Columbus to see the bedraggled Poncas on their forced march, and, later, by going to General Crook to urge him to go to bat for Standing Bear against his own superiors.

When he wrote of Bright Eyes's secret mission to Indian Territory, Henry Tibbles sang her praises, saying that she was the ideal envoy. After spending six "exceptional" years at the mission school, he wrote, Bright Eyes won high praise at the private school in New Jersey "for her brilliance, her willingness to work hard, and her pleasant, winning ways."[190] Bright Eyes had already exerted a powerful behind-the-scenes influence in the Standing Bear case, and now she and her father eagerly prepared to make the trip to Indian Territory. Apart from the covert motive for the journey, Tibbles says that Bright Eyes adored her uncle, White Swan, and she genuinely wanted to see her relatives who were languishing in the Indian Territory. Besides, it would give her the opportunity to celebrate her forthcoming birthday with her Ponca kin—she would turn twenty-five on May 26.

As no one knew what tactic the Interior Department would attempt next, every day was vital, so Iron Eye and Bright Eyes set off as soon as the Omaha committee gave the nod. They went south by train as far as they could into Kansas, then took to the road and walked into Indian Territory.

On May 20, when they reached the Ponca Agency, thirty-five miles south of Arkansas City, they were dismayed to find that the settlement there, at the junction of the Arkansas River and Salt Fork, was a shambles. It had scarcely any roads or paths, and the 550 Poncas confined to the reservation had been provided with six leaky shanty houses built by Indian Affairs. After more than two years, the majority of the tribe, who had been thrown out of fine log homes in the north, still lived in tents. Those tents were spread beside the Christian crosses and grave markers dotting a cemetery where many members of the tribe had been interred since arriving from the north. Here, under the new regime, the old "un-Christian" burial customs of the Ponca people had been terminated by Indian Affairs agent William Whiteman. Sorrowing members of the Ponca tribe would have lamented that many a departed Ponca was now wandering alone in the afterlife.

There was no church building here, and no school. For the past two years the children who had attended school at the northern reservation had gone without schooling. Agent Whiteman was meanwhile living in a large two-story wooden frame house, the first genuine residence to be erected at the site, built by white laborers from Arkansas City at a cost of $2,500 and paid for with government money. Henry Tibbles wrote that when Bright Eyes returned to Nebraska, she remarked that the handsome agent's residence "somehow looked strangely out of place among the tents and graves."[191]

Fortunately for them, Bright Eyes and her father arrived at the settlement when the agent was away. Agent Whiteman frequently went to Arkansas City on business, staying overnight at the Central Avenue Hotel, and by chance the paths of the Omaha pair and the agent did not cross. As the visitors discovered, the agent was keeping the Indian Territory Poncas cut off from the outside world. After a tearful reunion with White Swan, his ailing wife, and their other Ponca relatives at the settlement, Iron Eye and Bright Eyes learned that the Poncas knew nothing of Standing Bear's court victory. They didn't even know that Standing Bear had taken the government to court. Agent Whiteman had prevented newspapers from reaching the tribe, and he intercepted and opened all letters going in and out of the reservation, destroying any that he considered inflammatory. Under William Whiteman, the Ponca reservation was nothing more than a prison camp.

The Poncas told their visitors that in the middle of April the agent had suddenly announced his intention to build sixty new houses for the tribe. The amazed Poncas had not been able to work out why, overnight, he should become so uncharacteristically benevolent. Bright Eyes and Iron Eye knew why—the announcement had come after Andrew Poppleton and John Webster had petitioned the district court for the writ of habeas corpus for the Ponca runaways. Fearing publicity and closer scrutiny of how the Poncas in Indian Territory were being treated, Washington had instructed Whiteman to make rapid improvements on the reservation.

Behind closed doors, Bright Eyes and Iron Eye told the astonished Poncas the details of the court case, and of how Standing Bear was now a person in the eyes of U.S. law, entitled to live where he chose. To Chief White Eagle they also disclosed the secret reason for their visit. Elated by the wonderful change of fortune experienced by Standing Bear and his band, and excited by the possibility that the rest of the tribe might also return home to the Niobrara, that same day, May 20, old White Eagle discreetly dictated a long letter to Bright Eyes, addressed to Henry Tibbles.

In the letter, Chief White Eagle asked Tibbles to pass a message to lawyers Poppleton and Webster: "We had thought there was none to take pity on us. I thank you in the name of my tribe for what you have done for Standing Bear, and I ask you to go still further in your kindness and help us regain our land and our rights. . . . I want to save the remainder of my people, and I look to you for help."[192]

It seems that White Eagle then confided to Bright Eyes that Agent Whiteman was robbing the Ponca people at every opportunity. He would have told her how Whiteman purchased white man's horses at top prices and then expected the Ponca farmers to use them to pull their plows. What the Poncas needed were Indian ponies, purchased from other tribes. Indian ponies cost nothing to keep. Unlike white man's horses, Indian ponies did not need to be sheltered in stables or kept in corrals, and they did not have to be fed grain every day either. Over the winter, the Indians simply turned their horses loose, and they lived off cottonwood bark and came back next spring fit and healthy. White man's horses were of no use to Indians; they were a waste of good money. They were more expensive to buy than Indian ponies and more expensive to keep. Yet Whiteman had persisted in paying big money for horses and feed to Arkansas City suppliers.

And then there were Whiteman's other extravagances. White Eagle and his clan chiefs would have reeled off a string of instances where the agent had paid too much for goods for the reservation. They might have been Indians, but they were not stupid. They heard things, they saw things. Sometimes Whiteman would withdraw a contract from one man in Arkansas City a week after it had been awarded and give it to friends like agency trader Joe Sherburne at a higher price. Apparently Bright Eyes took up her pen once again and had the chiefs dictate statements about the agent's buying habits, and then had them sign these affidavits, which she witnessed.

That day or the next Whiteman returned to the agency to find Bright Eyes and her father staying with White Eagle. They had come from the north with official permission so there was nothing he could do about their presence, but he immediately realized that the pair had brought news of Standing Bear's victory to his otherwise ignorant Poncas. He was far from happy about that and knew that Washington would be equally unhappy. Rather than shy away from the agent, Bright Eyes boldly went to see him. For heartfelt reasons, as well as to promote her cover story for the visit, she asked permission for her uncle and sick aunt to return to the Omaha reservation with Iron Eye and herself. True to form, Agent Whiteman refused her request point-blank.

The day after Bright Eyes and her father arrived at the settlement a new drama was set in motion by Standing Bear's gigantic brother Big Snake. Excited and emboldened by the news of his brother's court victory and unable to see why Judge Dundy's ruling did not apply to the Poncas in the Indian Territory, Big Snake decided to test the Dundy decision. Perhaps Bright Eyes gave him the idea, but it's more likely she urged him to be patient, to wait for the next court victory she was working to achieve. But Big Snake was impatient.

Another issue had been simmering in Big Snake's breast, and it also had to do with his rights. Not long before, the government had sent eight Ponca children away to a new boarding school in a former army barracks in Carlisle, Pennsylvania, set up exclusively for Indians. One of those children was Big Snake's only son. Two of White Eagle's children had also been sent there. At Carlisle, the children were forced to cut their long hair and wear school uniforms. According to the *New York Observer* they were "governed kindly but firmly."[193] Unlike white boarding school students, they weren't allowed to go home over the summer but were hired out to white families around Carlisle as servants. Their lessons were taught exclusively in English, and they were permitted to write home just once a month, in English. Big Snake could not read English. He and his wife were pining for their boy. But more than that, Big Snake wanted to know what right the government had to take his son away from him.

Determined to prove he had rights too, just like Standing Bear, Big Snake gathered fellow members of the Soldier Lodge around him in a council. Together they discussed what they might do in light of his brother's successful judgment, and an idea occurred to them. The Southern Cheyenne, who for the past four years had been sharing a reservation with the Arapaho one hundred miles to the southwest, had offered to sell the Poncas Indian ponies to help make up for their heavy stock losses. But Agent Whiteman, intent on buying horses through his friends, had refused to allow the Poncas to make the purchase from the Cheyenne. The plotters decided to use this to their advantage and to act immediately.

That day, May 21, Big Snake and thirty other Ponca men went to Agent Whiteman, informed him they were going to the Cheyenne reservation to buy horses, declared they didn't need his permission to go, and then left the agency, knowing that Whiteman didn't have the physical resources to stop them. Setting off immediately, they made their way along the Arkansas River toward the Cheyenne-Arapaho reservation, leaving Agent Whiteman seething behind them.

Whiteman recognized this as a deliberate attempt by Big Snake to test the Standing Bear judgment and prove that *all* Indians were persons and could not be confined against their will on a reservation. Before he joined the Indian Affairs Bureau, Whiteman had been a small-town lawyer in Baxter Springs, Kansas, and was elected to a single term as Cherokee County attorney. Confident that Big Snake did not have a legal leg to stand on, he immediately sent a messenger to the telegraph office in Arkansas City.

A wire was sent to the commissioner of Indian Affairs in Washington containing a report from Agent Whiteman that Big Snake and thirty "renegades" had left the Ponca reservation to go to the Cheyenne reservation without his permission. Whiteman requested that the Ponca party be arrested on reaching the Cheyenne reservation and detained at the nearest Indian Territory military post, Fort Reno, "until the tribe has recovered from the demoralizing effects of the decision recently made by the United States district court in Nebraska, in the case of Standing Bear."[194]

This was the opposite of the truth, of course. Far from being demoralized, the Poncas had been uplifted by the Dundy decision. Whiteman wanted to keep the agitator Big Snake and his followers in the Fort Reno guardhouse, away from the rest of the tribe, for months if necessary, until all Poncas in the Indian Territory saw the folly of hoping to go home to the Niobrara and reuniting with Standing Bear's band. Already several Ponca leaders, including Lone Chief and even Standing Buffalo, were inclined toward accepting their fate and making the best of things here in the Indian Territory. If Whiteman could separate the troublemakers from the others, he was sure the rest of the tribe would soon fall into line.

Interior Secretary Schurz immediately asked the secretary of war to act in the Big Snake matter. The next day, May 22, General Sherman telegraphed General Sheridan in Chicago: "The honorable Secretary of the Interior requests that the Poncas be arrested and held at Fort Reno, in the Indian Territory."[195] Unlike Agent Whiteman, who wanted to lock up Big Snake and his followers for a prolonged period, Secretary Schurz urged that once they were in custody, Big Snake and his companions be returned by the army to the Ponca reservation at the Arkansas River as quickly as possible, before friends of the Poncas in the North heard about their arrest and instigated legal action on their behalf. "You may order this to be done," Sherman told Sheridan.[196]

To counter the claim that Big Snake could be expected to make—that the district court decision had given him the right to leave the Ponca reservation—General Sherman told General Sheridan in his telegram,

"The release under writ of *habeas corpus* of the Poncas in Nebraska *does not apply to any other than that specific case.*"[197]

Sherman was essentially right, since Standing Bear and his party had been released on a technicality. Had General Crook's orders required him to hand his prisoners over to the civil authorities and had General Crook complied, as he would have done, Standing Bear and his companions would have been taken before a judge, and that judge would have found that they were on the Omaha reservation illegally, and he could have been expected to order their return to the Ponca reservation in the Indian Territory.

Clearly the Interior Department and the War Department had closed ranks. Until challenged and tested in court, this was the stance they would take in all incidents involving Indians from this point on. As far as the government was concerned, Standing Bear's was an isolated case, and no other Indian had rights under the Constitution. Of all the Indians in America, only Standing Bear and his twenty-five Ponca companions were persons in the eyes of the law, and that was the way Carl Schurz and his colleagues intended it should stay.

General Sheridan in turn passed Sherman's order regarding Big Snake on to the military district commander at Fort Smith in Arkansas, which was both the military and judicial administrative center for Indian Territory. That officer passed the order to the commander at Fort Reno, a post four miles west of present-day El Reno in western Oklahoma that had the task of watching over the Cheyenne-Arapaho reservation and the Ponca reservation. Big Snake and his party were duly arrested on the Cheyenne reservation and taken to Fort Reno. By the beginning of June, Big Snake and his companions had been delivered back to the Ponca reservation by the army.

Bright Eyes and Iron Eye were still at the reservation when Big Snake's unhappy band was brought back under guard. They had no idea at the time that Big Snake's return had been made possible by another illegal order. Astonishingly, through ineptitude, arrogance, or misplaced pride, the Interior Department had requested, and the War Department had once again issued, an order that contravened the law. As in the Standing Bear case, General Sherman had ordered that Big Snake and his party be arrested, detained at a military post, and then returned by the army to the reservation from which they were deemed to have escaped. As the Dundy determination had made pointedly clear, Big Snake and his party could be arrested for being on the Cheyenne reservation without permission, but the law required that the commander at Fort Reno be ordered by the War Department to immediately escort his prisoners to "the civil authority of the territory or judicial district" in which they had been found—in this case, the federal marshal at Fort Smith, Arkansas—and handed over. The prisoners would then be brought before a judge at Fort Smith. Ironically, the judge would no doubt order them returned to their reservation, but the law would have been followed, to the letter.

Why the German-born Schurz deliberately and stubbornly ignored the law a second time defies comprehension. He was apparently determined not to admit that he had been wrong in the Dundy case. To him, to order Big Snake handed over to civil authorities would acknowledge that the judge had been right in the Dundy ruling, and that Schurz had indeed requested an unlawful act in the Standing Bear case. It can only be concluded that Schurz had been so stung by the Dundy judgment and took it so personally that he lost his perspective, his objectivity, and his respect for the law.

Had this latest illegal act by the authorities become public knowledge there would have been uproar among the Poncas' white supporters, and Henry Tibbles and his team would have been handed red-hot ammunition for their campaign. But Agent Whiteman acted quickly to ensure that didn't happen. The soldiers who returned Big Snake and his party to the reservation stayed at the agency for the time being and, backed by their guns, Whiteman kept Bright Eyes and Iron Eye separated from Big Snake and ordered the pair to leave before they had time to ask difficult questions. Smuggling White Eagle's letter and the affidavits about Whiteman's financial dealings off the reservation with them, Bright Eyes and her father said their tearful farewells to White Eagle, his wife, and the other

Poncas at the Arkansas River reservation. As they walked up the road toward Kansas and the train back north, they left behind a promise that good people in Nebraska would help the stranded Poncas.

Once the troublesome Omaha chief and his intelligent daughter were out of sight, Agent Whiteman again sealed off the Poncas living at the Arkansas River from the outside world. With Big Snake unaware that he should have been taken before a judge rather than returned directly to the reservation, with Bright Eyes and Iron Eye neither knowing nor imagining that the government had again acted illegally, and with no one at Fort Reno possessing the courage or the conviction to speak out about this latest travesty of justice, the details of the illegal handling of Big Snake and his colleagues would not become public knowledge for eight months. And by that time it would be too late. Much too late.

Big Snake, normally so gentle and conciliatory, was changed by this episode. He was now possessed by a notion—was he not, like his brother, also a person? And now that the white man's law had recognized his brother as a person, how could it be argued that Big Snake was not? Big Snake blamed Agent Whiteman for preventing him from exercising the right that he felt sure good white men would now accord him. Furious with Whiteman for having him brought back to the reservation like a runaway dog, he simmered with resentment, declaring that he would never again speak to the agent.

Whiteman was shaken by Big Snake's continued defiance. And he would have worried that Big Snake's Cheyenne reservation excursion might have jeopardized his job, just at a time when his agency was about to grow. For, without consulting the Poncas, Commissioner Hayt had decided to relocate another tribal group to the Ponca reservation in the Indian Territory—370 members of the fierce Nez Percé tribe from Idaho who tried to flee to Canada, fighting the U.S. Army all the way, before surrendering. As the *Arkansas City Traveler* commented, "With the addition of the Nez Percé trade will be increased considerably."[198] The editor knew that the Bureau of Indian Affairs would give Whiteman much more to spend in Arkansas City in support of the Nez Percé.

In early June, Whiteman invited his new friend Nathan Hughes, Arkansas City postmaster and newspaper editor, to pay him a visit on the Ponca reservation. When Whiteman regularly rode up from the Ponca Agency to the frontier town, he would invariably collect agency mail from Hughes and place advertisements with him to be run in the Wednesday *Traveler* seeking bids for the supply of stock, supplies, materials, and contractors for the Ponca reservation. While he was in town, Whiteman would jaw with the newspaper editor and complain about his Ponca charges.

Whiteman found a sympathetic ear in Hughes. The editor had no love for the Poncas, but he recognized their commercial worth to his town and was annoyed by attempts of their white allies in Nebraska to have them repatriated to their old reservation on the Niobrara. For their part, the Poncas did their best to befriend Hughes. Chief White Eagle even invited editor Hughes to watch the tribe's annual Sun Dance with its Soldier Lodge initiation ceremony—the same initiation that Henry Tibbles and General Crook had secretly undergone with the Omahas several years earlier.

The Poncas had kept up the Sun Dance tradition each summer since being taken down to Indian Territory, despite the fact that the Indian Affairs Bureau had banned the Ponca and the Omaha summer buffalo hunts after 1876. Hughes subsequently wrote a detailed and critical account of the "barbarous" Sun Dance ceremony for his *Traveler* readers. After describing the slits cut in the chests of the Ponca initiates, he commented, "Our only regret" was that the Poncas did not also "cut their fool heads off" while they were about it.[199]

Clearly Whiteman invited Hughes to the agency in June hoping he would run a story in the *Traveler* that might dampen any rumors about a disturbance at the Ponca reservation in late May—the unauthorized departure and enforced return of Big Snake and his thirty companions. Hughes was only too happy to oblige. In an editorial about the Ponca tribe that appeared in the Wednesday, June 18 edition of the *Traveler*, Hughes, an unabashed Republican, wrote glowingly of the state of affairs at the agency, from the fine agent's residence to four houses under construction, albeit for white agency employees, and one hundred acres of corn under cultivation.

Hughes also noted in his June 18 editorial, "We think that the restless spirit of the Poncas can be justly attributed to the influence of whites at their old reservation in the north. Certainly no tribe of Indians in the Territory has a more attractive agency, and no reservation a finer body of land." Whiteman assured Hughes that the "restless spirit" among the Poncas would soon be a thing of the past and the members of the tribe would settle down to a contented life in their new Indian Territory home.

That same month, twenty-five Poncas led by Walks Over the Other, Whistler, and Woodpecker slipped off the Indian Territory reservation. Following the route taken by Standing Bear and his escapees earlier in the year and selling their horses along the way to pay for food, they avoided detection and made it all the way to the Santee Agency in the Dakota Territory before swinging west to join Standing Bear on the Niobrara. Once they had arrived home, no orders came out of Washington for their arrest.

→ ←

While Bright Eyes and her father were in the Indian Territory, Tibbles put together the draft of a book, a hurried memoir of the groundbreaking Standing Bear court case, *The Ponca Chiefs, An Indian's Attempt to Appeal from the Tomahawk to the Courts*. It was little more than a compilation of documents relating to the case loosely linked by Tibble's brief narrative, but he hoped to find a publisher who would see a potential market in the many Americans who had followed the case in the press.

Meanwhile, in early June, Bright Eyes and Iron Eye returned to Nebraska after their Indian Territory mission. On the way back to their reservation the pair paused in Omaha to give Tibbles a report on the appalling conditions on the Indian Territory reservation, which he published in the *Herald* and presented to the Omaha committee. Most importantly, Bright Eyes handed White Eagles's lengthy letter to an impatient Henry Tibbles,

Standing Bear, in his formal attire, Washington, D.C., 1877, on his trip to meet with the Great Father, President Hayes. (*National Anthropological Archives, Smithsonian Institution*)

A confident Bright Eyes, age 25, circa 1880, "a lady of excellent attainments and bright intellect." (*Nebraska State Historical Society Photograph Collections*)

The shy Bright Eyes, a.k.a. Susette La Flesche, with her equally shy younger brother Woodworker, a.k.a. Francis (Frank) La Flesche, at the beginning of the speaking tour of 1879–80. (*National Anthropological Archives, Smithsonian Institution*)

General George Crook, described by William Tecumseh Sherman as the greatest manager the U.S. Army ever had, and the greatest Indian fighter the U.S. Army ever had, here in full dress uniform. (*Arizona Historical Society*)

Shown below: General George Crook in his more typical garb, a civilian campaign outfit, on his mule, Apache. (*Arizona Historical Society*)

Shown above:
Standing Bear and other Ponca chiefs, taken at I.S. Bonsall's Photograph Gallery, Arkansas City, Kansas, February 20,1877, during their inspection visit to Indian Territory with Edward Kemble and James Lawrence. (*Nebraska State Historical Society Photograph Collections*)

Standing Bear with wife, Susette, and their surviving daughter, Fanny, c. 1879, after the escape from Indian Territory. (*Nebraska State Historical Society Photograph Collections*)

Shown above:
After serving on the Union side of the Civil War, Thomas Henry Tibbles worked as a newspaper reporter and frontier guide, led a posse on the trail of outlaw Jesse James, and became a gun-toting Episcopal preacher. Shown here in his later years, Tibbles was assistant editor of the *Omaha Daily Herald* when he learned of the Ponca cause. (*Nebraska State Historical Society Photograph Collections*)

Dr. George L. Miller, publisher of the *Omaha Daily Herald* and T. H. Tibbles's boss in 1879. (*Courtesy of the* Omaha World-Herald)

Shown top left:
A friend of Buffalo Bill Cody, District Court Judge Elmer S. Dundy loved hunting, fishing, literature, and justice. (*Nebraska State Historical Society Photograph Collections*)

Shown top right:
President Rutherford B. Hayes, 1877. (*Library of Congress*)

Shown bottom left:
Andrew J. Poppleton, a passionate debater and one of Omaha's first attorneys, was part of Standing Bear's legal team. (*Nebraska State Historical Society Photograph Collections*)

Shown bottom middle:
John L. Webster, one of Standing Bear's attorneys, devised the strategy around the Fourteenth Amendment and sought Poppleton's help to convince a judge. (*Nebraska State Historical Society Photograph Collections*)

Shown bottom right:
A brigadier general for the Union during the Civil War, Carl Schurz, as secretary of the Interior, pressed for the removal of the Ponca. (*Library of Congress*)

Wendell Phillips, the Boston orator who helped Henry Tibbles launch his Ponca publicity tour of 1879. Phillips also wrote a dedication in Tibbles's book about the Standing Bear case, *Ponca Chiefs. (Library of Congress)*

Author Helen Hunt Jackson—H. H. as she was affectionately known to Standing Bear and Bright Eyes—joined the 1879 and 1880 tours in the East. *(Library of Congress)*

An advocate of a number of causes, Edward Everett Hale became a key member of the Boston Ponca Committee, later the Boston Indian Committee. *(Courtesy of the Bostonian Society/Old State House)*

ORDERS FROM SCHURZ.
The appropriations of Congress for the White River Utes were shipped last Fall. They destroyed their supplies during the attack on Thornburgh, and during the massacre at the White River Agency. The Indians can't destroy their cake and have it too.

NO MORE FOOLING

THE (INDIANS) INTERIOR DEPARTMENT COMING TO ITS SENSES.
SECRETARY SCHURZ. "Wilful waste makes woful want."

The 1880 *Harper's Weekly* cartoon by Thomas Nast of Interior Secretary Carl Schurz, which so amused Standing Bear when he was in New York City. *(Library of Congress)*

The Right Reverend
Robert H. Clarkson,
Episcopal Bishop of
Nebraska, founding mem-
ber of the Omaha Ponca
Relief Committee.
(*National Anthropological
Archives, Smithsonian
Institution*)

Samuel J. Kirkwood, who
chaired the Senate select
committee that
considered the Ponca
Commission's findings
and then presented his
own 1881 Ponca bill to
Congress. He became
Interior Secretary after
Carl Schurz. (*Library of
Congress*)

Senator Henry L. Dawes of Massachusetts, Ponca supporter, Schurz adversary, and sponsor of the well-meaning but ultimately disastrous General Allotment Act of 1887, also known as the Dawes Act. (*Library of Congress*)

Shown below:
Alice Cunningham Fletcher, allotting Indian land with Chief Joseph of the Nez Percé, 1889. (*Idaho State Historical Society*)

White Eagle, paramount chief of the Ponca tribe, who remained in the Indian Territory after Standing Bear's escape, photographed in Washington, D.C., on the 1877 visit to meet the president. *(Western History Collections, University of Oklahoma Library)*

Bright Eyes, photographed in New York City in 1880 after she had become nationally famous, from a postcard that included her Inshta-theamba autograph issued by photographers Price and Campbell. *(National Anthropological Archives, Smithsonian Institution)*

Big Snake, brother of Standing Bear, in Washington, D.C., 1877. Often described as a gentle giant, Big Snake was shot and killed at the Ponca Agency in Indian Territory on the orders of Agent William Whiteman. *(National Anthropological Archives, Smithsonian Institution)*

One Woman, a.k.a. Mary Gale La Flesche, Bright Eyes's mother. *(National Anthropological Archives, Smithsonian Institution)*

Standing Bear circa 1881. (*National Anthropological Archives, Smithsonian Institution*)

Yellow Horse, the brother of Standing Bear, who escaped with him from the Indian Territory, photographed late in his life in 1906. (*National Anthropological Archives, Smithsonian Institution*)

Standing Bear, his wife Susette, their surviving daughter Fanny, and their grandson and granddaughter, the children of Prairie Flower, late 1880s. (*Special Collections, Tutt Library, Colorado College Library*)

Shown below: Standing Bear with visitors at his farmhouse in the old homeland, Nebraska, late nineteenth century. (*National Anthropological Archives, Smithsonian Institution*)

Standing Bear posing with his "peace" pipe for photographer A. E. Sheldon, at his farm, several years before his death. (*National Anthropological Archives, Smithsonian Institution*)

who was anxious to receive the authorization it contained. He read it with relief and a rejuvenated sense of purpose. "Those words at last gave us clear, written authority to act for the stranded Poncas."[200]

But just as it was poised to launch on the next phase, the Ponca campaign hit a snag. Shortly after Judge Dundy's decision, Andrew Poppleton dropped out of the picture. Rather than offend Poppleton, who had helped win Standing Bear his freedom, Tibbles said nothing about how or why the esteemed lawyer withdrew from the crusading coalition. The precise reason is unclear, but in late May the *Herald* ran an article taking Poppleton to task over his interpretation of the historic 1857 Dred Scott case in his courtroom speech before Judge Dundy. The identity of the article's author wasn't revealed. If it was Tibbles, striving to display his thorough personal knowledge of the abolitionist fight, it certainly didn't endear him to Poppleton.

On the other hand, perhaps Poppleton was pressured by his employer, the Union Pacific Railroad; he continued to serve as the railroad's chief attorney for another nine years. Not that he deserted John Webster entirely. They would work together again, but for now he had other priorities, including a major property investment, a three-story brick office building under construction in downtown Omaha that opened the following year. The Poppleton Building still stands today.

For the moment, John Webster continued to be active in Standing Bear's interests behind the scenes, but he was more reticent than before to take a Ponca case to court. Bright Eyes and Iron Eye may have brought back written authority from White Eagle for the lawyer to act on behalf of the entire tribe, but Webster felt that, unlike his Fourteenth Amendment defense in Standing Bear's case, he did not have a legal hook to hang his hat on when it came to the rest of the tribe.

At the same time, word began to filter through from Washington that the opponents and exploiters of the Indians were mustering their forces, and one of their first targets would be the Omaha tribe, "as a reprisal for their help to the runaways," according to Henry Tibbles.[201] The word was that the bureaucrats and politicians were planning to legislate to

remove the Omahas from their reservation and herd them down to Indian Territory, just as the Poncas had been dispossessed. To make things
worse, Tibbles now discovered, after Webster read the fine print of the
treaty the Omaha tribe had signed with the U.S. government in 1854,
that it lacked a consent clause. Congress could relocate the tribe without its agreement.

There was yet another problem. Standing Bear and his band only occupied the island in the Niobrara where General Crook had settled them at
the whim of the government. For them to have permanent legal tenure, it
would be necessary for Washington to formalize their ownership of land
on the Niobrara. And no one in Washington was putting up his hand to do
that. It was time for the friends of Standing Bear to rethink their strategy
before the Omahas were sent south by an unfriendly Congress, and before Standing Bear was thrown off the Niobrara tract by the politicians
and made entirely homeless. Once those two pressing objectives had been
achieved, the campaigners could think about safeguarding the rights of all
Native Americans.

In mid-June, Tibbles, General Crook, and John Webster met with the
members of the Omaha Ponca Committee to decide what to do next. Tibbles later wrote, "We could see a hard struggle stretching out ahead." But
"we cared not a rap whether our campaign would land heavily on the toes
of the red tape Washington men, or those of the strong, ruthless Indian
Ring, or those of the political bosses."[202]

It was agreed that two things must be done for the campaign to succeed. First, a fighting fund had to be set up and substantial funds raised.
Tibbles says that they were anxious "to raise several thousand dollars
quickly" to combat the inexhaustible resources of their opponents.[203]
Some of this might pay for prominent but expensive lawyers further down
the road; the remainder would contribute to other campaign expenses.
Second, the campaign must not be confined to the West—it must be
taken onto the doorsteps of their powerful opponents in the East.

With a strategy in place, initial campaign tactics were devised. While
the committee organized fund-raising activities in Omaha, Henry Tibbles

volunteered to stir up support in the eastern big city press. His plan was to use his credentials as a newspaperman to win the ear of editors and reporters, showing them a wad of press clippings and written endorsements from leading Nebraska figures to back up his story.

The mission to the East was expected to last at least three months. It seems that the owner of the *Omaha Herald*, Dr. Miller, wouldn't give Tibbles a leave of absence—or perhaps the crusader didn't seek it. Tibbles, who had set his mind on the Ponca campaign, resigned his position with the paper. The Ponca committee would cover his transportation, accommodation, and food costs while he was in the East, but he would not be paid a salary. Whether Tibbles discussed any of this with his wife, Amelia, before he handed in his resignation is debatable. He later wrote that Amelia was fully supportive of this eastern enterprise and encouraged him to keep going when the going got tough. But she must have been shocked to learn that her husband was going to leave his little family for months at a time, with no support. Amelia would have to make do with their meager savings and charity from local church people.

Omaha journalists gave Tibbles a send-off party, at which they praised his morals, his determination, and his courage, and expressed their admiration for him. He later wrote that he found the greatest inspiration of all from them. "These men who knew my faults and failings as completely as my virtues had wished me God-speed in a worthy cause of which they understood every detail—and the memory of their words helped me through many hard moments."[204]

In late June, Henry Tibbles bade farewell to Standing Bear on the Niobrara and Bright Eyes and his other friends at the Omaha reservation, to his co-conspirators General Crook and John Webster, to the members of the Ponca committee in Omaha, and to Amelia and their girls, May and Eda, and then set off east. Conscious of the problems of credentials and credibility he had encountered during his wheat farmer relief appeal in the East five years earlier, this time Tibbles went armed with printed personal endorsements from General Crook, Bishop Clarkson, and leading Nebraska clergy.

Not content with these first-class references, Tibbles had gone down to Lincoln prior to his departure to see Albinus Nance, the new governor. Nance was a staunch Republican, a man who could have been expected to side with his Republican colleagues in Washington in the Ponca affair. But Nance was conscious of his local constituency and had one eye on his reelection chances in three and a half years. He knew that the state's influential Protestant church leaders were behind the Ponca campaign. As it turned out, Nance would be reelected. And Henry Tibbles went east that summer of 1879 carrying a ringing personal endorsement from the governor of Nebraska.

✦ PART THREE: THE CRUSADE ✦

The Indian Department may as well understand at once that the Ponca case has passed out of their control. It is a matter of simple justice which the people are determined to see righted.

Editorial,
New York Tribune, 1880

→ *Chapter 16* ←

THE POWER OF THE SPOKEN WORD

A S THE SUMMER of 1879 was beginning, Henry Tibbles headed east by train. He no longer had a paid job, but he did have a crusade, and throughout his life a cause would always be more important to him than a dollar. As he traveled, his mind went back to the highs and lows of the famine relief crusade of 1874. That campaign had cost him a great deal but had taught him even more.

As the crusader stepped down from the train in Chicago at the end of June to commence his Ponca campaign, it was with the conviction that he was far better prepared to do battle than he had been five years before. He hoped that this latest venture would exceed the successes of the 1874 crusade and raise waves of sympathy and barrels of funds for the Ponca cause without the stinging personal abuse his appeals for the famine victims had engendered. This time, surely, the merits of his cause would be self-evident, his credentials unimpeachable. Yet he knew that his Indian Ring opponents would be far more formidable than the Nebraska boosters who had tried to discredit him five years back. "Warned by what had happened then, I could easily guess what would lie ahead of me now," he later wrote.[205]

Churchmen on the Omaha Ponca Committee had prearranged with their brethren in Chicago for a large public meeting at Farwell Hall to give Tibbles the opportunity to address the people of Chicago as his first step in the new campaign. Before the meeting, Tibbles went around the city's

171

newspaper offices. After producing his endorsements and copies of Omaha newspaper articles and editorials about the plight of the Poncas, he was given a hearing by reporters at each paper. Presenting the facts as he knew them, he did his best to bring the continuing Ponca problem into the limelight.

The resulting press was favorable, if guarded. But it was enough, combined with the efforts of local church people and the brief fame of the Standing Bear court case, to ensure that the Chicago public meeting was well attended. As Tibbles nervously addressed the crowd in his halting but earnest fashion, he told the story of the injustices done to the peaceable Ponca people, and of the need to raise a fighting fund to ensure that Standing Bear's victory would not be a temporary one. When a collection was taken following Tibbles's speech, the sympathetic audience contributed $600 to the cause, and the following day the *Chicago Tribune* gave Tibbles's address favorable front-page coverage. The crusade was off and running.

Conscious of the accusations that had been flung at him about mishandling donations raised during his famine fund-raisers, Tibbles refused to touch a cent of the money contributed to the Ponca crusade. As he hurried on to Boston, the organizers of the Chicago meeting forwarded the funds directly to Revered Sherrill, treasurer of the Omaha Ponca Committee.

Boston was a key destination on Henry Tibbles's campaign tour. While New York City had more people, Bostonians boasted that their city had more class. It had fine public and private buildings, as well as highly respected institutions. Booming economically, with waves of immigrants arriving from Ireland, Canada, and Europe, it embraced modernity with an efficient streetcar system and imaginative urban expansion projects. Like New York, it had introduced hansom cabs from London several years back, considered the mark of an international city. While Chicago and New York tussled for recognition as the commercial capital of America, Boston, with its satellite towns such as Cambridge, home to Harvard University, just across the Charles River, was indisputably the intellectual capital, with more eminent writers, publishers, and philosophers per square mile than any other region in the country. There were people in Boston who could influence and shape the opinions of an entire nation, and it was these people Henry Tibbles wanted to reach.

By the time Tibbles arrived in Boston it was July. As he knocked on the doors of the eminent people of the city, he found that just about everybody who was anybody in Boston had left town for the summer and gone to the country or the seashore. He became increasingly dispirited, until a letter reached him from Amelia back home in Omaha. "My wife, whose sympathies were strongly with this work, brought me fresh courage," Tibbles later wrote. "Just as fearlessly as she had ridden the wild horse or braved the shootings in our gospel tent, she now was facing this new venture which might wreck our own fortunes for good and all."[206]

The next door the crusader knocked on belonged to Delano A. Goddard, editor of the *Boston Daily Advertiser*. Goddard was captivated by the Poncas' story and by the rustic who told it. He promised the paper's backing and introduced Tibbles to the son of the late Nathan Hale, the *Advertiser's* founder. A grandnephew of a Revolutionary War hero, the bushy-bearded fifty-seven-year-old Edward Everett Hale had gained national fame as a successful novelist and liberal theologian at the forefront of the social gospel movement. Hale was an advocate of worthy causes ranging from the education of poor black people to worker housing and world peace, and the Poncas' story attracted his attention and his strong sympathy.

Within days, Hale had written a powerful editorial entitled "Indians and the Law" supporting the Poncas, and Goddard ran it in the *Advertiser* alongside a page 2 article penned by Goddard himself describing the mistreatment of the tribe. The article and editorial, in Tibbles's words, "broke the Boston ice" for him.[207] Hale, an ordained Congregational minister, introduced Tibbles to other churchmen in the city. Consequently the day the Ponca material appeared in the *Advertiser*, July 30, he was able to address the directors of the Society for Propagating the Gospel Among the Indians and Others of North America (SPGAIONA), when they met at the offices of an insurance company. Founded in Boston by Baptists in 1813, this group had extensive influence and resources.

Impressed by Tibbles's address and his dedication, the SPGAIONA quickly swung behind the Ponca cause, with the society's directors forming a committee of five leading citizens, including Edward Everett Hale himself, to organize a large public meeting at Tremont Temple on August 5 at which Tibbles and other Indian rights advocates would speak. In the meantime, Tibbles would have to kick his heels around Boston.

The Gospel Society Committee did its job well, for the affluent and the influential flooded back into the city from their summer homes for the meeting. As chief speaker they secured Wendell Phillips, a famous abolitionist considered one of the finest orators of his day. Phillips, renowned for delivering speeches without a single note, sent Tibbles word that he wanted him to speak first. Once Phillips heard what the Westerner had to say, he would make his own appeal to the audience.

Tibbles arrived at the large basement meeting hall well in advance of the advertised starting time of noon, nervous and clutching a thick pile of letters, newspaper clippings, and documents relevant to the Ponca case. The hall was slowly beginning to fill when he walked onto the stage. A line of chairs had been arrayed for the five organizing committee members and the evening's two speakers. At one end of the line sat Wendell Phillips. Sixty-seven-year-old Phillips, with thinning gray hair, clean shaven except for distinctive sideburns high on his cheeks, wearing an expensive suit, silk vest, and large bow tie, nodded to the Westerner. Tibbles nodded back. He had met Phillips years before but guessed he would not remember him. Terrified of sitting next to the famous man, the out-of-towner went to the far end of the line of chairs and took a seat beside one of the less daunting committee members.

The committee member, B. W. Williams, proprietor of a lecture bureau, shook Tibbles's hand and indicated where he was to stand when the time came for him to speak. Williams, who like Edward Everett Hale was an ordained minister, had been inspired by the example of an enterprising Bostonian, James Clark Redpath, who some years earlier had set up a lyceum bureau in the city and proceeded to make himself rich. In these days before radio, television, movies, and the Internet, a public whose appetite for entertainment was whetted by books, newspapers, and magazines wanted to see and hear the famous people whose work they read, and about whom they read. Before the Civil War, lyceum societies had sprung up all over the country, with members at first giving lectures to each other on various intellectual subjects. Before long, they began bringing in lecturers of note, and a speakers circuit had grown, particularly in the Northeast, with fees often being paid to the orators from either donations or door charges. Seeing the moneymaking potential, J. C. Redpath had set up as an agent for these speakers. Famous authors were his mainstay, but in time he represented every kind of stage and musical act, with his vast client list ranging from writer Mark Twain to theater and circus impresario P. T. Barnum.

As Redpath experienced quick success, other agents competed with him in Boston, Chicago, and New York. In Boston, B. W. Williams ventured into the field, setting up the Williams Lecture and Musical Bureau. The bureau soon proved profitable, although Williams's firm and the other agency in Boston, the Midland Lyceum Bureau, were dwarfed by the Redpath operation. After Redpath sold out to his partners in 1875, it blossomed into two agencies, the Boston Lyceum Bureau locally and the Redpath Lyceum Bureau of New York, which shared a catalog of famous clients.

Seated on the Boston stage, Henry Tibbles was soon deep in conversation with the speakers agent. Williams knew all the notables in the audience and pointed them out to Tibbles as they took their seats. "Poets, historians, scientists, lecturers," Tibbles wrote. "In they walked until I got thoroughly frightened."[208] Soon the hall was full to overflowing and Willams was on his feet and moving to the lectern. To get the proceedings under way, Williams introduced the mayor of Boston, Frederick O. Prince.

A handsome man with short dark hair and a distinctive gray walrus mustache, Mayor Prince would soon become a prominent player in the pro-Ponca movement in New England. He launched the Massachusetts campaign with a rhetorical broadside of the kind that had made his name in the Boston political arena. Prince declared that he was surprised that in a country which boasted so much philanthropy and refinement there were men who dared to defy public opinion with an act against the peaceable Ponca tribe of Indians that exceeded in its cruelty all other wrongs perpetrated by the strong against the weak. Then, to explain the tale of atrocity in detail, he had the pleasure to introduce courageous Omaha newspaper editor T. H. Tibbles.

As applause filled the hall, Henry Tibbles nervously came to his feet. He later wrote that, conscious of the eyes of all these learned Easterners focused on him and of the famous Wendell Phillips waiting to be inspired by his inexpert speech, he was trembling so badly he could hardly walk. Clutching his batch of support materials, Tibbles made his way with difficulty to the lectern and then stood looking out over the sea of expectant Bostonian faces. In sudden terror, his mind went blank. His hand shook so much that he lost his grip on his collection of papers. The documents dropped from his hand, hit the floor, and spread in all directions. He looked down at the papers for a horror-struck moment, then, with hardly a thought, kicked them away with his foot. He returned his gaze to the silent but sympathetic crowd, girded his courage, and took the plunge into oratory.

"I take it this audience doesn't wish me to read from those official documents," he began, indicating the papers on the floor. "They're at the service of any person present. What you wish is to hear some salient facts upon which you can form a judgment." He then proceeded to give them the facts about the Ponca tribe and the gross mistreatment they had received from the government that represented them. "I make no assault upon any individual," he assured his listeners. "I assault the system."[209]

After giving a heart-wrenching account of the plight of the Poncas, Tibbles moved on to suggest measures that he felt needed to be introduced to change the system of which he was so critical. He said that all Indians must be granted the protection of the courts, as Standing Bear had been. And he supported the principle President Hayes had espoused for the past few years of "severalty" for Indians, in which a plot of farmland was granted to each adult male Indian, instead of the present system of collective ownership of a reservation by an entire tribe, so that any Indian could be a landowner in the same way that individual whites owned their land. With individual land ownership would come citizenship and the protection under law that was currently denied Indians.

Whether he had discussed the severalty concept with Standing Bear, Iron Eye, or Bright Eyes is unclear, but they seem not to have opposed it at that time. In principle, there was a valid rationale to President Hayes's idea. By making an individual Indian a landowner in the eyes of the law, the government could neither control nor tamper with his land the way it currently tampered with and controlled the reservations, which, while technically reserved for exclusive Indian use, were still treated as federal land.

The right of an Indian to be represented in court was the central tenet of the original district court petition by attorneys Webster and Poppleton and of the campaign that Tibbles had now brought East. When the newspaperman reminded his audience why Judge Dundy had found in Standing Bear's favor and expressed the judge's liberal sentiments with the words, "Any human being that God ever made can come into my court," the audience burst into loud, sustained applause.[210]

To Tibbles's relief, when he finished his disorganized though heartfelt speech he received another wave of warm applause from his audience. Smiling gratefully, he turned and began to retrace his steps to his seat, with the sound of clapping following him. In the process, he crossed paths with Wendell Phillips, who was walking to the front of the stage to take his turn at speaking. As they passed, Phillips paused briefly and said in Tibbles's ear, "Don't go away after the meeting until I have the opportunity to speak to you."[211]

Phillips then took center stage and proceeded to deliver an off-the-cuff speech that Tibbles later described as "a masterpiece."[212] Phillips had given his first speech forty-two years before at Boston's famous Faneuil Hall, protesting the murder of an abolitionist. He was just twenty-five years old at the time. He was immediately recognized as a brilliant orator who could stir the hearts and minds of any audience, and he had never lost his touch in the thousands of speeches he had given since. Now, after echoing the Nebraskan's sentiments about the Poncas, the failings of the existing system, and the depredations of the Indian Ring, receiving "liberal applause" every time he praised the Indians or condemned the ring, Phillips declared that Indians needed access to the courts to protect their property.[213]

Phillips then proposed a set of resolutions in favor of the Poncas, which included the establishment of a committee of ten ardent and influential Bostonians to provide ongoing moral and financial support to work conducted on behalf of the tribe. The proposal was loudly and enthusiastically endorsed by the gathering, without a single dissent, and the Boston Ponca Committee was born. A mirror of the Omaha committee, it would in time include Mayor Prince, the Speaker of the Massachusetts House of Representatives, a professor of constitutional law at Harvard University, and several Boston publishers, as well as the constant Edward Everett Hale.

Wendell Phillips then turned his attention to the last speaker and proceeded to paint Henry Tibbles as the bravest man in America for taking on such formidable opponents in aid of a peaceable yet downtrodden Indian tribe. The experienced orator delivered his words in such a passionate, theatrical way that the audience came to its feet as one, applauding and cheering. Hundreds rushed onto the stage to drag a stunned Henry Tibbles to his feet and grasp him by the hand. Time and again, Bostonians congratulated Tibbles for his courage and pledged to do all they could to improve the treatment the Indian peoples received. Phillips waited patiently in the wings for the last handshake and the last promise and then, as the hall emptied, he walked up to Tibbles and said, "Come take dinner with me."[214]

Phillips took the elated crusader to a modest little restaurant on a side street. As they sat across a table after placing their orders, Phillips looked

at Tibbles for such a long time without saying a word that the newspaperman began to squirm with embarrassment. Finally, Phillips said, "I don't
know what to say to you."

"I wish you would say something!" Tibbles returned with a laugh.

Phillips laughed too. Then he said, "I suppose Boston would not say
you were an orator according to its standards, but you influenced that audience in a way I could not. I never saw a Boston audience act in just that
way before."

Phillips's demeanor changed as he leaned a little closer and passed on
a friendly but serious caution, telling Tibbles not to be seduced by the reaction of the audience that evening. It would be easy to think that the
righteousness of the cause would guarantee it would always be like this,
he said, that it was just a matter of fronting up to audiences in a few major
cities and then in Washington for the government to bend to the will of
the Poncas' supporters and change the system.

Phillips assured Tibbles he was not trying to talk him out of continuing
the Ponca crusade. "I want you to go on with this work. You have the facts
and a peculiar way of presenting them that take hold of the hearts of people." But the obstacles would be immense, his opponents fierce. "I know
the Indian Ring." He glanced at Tibbles's thick, black hair. "Your hair will
be gray before the first law is passed that does away with the present system. Men of national reputation will attack you." But, despite the slings
and the arrows, he said, Tibbles must continue with his crusade. As they
parted after dinner, Phillips wished Tibbles well and invited him to call on
him at any time if there was assistance he could render.[215]

During the next few days, Tibbles met with the new Boston Ponca
Committee to discuss tactics. They agreed he must continue delivering
his Ponca lectures, rough and ready as they were. It was also felt that a
book or pamphlet about the Ponca cause should be sold, with proceeds
going to the cause, and committee member John S. Lockwood, a publisher, expressed interest in putting it out. Tibbles mentioned the book he
had already drafted, *Ponca Chiefs*, telling Lockwood that it contained all

the Standing Bear material he'd collated, including his own press articles and the many relevant documents provided to him by Standing Bear, Bright Eyes, and others. It was agreed that once Tibbles returned to Omaha he would finalize the manuscript and then mail it to Lockwood.

As for lecturing, over dinner Wendell Phillips had recommended that Tibbles secure himself a lyceum agent. These agents, he would have told his new friend, were the best avenue to speaking engagements at leading venues in New England and elsewhere. They knew how to attract big crowds, and they knew how to make money—and the Ponca cause needed both. Following that first Boston speech, Tibbles received an invitation to visit his companion on the platform that night, B. W. Williams, member of the Boston Ponca Committee and, more importantly, B. W. Williams the agent.

Recommendation and invitation meshed, and within days of his Boston address Tibbles was in the office of the Williams Lecture and Musical Bureau. While he didn't run the largest agency, Williams was no less entrepreneurial than his opposition at the Boston Lyceum Bureau and the Midland Bureau. He knew that a speaker didn't have to be famous to attract a crowd. Lyceum audiences were hungry for enlightenment and entertainment. While religious speakers were always popular, a lecturer at the other end of the scale doing good business was Carleton Hughes, a former clerk in the dead letter office in Washington, who revealed the secrets of thousands of ill-addressed letters that found their way to the office, some containing thousands of dollars, and the often incredible efforts of the post office to find either addressee or sender.

Inspired by what he had seen at Tibbles's first outing and some subsequent good press (on August 11 the *Chicago Tribune* called Tibbles "the heroic Editor of Omaha"), B. W. Williams recognized the crowd appeal of Tibbles's subject. But, like Wendell Phillips, Williams did not find Tibbles a particularly enervating speaker. Tibbles had the facts and he had sincerity, but, in Williams's eyes, this campaign needed an additional speaker, one who could deliver a Wendell Phillips entrée on the heels of a Tibbles appetizer.

Then one of them, either Williams or Tibbles, made a suggestion. Tibbles did not to claim it as his idea, and it probably came from astute businessman Williams: What if Standing Bear himself addressed their audiences? What could serve the Ponca cause better than to have the chief speak for himself? For the vast majority of people who could be expected to flood to the speaking engagements, this would be the first real live Indian chief they had ever seen. The sensational Wild West dime novels of Buntline and Ingraham were being devoured by a public enamored with both the perceived barbarism and the romance of the Indian way of life. Buffalo Bill's Wild West traveling shows would soon tap into this same public fear cum fascination. And of course Standing Bear had already achieved national notoriety as a result of his court victory. His name alone on a poster promoting a speaking engagement was guaranteed to attract attention, much more so than Tibbles's name.

Tibbles probably worried that Standing Bear would need an interpreter and so would not have the impact of an English speaker, but Williams would have reminded him that even with an interpreter Standing Bear had created a dynamic effect when he spoke in Judge Dundy's courtroom. So, there in the Boston office of the lecture bureau, Tibbles took it on himself to sign a contract with Williams on his behalf and on Standing Bear's behalf, agreeing that he and the Ponca chief would tour the cities of the East to promote the Ponca cause at a series of public meetings. Williams agreed to organize, promote, and manage the engagements at cities that he nominated.

There would be an added attraction. Unlike most lecturers doing the rounds, the Ponca speakers would not charge admission to their addresses. Audiences would be asked for donations, which would go to the Ponca fighting fund. Expenses would be deducted—Williams's promotional costs, as well as the costs for the transportation, food, and accommodation of the touring party. After that, in a normal commercial arrangement Williams would retain a percentage of the take as a commission and pass on the balance to the speakers. In this case Williams would not be taking a commission for his services. But even though he didn't take a fee, in the long run he could still profit handsomely from the deal. If Standing Bear and Henry Tibbles proved to be the drawing card the agent expected them to be, the profile of the Williams Lecture and Musical Bureau would skyrocket, and Williams could be expected to attract plenty of new speakers and paying customers.

As Henry Tibbles headed back home to Nebraska in early September with the Williams bureau contract in his pocket, he was thinking about how he would convince Standing Bear to make the trip east with him. As he sat in train carriages rocking west, he would have told himself that he would need to take along an interpreter. The most natural choice was of course Bright Eyes. She was committed to the cause, and she had proven an excellent translator up till then, one with whom Standing Bear was comfortable and one he trusted. Not all interpreters could be relied on to translate with accuracy or sensitivity. But there could be a problem. As Tibbles knew, protective Iron Eye would not like the idea of his eldest daughter going east with two men. Iron Eye, like Standing Bear, would need some convincing about this speaking tour.

When Tibbles arrived back in Omaha on September 6, he was formulating some persuasive arguments for his Indian friends.

Chapter 17

THE FOUR CRUSADERS

IRONICALLY, IN HENRY Tibbles's absence, a noted Boston lecturer had come through Omaha on a speaking tour during the summer. After he met Bright Eyes and was greatly impressed by her, the lecturer had urged the Omaha Ponca Committee to send her east to plead for the Ponca cause. As soon as Tibbles arrived back in town in early September, Bishop Clarkson and the other committee members assailed him with the idea, even before Tibbles could reveal that he was carrying a signed contract for a speaking tour for Standing Bear and himself. Realizing that he could very easily alienate the committee members if he revealed he'd committed to the Williams contract without first consulting them, he knew he would have to handle the subject of a speaking tour very delicately.

First, there was the matter of Bright Eyes's involvement. Tibbles says that he resisted the idea at first. While he himself had been thinking of taking Bright Eyes along as interpreter, he had not envisaged her as one of the featured speakers alongside Standing Bear and himself. At the forefront of his mind was a doubt that she could overcome her shyness in the face of large groups and succeed as a speaker. As the committee members pushed for Bright Eyes to be approached with the proposal of going East to speak on behalf of the Poncas, Tibbles had no choice but come clean about the deal he had done with the Williams bureau. Showing the committee members his Williams contract, Tibbles suggested that Bright Eyes would make an excellent translator of Standing Bear's speeches, but he continued to resist putting her on stage on her own.

The bishop and the other committee members were ahead of him. They had already convinced both Bright Eyes and Standing Bear to speak at a large public gathering organized by Reverend Harsha at the Omaha Presbyterian Church. This would be Bright Eyes's big test. If she failed here, they said, there would be no point putting her through the trauma of solo appearances in the East. Standing Bear was supportive of the idea. He liked and respected Bright Eyes, and he could see her as a strong advocate for his people's cause. So it was agreed that a decision would be made after Bright Eyes addressed the Omaha audience.

The day of the test speech came, and when Tibbles met Bright Eyes, her family members, and Standing Bear outside the packed Omaha church, the diminutive speaker was clearly very nervous. Reverend Harsha, Reverend Sherrill, Bishop Clarkson, and other Omaha clergymen, along with a large band of church ladies, escorted their two guests of honor into the building, and Tibbles followed along behind. To Henry Tibbles's astonishment, when they saw Bright Eyes, the members of the large congregation jumped to their feet and clapped, cheered, and waved handkerchiefs in the air as she was led through the throng onto the platform at the front of the church.

As her friends and family gathered with Standing Bear behind her, the ministers guided Bright Eyes to the front of the platform, beside the pulpit, and the crowd resumed its seats. Typically dressed in a long dark dress and gloves, with her hair tied back, tiny Bright Eyes stood there, looking out over the faces of the silent, reverent audience. Every chair and bench was occupied. The walls were lined with more people, standing. The church doors had been left open, and many people who could not fit inside crowded the doorway or spilled back out over the church steps.

"There stood the little figure, trembling," Tibbles later wrote, "and gazing at the crowd with eyes which afterwards thrilled many audiences. They were wonderful eyes. They could smile, command, flash, plead, mourn, and play all sorts of tricks with anyone they lingered on."

For a long time she didn't open her mouth, drawing the rapt attention of the crowd like metal to a magnet. Obviously frightened by the size of her audience, Bright Eyes looked like "a bird in a net."[216] Yet she never lost her dignity. And her obvious fear made her appear vulnerable to her audience and won their sympathy all the more. When she finally spoke, it was in a surprisingly rich, strong voice that carried all the way to the people on the steps outside. Tibbles had his notebook at the ready and recorded her words.

"Why should I be asked to speak?" she began. "I am but an Indian girl, brought up among the Indians. I love my people; I have been educated and they have not. I have told them that they must learn the arts of the whites and adopt their customs. But how can they, when the government sends the soldiers to drive them out?" She paused a moment, suddenly conscious that her listeners were hanging on her every word, before resuming.

"The soldiers drove Standing Bear and his wife and children from the land that belonged to him and his fathers before him—at the point of the bayonet. And on the way his daughter dies from the hardships of the journey. The Christian ladies of Milford, Nebraska, come to the Indian camp, pray for the dying girl, and give her a Christian burial." She took a deep breath. "Oh, the perplexities of this thing they call civilization! Part of the white people murder my girl companion and another part tenderly bury her, while her father stands over her grave and says, 'My heart breaks.'"[217]

She fought back tears. Her voice faded away. She swayed, then clutched at the pulpit for support as the strength went from her legs. There was a gasp from the audience. Women on the platform hurried forward and swarmed protectively around her, then led her away. Tibbles says that even though Bright Eyes had not been able to complete her first public address, the effect of her brief appearance had been electric. Women were crying, men were shouting, some even swore. "There in church, with the bishop on the platform," Tibbles recorded.

"If I were Standing Bear," Tibbles says one of the leading citizens of Omaha yelled, "I would let the courts go hang. I'd take my tomahawk and scalping knife and follow the trail of the secretary of the Interior. Then I'd settle the thing right there!"[218]

The meeting broke up amid this mood of heightened emotions. When the Ponca committee met soon after, the members agreed that even though Bright Eyes broke down before she could finish, she had a unique ability to stir an audience. Today we would say that she had that indefinable and elusive quality, charisma. Tibbles too recognized her star quality and gave up his objections to her taking the stage as a speaker in her own right on the eastern tour.

Following that Presbyterian Church meeting, after Bright Eyes had recovered, Tibbles asked Standing Bear if he would come east with him on the speaking tour he had already contracted in both their names. In all probability he posed the question through Bright Eyes. Tibbles would have expected the chief to be reticent and take some convincing, but, only days before, Interior Secretary Schurz had issued a statement to the press in which he had described Standing Bear as "morose, sullen, and indolent."[219] These were fighting words as far as Standing Bear was concerned (once they were translated and explained to him), and he readily agreed to make the speaking tour, knowing his participation could help bring the Ponca tribe back together on the Niobrara.

Then there was Bright Eyes. When the Omaha committee put the idea to her of also becoming one of the speakers on the eastern tour, she refused to even consider it at first. It would mean resigning her post as school principal, a job that she absolutely loved, and there was no guarantee she would ever regain it or anything like it. And then there was her father. He utterly disapproved of the idea of her going east on the tour.

Within days, as the disappointed Omaha committee rethought its tour plans, news reached Omaha that a bill was likely to be introduced in the next session of Congress by Carl Schurz's Republican colleagues to authorize the immediate removal of the Omaha tribe from Nebraska to the Indian Territory. This rocked all concerned.

Tibbles hurried to Joe's Village to discuss the news with Iron Eye, and to again put the proposal that Bright Eyes be encouraged to go east and lecture—on behalf of both tribes now. He told Iron Eye that now the Omahas were also under threat it had been decided by the committees in both Omaha and Boston that they would change their names. They would now be the Omaha Indian Committee and the Boston Indian Committee, and they would devote their energies and their funds to helping both the Omahas and the Poncas.

In the face of the new threat from Washington, Iron Eye now gave way. "Bright Eyes may go east to lecture," he conceded, "if her brother Woodworker (Francis, a.k.a. Frank, La Flesche) goes with her."[220]

Bright Eyes ceased to protest. For the good of her people, she would pluck up her courage and join Standing Bear on the podiums of the daunting cities of the East. Telegrams were sent off to the Williams bureau and the Boston committee to inform them that both Bright Eyes and Standing Bear would be coming on the tour, and the Omaha committee went into planning mode.

The committee discussed in fine detail the program that each lecture would follow. It was agreed that Tibbles would speak first, talking about what had induced him to take up the cause of the Ponca and Omaha peoples. He would then introduce Standing Bear, whose speeches would be translated by Bright Eyes or her brother. Standing Bear would tell a simple story of the inhuman treatment dealt out to his peaceful tribe, to his family and himself. Bright Eyes would step up to the lectern and give her speech last of all. Her address would be the call to arms. The preceding speakers had detailed the injustice; she would speak of how the people of America could help right the wrong.

The committee decided that when they were traveling or between engagements Frank and Standing Bear were to wear European clothing. This was Frank's normal style of dress anyway, and he wore his hair reasonably short as a matter of course. Standing Bear would continue to keep his hair long—below his shoulders in tribal fashion—and on stage he would wear his buckskins, feathers, beaded belt, claw necklace, and red blanket. Bright Eyes would wear plain, dark, ladylike dresses, a white lace scarf, and gloves.

The Williams bureau telegraphed that the party's first engagements had been booked for Boston in late October and early November, with other New England centers to follow. The excitement and the nervousness grew in various parts of Nebraska as the touring party's departure day drew near—in Omaha, on the Omaha reservation, and at Standing Bear's little settlement on the Niobrara. Standing Bear had been east of the Missouri just once, on the chiefs' disappointing trip to Washington, while the last time Bright Eyes had been east it was to a school in New Jersey, alone among white girls, many of whom would not have been warm toward an Indian girl in their midst. But she would have put bad memories behind her as she made her last farewells on the Omaha reservation, to the other members of the tribe, to her younger half brother and numerous sisters and half sisters, to her mother and stepmother.

The stories told about Bright Eyes never mentioned her mother, Mary Gale La Flesche, whose tribal name was the One Woman, nor of Iron Eye's other wife, Tainne, an Iowa. Both lived in Iron Eye's large house on the reservation at the same time with all their children. Iron Eye had a third, unnamed wife, but he had sent her away sometime before this. Tainne died after four years, but the One Woman lived for another three decades. She would have been a strong influence in Bright Eyes's life. Perhaps Bright Eyes was also close to Tainne; we don't know.

The patriarchal Indian social system that kept women in the background differed little from white society; white American women did not yet have the right to vote, and they were expected to play a subordinate role to their menfolk. Henry Tibbles makes no mention of Bright Eyes's relationship with her mother or stepmother, but we can imagine a tear-filled parting one day in early October as the family's eldest girl set off to walk and talk among the white people of America in the smoke-filled cities of the eastern states, to plead for America's help to save the Ponca and Omaha people.

Tibbles made no mention of his wife, Amelia, when he wrote of the preparations for the tour. He assumed that Amelia would be supportive of his latest venture, as always, and made no reference to discussing it with her or to parting from her or his girls Eda and May that fall.

Suddenly the October departure day was on them. Standing Bear, Bright Eyes, and her brother came down to Omaha to link up with Tibbles, and the eclectic little band, sent off by the Indian committee and the church people of Omaha, headed east. To set them on their lecturing feet the crusaders were being accompanied to Chicago by Bishop Clarkson and Reverend Harsha of the Presbyterian Church. The churchmen would introduce them to the audience at their first Chicago engagement, which was being organized by the Presbyterians. After that, the quartet would be on their own.

The four crusaders had no idea how they would be received. Already the first rounds in a Ponca press war had been fired in the East ahead of their arrival. Some papers such as the *New York Times* had come out with pro-government articles declaring that the Poncas in the Indian Territory were "prospering fairly" and "contented."[221] As Henry Tibbles had feared, other papers criticized him personally, referring to his previous farm relief crusade and characterizing him as an adventurer. Pro-Ponca papers such as the *Boston Advertiser* responded with stories about the true state of affairs in the Indian Territory and defended Tibbles's role, pointing out that all funds raised by him went directly to the fund administered by the Reverend Sherrill in Omaha.

Expecting much more mud to be flung their way in the coming months, the crusaders would have been hoping and praying that despite the opposition orchestrated by the Interior Department they could draw enough attention to their cause to prevent the Omahas from being dispossessed and to allow the Poncas stranded in the Indian Territory to be brought home to the Niobrara.

Chapter 18

THE DARK DAYS OF OCTOBER

I N   T H E   S E C O N D half of September, while the four crusaders were busy preparing to head east, their chief opponent, Secretary of the Interior Carl Schurz, was far from idle. Henry Tibbles's efforts on behalf of the Poncas in Boston during the summer caused a stir that sent shock waves all the way to Washington. The eminence of the members of the Boston Ponca Committee, the strongly pro-Ponca editorial by the respected Edward Everett Hale and later supportive articles in the *Boston Advertiser*, as well as the vocal support of Wendell Phillips and Mayor Prince, all combined to sink the secretary's strategy of slurring Standing Bear and Henry Tibbles to discredit their Ponca campaign. Other measures would be necessary if this wave of sympathy for the Poncas was to be countered. Schurz went on the offensive.

In its September 24 edition, the *Arkansas City Traveler* reported on the front page that Secretary Schurz had just issued "a long and elaborate statement concerning the true condition of the Poncas." Distributed to the press throughout the country to appear in papers from the *New York Times* to the *Omaha Daily Herald*, this statement contained the first public admission by the Interior Department that the Poncas had good reason for complaint. A version of this statement was included in the Interior Department's report to Congress for the year 1879. Not surprisingly, the statement was worded in a way that skewed the truth in the defense of Secretary Schurz and spread the blame among entities ranging from the

Sioux Indian tribes to Schurz's predecessor at the department during the Grant administration, Zacharia Chandler.

> Mr. Schurz says that by the treaty of 1868, this (Ponca) reservation, situated in Dakota, was ceded to the Sioux, who are now in actual possession of the same. This cession was the result of a blunder of a former administration, and as the Sioux insisted upon their property rights, a removal of the Poncas became necessary. This removal was accompanied by a combination of disasters and mishaps; but the sum of the whole matter is comprised in the statement that the Ponca Indians, on their new reservation in the Indian Territory, are prospering fairly, and are not only contented, but are on the road to civilization.

The unidentified Washington-based author of this article proceeded to add his own comment to the story about the Schurz statement. "This careful presentment of the case may not please the sentimentalists who have been so vociferous over the wrongs of the Poncas. But it bears the unmistakable impress of absolute truthfulness."

Carl Schurz didn't stop there. As soon as his statement had been circulated, he departed Washington and headed west. On October 1, the *Traveler* reported that Secretary Schurz had just passed through Arkansas City on his way to inspect all the Indian reservations in the Indian Territory. On October 22, the same paper reported that Schurz had returned from the Ponca reservation and was heading back to Washington after concluding his tour of Indian Territory reservations. In Arkansas City, the secretary announced that a school would be built at the Ponca agency, but apart from the present lack of school facilities, according to the *Traveler*, Carl Schurz "expressed himself highly pleased with things at the Agency."

Schurz was supremely confident of his position in the Ponca affair. If worse came to worst, he could call on the support of President Rutherford B. Hayes. The president was careful to refer to Schurz in public as "General Schurz,"[222] respecting his Union army rank of brigadier general, but in private he called him Carl.[223] More than a political supporter, Schurz was a close family friend who went out of his way to aid and advise Hayes and his son, Webb C. Hayes, the president's personal secretary. Schurz knew that the president would resist any accusation against him and would staunchly stand by his Interior secretary.

As Schurz returned to Washington, satisfied that he had been seen to give prompt attention to the Ponca tribe and that he had shored up his position against the complaints coming out of Boston, he had no idea that Henry Tibbles and three Indian companions were also heading east and were about to launch a powerful new assault against him.

→ ←

As they set off from Omaha in the second half of October, Tibbles and his fellow crusaders received a telegram from Williams, their agent, telling them he had arranged lecture engagements at Pittsburgh en route to Boston. First stop was Chicago, where on October 19 they made their inaugural speeches at the Second Presbyterian Church. Introduced by Bishop Clarkson, the crusaders were followed by Reverend Harsha. Raising several hundred dollars, the event was a success but not a triumph. After a brief stay at Chicago's Palmer House hotel, the quartet bade farewell to the two churchmen and took the train to Pittsburgh in the last week of October. Now the crusaders were truly on their own.

There was no Indian committee in Pittsburgh, so their reception was low-key. Tibbles says nothing about the venues at Pittsburgh or the size of the crowds, nor about how the speeches made by Standing Bear and Bright Eyes were received. He only says that while he was sitting on the platform during the last of the engagements, listening to either Standing Bear or Bright Eyes speak, a telegram from Williams was handed to him. It instructed the party to take the next train to Boston without delay. They departed Pittsburgh the next day.

When they stepped off the train at Boston early on the morning of
Wednesday, October 29, exhausted after a three-hundred-mile journey
from Pittsburgh, they were met by a beaming B. W. Williams with the
news that, thanks to Mayor Prince, the members of the party were to
be the guests of the city of Boston for an entire week. They were to be
put up at the Tremont House, one of the city's best hotels, at the
Boston city council's expense. And later that same morning the mayor,
members of the council, and one hundred prominent citizens would
hold a grand reception for them in the hotel ballroom. Then, come Saturday night, there would be a great public reception for them at Horticultural Hall, with all of Boston invited to attend and extend a welcome
to the Ponca crusaders. With this coup of organization, Williams had
excelled himself.

After breakfast at the Tremont House, the crusaders found themselves
the toast of the town in the hotel ballroom later that morning. Introduced
by Mayor Prince, Tibbles, Bright Eyes, and Standing Bear each spoke
briefly, before the guests thronged around Standing Bear and Bright Eyes,
keen to meet and talk to them. As Henry Tibbles and Frank La Flesche
hung back, marveling at the reception, Bright Eyes and Standing Bear
were surrounded by people who wanted to shake their hands and wish
them well. When they finally broke away to eat lunch in the hotel dining
room, the four of them were "amazed and delighted" by the reception they
received from Boston's movers and shakers.[224]

The people of Boston had a long history of taking colorful guests to
their hearts. Almost half a century before, in 1834, famous Tennessee
frontiersman and congressman Davy Crockett had come to the city, also
on a speaking tour of New England, and had found a similarly warm welcome. "The citizens of Boston generally are uncommon kind and civil,"
Crockett was to write after his visit. "I was entertained like a prince."
Crockett came away with the opinion that the people of New England
"have more kind feelings to one another, and live in more peace and harmony than any people I ever was among."[225]

Over the next two days the campaigners met with the members of the Boston Indian Committee and gave press interviews as they prepared for their largest event yet, the huge public reception planned for Saturday night. The *Boston Advertiser* had featured their arrival in two editions that week, and editor Goddard promised a stirring editorial for Saturday's issue to ensure a large turnout for the Horticultural Hall reception.

As Tibbles, Standing Bear, Bright Eyes, and Frank La Flesche lingered over an alcohol-free lunch at the Tremont House on Saturday, November 1, chattering excitedly about the overwhelming welcome Boston had given them so far, about the grand event coming up that evening and the campaign that lay ahead, Tibbles says that they "almost dared to hope that we should win the dreaded fight very easily."[226] Their spirits were high. None of them ever touched a drop of alcohol, but that heady day they were so happy it was almost as if they were drunk. Standing Bear, it turned out, liked to make dreadful puns, which were even worse in translation. "That afternoon," says Tibbles, "we laughed at everything, especially Standing Bear's many puns."[227]

They were still at the table when, around 5:00 P.M., Agent Williams walked into the dining room, ashen-faced. He looked ghastly as he slowly approached them. The jolly mood of the quartet evaporated as they realized something was amiss. Tibbles noticed that Williams held several telegrams in his hand. He asked what was wrong. Williams fidgeted with the telegrams as he advised in a faltering voice that one was fresh off the line from Kansas. The other, "followed you from Chicago round by Pittsburgh" and was "three days old now."[228]

No one could imagine what news the telegrams could contain to make the lecture bureau chief look so distraught. They would have thought the speaking tour had been canceled for some reason, perhaps as a result of some act by the government.

Williams faced Tibbles, hardly able to look him in the eye. "I have some very bad news," he said. "You and Standing Bear must prepare yourselves for heavy blows."[229] He then proceeded to tell Tibbles that, the previous day around noon, Standing Bear's brother Big Snake had been shot and killed at the Ponca agency in the Indian Territory on the orders of Agent William Whiteman. But there were tidings even worse than that. As Williams held out the telegrams, he informed Henry Tibbles that the second message had been sent from Omaha three days before, bearing the news that his wife, Amelia, was dead.

→ *Chapter 19* ←

THE SHOOTING OF BIG SNAKE

I N THE EARLY hours of Thursday, October 30, 1879, Lieutenant
Stanton A. Mason, a sergeant, and twelve troopers from Company H
of the 4th Cavalry Regiment quietly dismounted at the Ponca agency at
the junction of the Arkansas and Salt Fork Rivers. After concealing their
horses behind the agency's commissary store, the cavalrymen slipped into
the house of Indian Affairs agent William H. Whiteman.

Ever since Big Snake had been brought back to the Ponca reservation
in the spring, Agent Whiteman had been sending reports to the Bureau of
Indian Affairs in Washington that Big Snake was "extremely sullen and
morose" and was having "a very demoralizing effect upon the other Indians."[230] Whiteman later claimed in one breath that throughout the summer Big Snake repeatedly threatened to kill him, while in another he said
that Big Snake had not spoken a word to him since his enforced return. In
the third week of October, Whiteman sent a telegram to Commissioner
Hayt, telling him that the Ponca had attempted to murder two men on the
reservation and begging the commissioner "to arrest Big Snake and convey
him to Fort Reno and there confine him for the remainder of his natural
life."[231] On October 25, the Interior Department gave approval for Big
Snake to be arrested, and the interdepartmental wheels began to turn, resulting in the dispatch of Lieutenant Mason and his men from Fort Reno.

After Lieutenant Mason arrived at the agency, he and Whiteman discussed the best way to carry out the arrest of Big Snake. Whiteman told

the cavalry officer that he owed a number of Ponca tribesmen money for special work they had carried out for the agency, and Big Snake was one of them. Government money only came into the agency spasmodically. The agent and his white employees were themselves only paid several times each year, and earlier that year the Bureau of Indian Affairs had fallen six months behind in its salary payments to the Ponca agency. By June, money for salaries and expenses had finally been brought up to date, and now in October the latest pay packet had just come out from Washington. This meant that if Whiteman were to send out a message that he would be paying all outstanding moneys to the Poncas the next day, Big Snake would almost certainly come into the agency. Whiteman proposed to Lieutenant Mason that if the soldiers were to lie in wait for the big man they should be able to surprise and arrest him.

Lieutenant Stanton Mason was, according to Nathan Hughes, acerbic editor of the *Arkansas City Traveler*, "one of the most gentlemanly officers it was ever our pleasure to meet."[232] What Hughes might categorize as a gentleman is open to question—he also described William Whiteman as a gentleman. Lieutenant Mason passed through Arkansas City from time to time in the course of his duties, and Hughes befriended him. According to the editor, "Mason is a good officer, a man of courage, and will carry out instructions to the letter."[233] In this case, Lieutenant Mason's instructions were to bring Big Snake back to Fort Reno in handcuffs, and that was what he intended to do, with a minimum of fuss. Mason agreed to Agent Whiteman's plan.

The agent's message regarding payment for special work was duly circulated by runners during the day. Throughout the following morning men of the Ponca tribe arrived at the agency office in ones and twos to collect their earnings and then purchase goods from the agency trader, Joe Sherburne. Inside the office, the Poncas dealt with several men—Whiteman, the agent's clerk A. R. Satterthwaite, Sherburne, and the interpreter employed by the agency, Batiste Barnaby, an Oto. All went without incident through the morning, as Whiteman paid each man what was owed him, always with one eye on the door in case Big Snake appeared.

A little before noon on Friday, Big Snake walked into the agency office, accompanied by another Ponca clan chief, Hairy Bear, who had moved up in the clan hierarchy, apparently via the death through natural causes of its previous leader, one of the chiefs who had accompanied White Eagle and Standing Bear on the 1877 inspection tour of Indian Territory.

Whiteman told Big Snake and Hairy Bear to take a seat for a moment, then left the room. Moments later, he returned with Lieutenant Mason, his sergeant, and seven enlisted men armed with loaded cavalry carbines. Big Snake and Hairy Bear were sitting waiting for the agent. As Stanton and the main body of soldiers quickly surrounded the two Indians, the remaining five enlisted men appeared outside the agency building and barred the door, with carbines at the ready, to prevent other members of the tribe from entering the office to help Big Snake.

Big Snake's companion, Hairy Bear, jumped to his feet at the sight of the armed soldiers, but Big Snake kept his seat and eyed the troopers with disdain, realizing that he had been lured into a trap. Through interpreter Barnaby, Lieutenant Mason informed Big Snake that he was under arrest. Big Snake remained calm, asking why. Agent Whiteman then said that one of the charges against him was that he had threatened the agent's life. Big Snake patiently denied the claim.

"Tell Big Snake to come along," Lieutenant Mason instructed the interpreter. "Tell him to get up and come with us."

Big Snake did not budge from his chair. "Tell me what I have done," he said to the officer. "I have killed no one, I have stolen no horses, I have done nothing wrong."

The lieutenant briefly conferred with Agent Whiteman to one side, while Big Snake sat defiantly with arms folded. Mason once more addressed the Ponca through the interpreter. "You tried to kill two men, and were pretty mean."

Big Snake shook his head and denied the trumped-up charge.

Now Agent Whiteman intervened, instructing the interpreter to tell Big Snake that he had better go with the soldiers; he would learn more about the charges against him once he reached Fort Reno.

Big Snake shook his head. "I have done nothing wrong." He glared at Whiteman. "I will die before I go."

Hairy Bear, seeing Big Snake's defiance on the one hand and the soldiers' determination to arrest him on the other, tried to reason with his friend, telling him that the officer was not going to arrest him for nothing, and he had better go along with him. "Perhaps you will come back to the reservation all right," he added. "You have a wife and children," he reminded him. "Remember them, and do not get killed."

"Get up," Lieutenant Mason commanded once more. "If you do not go with us, something might happen."[234]

Slowly Big Snake rose to his feet and stood towering over the soldiers. Agency trader Joe Sherburne, who had been watching all this take place from the background, later testified that Big Snake now threw off the red blanket he had been carrying over his shoulders. This act, to Sherburne, was Big Snake's way of showing that he was not armed. But the soldiers around him, no doubt thinking that he meant to fight, would have immediately tensed.[235]

Big Snake turned to Hairy Bear. "I do not want to go," he told him. "If they want to kill me, let them do it, right here."[236] Hairy Bear was impressed by his friend's coolness and determination in the face of the Bluecoats but terrified for him at the same time. Meanwhile, the interpreter translated Big Snake's words, which only generated impatience from Lieutenant Mason.

"There is no use in talking," the lieutenant said. "I came to arrest you, and I want you to come with me."[237] Mason stomped out the door to the troopers outside. When he returned, he was carrying a pair of handcuffs. Mason and one of his men then tried to take hold of Big Snake by the wrists, but the Indian effortlessly pushed the two of them away. Mason, angry now, instructed four of his men to secure the man while his sergeant applied the handcuffs. The soldiers lay aside their carbines, but when they advanced on Big Snake, all five were thrown off, as if they were rag dolls. Again they tried, and again the soldiers found themselves repelled by the giant.

There was a pause, with the soldiers puffing and panting, and now Big Snake calmly resumed his seat and folded his arms. Lieutenant Mason snapped an order, and now the sergeant and five of his men fell on the seated figure. Even as it appeared they had the man under control, Big Snake rose up to his feet with the soldiers hanging onto him. With a monumental effort he then heaved them off him, sending all six sprawling across the floorboards.

The two remaining troopers had been standing, carbines in hand, watching this circus, and now one stepped up to Big Snake, swinging his weapon. With a sickening crunch, he crashed the butt of his carbine into the Indian's face. Moments later, the second soldier came from the side and brought the barrel of his carbine down across Big Snake's temple. The Ponca staggered and fell back against the wall. But he would not go down. With blood streaming down his face, he straightened again.

Hairy Bear later testified to what he witnessed and heard that day: he saw one of the soldiers level his carbine and point it at Big Snake, who was only feet away from him. Gripped by fear for his friend, unable to watch what he knew must come next, Hairy Bear looked away. He heard a shot. And then he heard Big Snake crash to the floor, dead.

The shooting of Big Snake at first panicked Lieutenant Mason and Agent Whiteman. The man was the brother of the nationally famous Standing Bear, after all, and they both knew how his death might look to Standing Bear's white friends—as a payback by the government for Standing Bear's daring to take the authorities to court and win. The pair must have talked long and hard about what to do, for it was not until the next afternoon that a trooper arrived at the Arkansas City telegraph office to send a message to Washington telling of the shooting—a message that Whiteman and Mason would have labored over at length.

From the telegraph office the news spread rapidly around Arkansas City, and it was the talk of the town that night and the next day. Meanwhile, someone in Arkansas City sent a telegraph message to the *Boston Daily Advertiser* with the report that Big Snake had been shot on William Whiteman's orders. Perhaps it was the telegraph operator himself, excitedly sending the news out broadcast. Maybe it was a local clergyman sympathetic to the Poncas, intent on letting the increasingly well-known Boston committee know what had taken place.

From whatever source, the news flashed north to Boston during the late afternoon. Once it reached the *Advertiser*, the telegram was quickly passed on to B. W. Williams. And this was the message from Kansas that Williams carried into the Boston hotel to the Tibbles party at around 5:00 P.M. that Saturday.

The following Monday, as the news of Big Snake's death broke in the press, the Department of the Interior issued a statement that "Standing Bear's brother, Big Snake, a bad man" had been "shot accidentally" at the Ponca agency in the Indian Territory.[238]

On Wednesday, November 5, the *Arkansas City Traveler* informed its readers,

> On Saturday night and Sunday our city was rife with rumors of "heep big Injun" troubles at the Ponca Agency, which upon investigation proves to have grown out of an attempt to make an arrest. It appears that a squad of soldiers had an order to arrest an Indian for various misdemeanors, who refused to submit to the law's requirements and resisted. He was pled with, both by the soldiers and prominent Indians of the tribe, but all to no purpose, and, becoming enraged, he attempted violence and was, in the melee that followed, shot by one of the soldiers. No blame is attached to anyone, and in half an hour's time everything was as quiet as if nothing had occurred.

The message received in Boston said that Big Snake had been shot on Agent Whiteman's orders. Despite the contradictions and controversy surrounding the shooting of Standing Bear's brother, Secretary Schurz did not order an Interior Department inquiry. As far as Carl Schurz was concerned, the matter was closed.

Chapter 20

THE ROAD TO FREEDOM

H ENRY TIBBLES WAS devastated by the news of his wife's death. The telegram from Omaha, which had taken three days to reach him, told of how Amelia had taken ill with severe pain. The ailment was not diagnosed immediately, and next day it was realized that she was suffering from appendicitis. Her appendix ruptured within hours, and twenty-four hours after becoming ill Amelia died from peritonitis.

After receiving the news at his Boston hotel, Tibbles left the luncheon party in a state of shock and went to his room. There, he wrote later, he prostrated himself on his bed in grief, hardly aware that his companions were in the room with him. Standing Bear knelt beside him seemingly in silent prayer for some minutes before he reached out and laid his large hands on Tibbles's head and began to pray aloud in his native tongue.

With Frank La Flesche translating, Standing Bear then said to him emotionally, "My friend, you have lost the one you love most. I knew her, too. She was beautiful and good. Your heart is very sad. A wife is closer to a man than a brother. We both suffer. But remember those others who suffer and die in that strange land. Do not go back home. Do not stop trying to help my poor people. They have no one to help them but you. Many husbands have seen their wives die, down in that hot country. They have no missionary to tell them of the good words God has spoken to those who have trouble. You can read God's book, and kind people will say words to comfort you. You suffer greatly, but they suffer more. Promise me that you will not forsake them."[239]

Tibbles looked around at the Ponca chief. He later wrote, "What could I do but take his hand and promise?"[240] Within hours, two more telegrams arrived from Omaha, this time sent directly to Boston. One told Tibbles that Bishop Clarkson had buried Amelia in Omaha that same day. Another came from attorney John L. Webster, telling Tibbles not to worry about his girls Eda and May, as he had immediately placed them in a private boarding school at Omaha under the personal supervision of Bishop Clarkson.

We can be sure that Bright Eyes commiserated with Tibbles that evening and that Tibbles quickly wrote to his daughters, but he did not mention doing so in his later writings. Before Tibbles had time to wallow too deeply in his grief, B. W. Williams summoned the other members of the Boston Indian Committee to the Tremont House, and there, within an hour or so of the double dose of terrible news reaching Tibbles and Standing Bear, the committee met with the members of the lecture party.

The committee members expressed their profound sympathy to both grieving men, but they urged them not to lose sight of the fact that the Ponca cause was of primary importance. They reminded Tibbles and company about the huge public reception at Horticultural Hall in a few hours, with thousands of Bostonians expected to turn out. The committee was unanimously of the view that all four members of the quartet should attend the reception, and the three speakers should all say at least a few words to the crowd. Tibbles resisted the idea, feeling that he simply could not face the ordeal of the public appearance with his heart dragging on the ground. "A soldier on the fighting line," one of the committeemen responded, "if his brother falls or his wife dies, still must keep his place in the battle."[241]

Still Tibbles resisted. Then Standing Bear reminded him that he himself had never given up, even though he had lost three of his four children. "I am older than you," he went on to say, "and I have suffered more. Now my brother is dead. He did not die of disease, but was cruelly murdered. All these things I bear. Your wife was dear to me. I know how sore your heart is, but do go to the meeting and say one word for those who suffer and die with no one to pity. If you can do that, it will make your burdens lighter, not heavier."[242]

So Tibbles accompanied Standing Bear, Bright Eyes, and Frank to the public reception that evening, to find a massive crowd gathered at Horticultural Hall. Boston was a city of 250,000 people by 1870, with 75,000 more women than men in 1879 as a result of Civil War casualties a decade and a half before. The Ponca cause strongly appealed to women with a sense of justice and morality, and there can be no doubt that women made up much of the crowd that night, with a small number of male chaperones to each group.

Very few of those attending knew of the death of Tibbles's wife and Standing Bear's brother. Had they known, their sympathy for the campaigners would probably have overwhelmed Henry Tibbles, who was only going through the motions. He spoke a few words to the crowd, although, as he later wrote, he would remember nothing of it. "My mind was not at the meeting—it was living over, moment by moment, eighteen hard, brave, wonderful years (with Amelia) that now were done."[243]

The public reception that night was a huge success, as the Boston papers enthusiastically reported in coming days. That reception, combined with the news of the party's double tragedy, won the Poncas thousands more fans. "Boston now was really stirred up," Tibbles would write.[244] During the following week in the city he could not walk down the street without being approached by an endless parade of complete strangers who wanted to pass on their sympathies, shake his hand, and wish him and his Indian friends well. Staff at the swanky Tremont House continually had to move away countless people who gathered outside the hotel to catch sight of the new celebrities.

The speeches at the massive Boston reception that night set the scene for grueling months of speeches by the crusading quartet throughout New England and then across the length and breadth of New York, Pennsylvania, and Maryland, and into the very lion's den itself—Washington, D.C.—before they could go home to Nebraska. Tens of thousands of

Americans came to see and hear a former frontier newspaper editor, an Indian chief, and a so-called Indian princess describe a great injustice—a great trampling of human rights—and explain how ordinary Americans could right the injustice, with their financial support and their vocal support for legislation to bring the Indian peoples under the protection of the law by recognizing them as citizens. At some venues, thousands were turned away because there was no more room inside.

The speeches changed little from engagement to engagement. Bright Eyes polished and modified her presentation over time, as she developed the theme that law was liberty, and that without the protection of law Native Americans had no liberty. "If we cannot get the protection of the law," she said of her own Omaha people in 1879, "we shall be driven from our reservation. And then what will become of my father and my mother and my sisters?"[245]

On the night of November 1, Bright Eyes, reading her address in a "modest, natural manner," told the vast Boston audience that when Inspector Kemble had taken the ten Ponca chiefs south to inspect Indian Territory two years earlier, her mother, the One Woman, worried that they would be left in a strange place from which they could not find their way home.[246] Bright Eyes said she'd laughed at this, telling her mother that the U.S. government would never "treat the chiefs of a nation with whom it made treaties in that dishonorable way."[247] And yet her mother had been right; that was exactly what the representatives of the U.S. government had done. Now, as she and her fellow crusaders took the story of the injustices done to and threatened against the Ponca and Omaha peoples to the American people, Bright Eyes was helping her brothers and sisters find their way home. "All we ask of your government," she said that night, "is to be treated as men and women, to be allowed to have a voice in whatever concerns us."[248]

Standing Bear's line remained consistent. That night in Boston when he and Henry Tibbles set aside their personal tragedies and set the stamp on the long hard campaign that lay ahead, he spoke, according to a reporter for the *Boston Daily Advertiser*, "with great animation and earnest eloquence, using vigorous gestures" as he would on hundreds of similar occasions in the months and years ahead.[249]

"I am the Ponca people," he told his audiences. "I have been here 2,000 years or more."[250] He sadly he told America of the forced march of his people to Indian Territory and remarked, "When people want to slaughter cattle they drive them along until they get them to a corral, and then they slaughter them. So it was with us."[251]

He told them of his personal tragedies. "My children have been exterminated, my brother has been killed."[252] And he told them of his attachment to the land of his forefathers beside the Swift Running Water. "My friends, if you took me away from this land it would be very hard for me. I wish to die in this land. I wish to be an old man here. I have not wished to give even a part of it to the Great Father. Though he were to give me a million dollars I would not give him this land."[253]

The simple honesty of the Indian chief's delivery, the undeniable human tragedy of his story, and the unpretentious nobility of the man himself sent ordinary Americans away from the Boston reception that night (and from meetings like it up and down the Northeast in coming months and years) with a heartfelt conviction that progress at the price of someone else's pain and suffering is not progress at all. It is a crime. Though the proponents of progress and America's "manifest destiny"[254] fought them every step of the way, the road on which Standing Bear, Bright Eyes, Frank La Flesche, and Henry Tibbles embarked that first November night after that dark, dark October of 1879 seemed certain to lead to victory, justice, and equality for Standing Bear and his people.

→ *Chapter 21* ←

THE WEDDING

A S THEIR STRUGGLE continued, Bright Eyes and Tibbles became
increasingly close. Their crusade threw them together, as they
shared their triumphs and defeats, their newfound national celebrity, and
the vitriol cast their way by their opponents. They shared hotels, restaurants, and railroad carriages for days, weeks, and months on end, as year
after year they and Standing Bear had toured the eastern states promoting
Indian rights, with the three Indians in the party liable to arrest at any
time as wards of the state on the loose.

They had hoped that the five-month tour of 1879–1880 would see
them achieve their goals—land title for the Poncas on the Niobrara, the
Indian Territory Poncas returned to their homeland, guaranteed tenure to
their Nebraska lands for the Omaha tribe, and their call for equal rights
for all Indians adopted by Congress. They'd been encouraged by the fact
that Interior Secretary Schurz had instructed the attorney general not to
proceed with the appeal against the Dundy decision (Lambertson had
moved for a dismissal on January 5, 1880). Schurz wanted the Ponca case
to die and be forgotten; another court hearing would only have given the
crusaders more national publicity. Determined not to be forgotten, they'd
thrown everything into their speaking campaign.

Bright Eyes, who did not have a strong constitution in the first place,
collapsed several times on the arduous tour. Tibbles begged her to ease up
but she wouldn't, fearing that her people might suffer if she thought of

herself. But when Tibbles discovered that beneath her glove her right hand was black and blue from all the handshaking that followed each speaking engagement, he instructed the tour manager provided by the Boston committee to quietly ask the people in line to meet her to shake Bright Eyes's hand gently. Even so, by April 1880, after almost half a year of continuous lecturing, the crusading quartet looked and felt totally "battered," as Tibbles wrote in *Buckskin and Blanket Days*. On a train to Baltimore, their exhausted state shocked a fellow passenger, Mrs. Mary Porter Tileston Hemenway.

Without saying a word to the party, the fifty-nine-year-old Mrs. Hemenway, widow of wealthy Boston merchant Augustus Hemenway, and a noted philanthropist, got off the train at Baltimore and wired the Boston Indian Committee that she would pay for the crusading quartet to spend ten days resting up at a popular Virginia seaside resort town, Old Point Comfort. Courtesy of Mrs. Hemenway, Bright Eyes, Standing Bear, Frank La Flesche, and Henry Tibbles enjoyed a ten-day break during the second half of April, before finally returning to Nebraska.

They went back west with the knowledge that an Indian bill containing provisions for Standing Bear's band to be granted tenure to land on the Niobrara had been presented to the Senate by Massachusetts senator Henry L. Dawes, longtime chairman of the Senate Indian Affairs Committee, and was about to be approved (the bill passed the Senate on April 30). They also knew that earlier that month attorneys John Webster and Andrew Poppleton had teamed up once again and gone back to the district court on behalf of the entire Ponca tribe, this time to literally sue the Sioux—for restoration of the land that had been taken from the Poncas by the treaty of 1868. That case was heard later in the year.

Back home by May 1880, the members of the quartet tried to pick up the pieces of their old lives. Standing Bear went home to his wife and daughter on the island at the mouth of the Niobrara, where they were living in a tent. He worked his fields and helped his family and the rest of his little community keep their promise to the government that they would fend for themselves. Bright Eyes, unemployed since she had resigned the job she loved at the Omaha reservation government school, went to work in the fields with her family, as did her half brother Frank. Tibbles was reunited with his tearful daughters for the first time since the death of their mother.

Once the dust had settled, Tibbles met with General Crook, John Webster, and the members of the Omaha Indian Committee to review the 1879–1880 campaign. They had to agree that the campaign had achieved some notable successes. There was the matter, for example, of William Whiteman, the detested Indian Affairs agent on the Ponca reservation in the Indian Territory. When the crusaders reached Washington in December 1879, Bright Eyes presented the Bureau of Indian Affairs with statements she collected from White Eagle and others about Whiteman's financial mismanagement. Pessimists would have been sure that the bureau would dismiss the accusations contained in those statements. But just days before Christmas, Special Inspector Pollock and Mr. Pugh from the Interior Department suddenly arrived at the Ponca agency in the Indian Territory and demanded to see Whiteman's account books. A week later, the Bureau of Indian Affairs announced that William H. Whiteman was retiring, effective forthwith.[255] The Poncas' Indian Territory jailer had been undone.

Following Whiteman's dismissal, Nathan Hughes wrote in the *Arkansas City Traveler*, "A very bitter fight has been waged against Whiteman, and he alleges that no defense has been allowed him. The charges are based on affidavits of exorbitant prices paid for supplies purchased in open market and have no connection with the charges or influence of those who have been striving, since the death of Big Snake, for the Agent's removal. Whiteman is a gentleman of good address, a fine lawyer, and it has always been a wonder to us why he accepted an appointment as Agent at a very moderate salary."[256]

The reason Whiteman had accepted that "very moderate salary" was unearthed by the men from Washington—Whiteman had been accepting kickbacks from local contractors while overpaying for their goods and services. The amount involved was never revealed. Eight years before, the

Indian Affairs agent at the Arapaho agency had embezzled $30,000 of the $90,000 allocated to the tribe by the government. One of his suppliers alone sold goods to the agency at a profit margin of 125 percent and then split the take with the agent.

Whiteman's was the crusaders' first proverbial scalp. Within weeks, there were others. First, during early January 1880, Indian Affairs Commissioner Ezra Hayt announced that a member of his board of commissioners, a churchman by the name of Barston (described by John Bourke as a "whining, psalm singing hypocrite"), was dismissed for illicitly supplying stoves to the bureau for use on Indian reservations.[257]

The Indian Affairs corruption scandal was fanned by newspapers such as the New York Daily Sun, whose publisher, Charles A. Dana, pioneered the human interest story. Dana was a strong critic of Rutherford B. Hayes and his claim to be rooting out corruption from Washington's corridors of power. The Sun referred to Hayes as "His Fraudulency the President."[258] As the press applied the heat, the scandal spread—upward. Within weeks, Interior Secretary Schurz announced the dismissal of Commissioner Ezra Hayt for corrupt practices. The establishment was rocked by Hayt's fall. The pro-Indian lobby was jubilant.

The crusaders had other successes during this period too. Sitting in the Boston audience on November 1, 1879, had been forty-nine-year-old writer Helen Hunt Jackson, a correspondent who wrote under the byline of H.H. for the New York weekly Independent. Within days Jackson had approached Henry Tibbles about joining the crusaders on tour. Jackson became the fifth member of the team, a mentor for Bright Eyes and a motivator for them all. Both Standing Bear and Bright Eyes soon became extremely fond of H.H. She would have been present later that month when Bright Eyes became the first woman ever to speak at Boston's famous Faneuil Hall and Standing Bear, the first Native American to do so.

Through contacts such as Edward Everett Hale the crusaders made many famous, influential friends. At the Cambridge, Massachusetts, home of a Boston committee member, influential book publisher Henry Houghton, the members of the crusading party were introduced to a host of household names. The most famous of them all, a white-haired old man, waited impatiently for them at the top of Houghton's front steps; Henry Wadsworth Longfellow was world famous for his poems *The Wreck of the Hesperus, Paul Revere's Ride,* and, most notably, *The Song of Hiawatha,* a story of Chippewa chief Hiawatha and the beautiful Indian maid Minnehaha.

As Bright Eyes came up the steps to meet Longfellow, he took her hand and said, *"This* is Minnehaha!"[259] Longfellow monopolized Bright Eyes for an hour before allowing other noted guests such as Oliver Wendell Holmes and James Russell Lowell to talk to her that night.

Yet, for all their notoriety and new friends, the crusaders had not achieved any of their primary goals. Before losing his job, Commissioner Hayt had recommended to Congress that the Indian Territory Poncas be paid compensation for their lands on the Niobrara, but White Eagle and most of his people didn't want that. They wanted to go home to the Niobrara, as Standing Bear and his little band had. Meanwhile, Interior Secretary Schurz had stated his determination to keep the Poncas in the Indian Territory, in order to prevent other relocated tribes from agitating to be returned to their homelands. In a string of letters, statements, and press interviews he defended his position and his handling of the removal of the Poncas, blaming the previous administration, Congress, even Inspector Kemble, finding fault with everyone but himself.

The crusaders' hopes had been fanned when Senator Dawes first introduced his Indian bill to the Senate. The Dawes bill was referred to a five-man Senate select committee, and in February 1880 one of the first witnesses to give evidence to the committee was Standing Bear. The Dawes Bill was passed several months later.

Once the crusaders read the Dawes legislation, they realized there was a major problem with it. While a provision of the bill stated, "Each member of the Ponca tribe of Indians now occupying a part of the old Ponca reservation, within the limits of said great Sioux reservation, shall be entitled to allotments upon said old Ponca reservation," it also required that for the allotment process to go ahead three-fourths of all male Sioux must agree, in a referendum arranged by the Interior Department, to cede the land back to the Poncas.[260] That referendum was to take place whenever the Interior secretary saw fit. As the crusaders knew all too well, Interior Secretary Schurz did not see fit and would never see fit if he had his way. Apart from Schurz's concession that the Poncas had genuine grievances, all the momentum of the crusaders' 1879–1880 campaign seemed to come to a shuddering halt at Carl Schurz's door.

In June, Tibbles, restless and worried about what the Interior secretary might do behind the crusaders' backs, went down to the Poncas in the Indian Territory without permission, taking Omaha interpreter Henry Fontanelle along with him. Once he linked up with White Eagle and his Poncas, Tibbles updated them with regard to all that was being done on their behalf in the East and wrung a promise from them that under no circumstances would they sign any documents presented to them by the Interior Department before they were checked by lawyer John L. Webster.

Inevitably Tibbles was caught by Indian Affairs men and thrown off the reservation. Tibbles's brief arrest was a source of great propaganda for the Interior Department, which could now paint a leading Ponca crusader as a lawbreaker. In August 1880, the *Council Fire*, which supported the Interior secretary, had declared Tibbles "a professional adventurer" and accused him of "wild and untruthful utterances and suspicious actions in connection with this Standing Bear case."

But not every step the crusaders took during this period was a backward one. While Tibbles went south, Standing Bear went north to the Rosebud agency of the Brulé Lakota Sioux in Dakota Territory, visiting with Spotted Tail, powerful paramount chief of the Brulé. For hundreds of years the Sioux had tormented the Poncas, and there was no guarantee that they would vote to give the Poncas back even a portion of their old homeland if and when Secretary Schurz set the referendum in motion. Yet, after Standing Bear put his case to the Sioux chief, Spotted Tail called a council of his clan chiefs, who agreed the Brulé would support the return of land to Standing Bear's band if the government held the referendum.

In the fall of 1880 the Omaha Indian Committee and Boston Indian Committee concluded that it would be necessary to put pressure on Secretary Schurz to set the Sioux vote in motion. They decided to restart the public campaign in the East, meaning that the four crusaders would have to go back on the lecture circuit. That November, while Webster and Poppleton prepared to present their case against the Sioux in court the following month, Standing Bear again parted from his wife and daughter at the Niobrara, Bright Eyes and her brother Frank came down from the Omaha reservation, and Henry Tibbles said good-bye to his daughters—having brought his sprightly seventy-eight-year-old widowed mother, Martha Tibbles, west from Ohio to care for Ida and May while he was away.

Lyceum agent B. W. Williams quickly booked a speaking tour for 1880–1881 that took in much of the Northeast once again, involving engagements on at least five days of each week and frequently on seven. The team started the tour in New England, scene of their great triumphs during the previous season. In Boston they were joined for the second year running by their writer friend Helen Hunt Jackson (H.H. as they affectionately called her), who came east from her home in Colorado to travel with the crusaders during the current tour.

One Friday night in November 1880, Tibbles, Standing Bear, and Bright Eyes addressed a packed house at Worcester, Massachusetts, as the new tour gathered momentum. In the supportive audience that night sat Senator George F. Hoar, a Worcester resident. Stirred up by what he heard at the meeting and read in the press the next day, the bookish Senator Hoar wrote to President Hayes at the White House, enclosing a press clipping about the meeting and expressing his concern at the wrong done the Poncas by the government. "I feel profound anxiety that the order for redressing this wrong should come from you," he wrote, "not from a Senator or the Congress."[261] Hoar also pointed out that the press was assigning the blame for this terrible wrong to Hayes's Interior secretary.

An irritated President Hayes replied swiftly: "As soon as practicable I will give the matter attention, and will be glad to confer with you when you return [to Washington]. I suppose General Schurz has been most shamefully treated in this affair, but I may be mistaken. I will look into it carefully."[262] Hayes promptly discussed the senator's letter with Schurz, who convinced the president that the problem with the Poncas had been caused by Congress; his department had only complied with the laws and treaties endorsed by Congress.

Senator Dawes also heard the hullabaloo in his home state, and he approached the Interior Department to find out what it intended to do about the Poncas. He was told that Secretary Schurz planned to bring the Indian Territory Ponca chiefs to Washington in December to resolve their complaints. Dawes didn't like the sound of that and wrote the president to tell him so. Hayes wrote back, "While I am confident that there is no foundation to your apprehension of wrong-doing to the Poncas in case they visit the Interior Department next month, I will nevertheless give heed to your caution and see that nothing unfair or inconsiderate is done."[263]

Meanwhile, in late November, Webster and Poppleton went to court in Omaha to pursue the Ponca action against Chief Red Cloud and his Sioux. Once again, they appeared before Judge Elmer S. Dundy. On December 4, a news report emanating from Omaha flashed around the nation via telegraph: "Judge Dundy in the United States Circuit this morning decided in the Ponca Indian case—to recover their old reservation and establish a title thereto—that the Ponca tribe of Indians have legal estate in the reservation, and are entitled to possession thereto. This case is the first on record where one Indian brought suit against another in the courts of the United States, and has aroused deep and widespread feeling on account of the wrong done the Poncas."[264]

Although this victory was celebrated by the Indian lobby, it hardly raised an eyebrow in middle America. Unlike Standing Bear's original victory over the government, this latest case was generally perceived as a tiff between Indians that was of no concern to whites. But it didn't go unnoticed in Washington. Spurred by the ruckus being raised by the crusaders on tour, the increasingly embattled President Hayes now came under intense pressure from the press and church groups to set up an independent commission to look into the Poncas' complaints.

On December 8, Hayes wrote in his diary, "A great and grievous wrong has been done to the Poncas." But he added that he didn't blame Carl Schurz; rather, he blamed Senator Dawes for not bringing the problem to his attention earlier—following the line put to him by Schurz two weeks earlier. This was despite the fact that Standing Bear and White Eagle personally informed Hayes of the mistreatment of the Poncas when they were at the White House two years previously.

President Hayes agreed to set up a four-man Presidential Ponca Commission, which met for five weeks from December 18 to ascertain the facts surrounding the Poncas' removal from the Niobrara and their present condition and to recommend ways the government could redress their situation.

But before President Hayes could announce the composition of his commission, General George Crook had a word in his ear. Officially Crook went to Washington to attend a December 15 White House dinner for thirty-six in honor of former president Ulysses S. Grant. Before the alcohol-free dinner, Crook took his old friend and one-time subordinate Hayes for a stroll across the grass from the White House to the Washington Monument, construction of which was then nearing completion. Together the pair climbed the 898 clanging metal steps to the top and surveyed the city from a vantage point that no one other than those associated with the construction had previously enjoyed.

Three days later, when the president formally named the members of his Ponca Commission, General George Crook was its chairman, replacing an earlier candidate.[265] It seems the price for Crook's participation was a promise from Crook to Hayes that the commission's final report would avoid criticizing the government or its individual employees and would stick to determining whether the Poncas' grievances were legitimate and, if so, recommend what should be done to redress those grievances.

On paper Crook seemingly had two allies among the commission's four members—his subordinate, Brigadier General Nelson Miles, and Walter Allen, a reporter from the *Boston Advertiser* nominated by the Boston Indian Committee. The fourth commissioner was William Stickney, a member of the Indian Bureau's board of commissioners, considered a representative of the enemy by the friends of the Poncas. General Crook's ADC, John "Ink Man" Bourke, was appointed recorder (secretary) to the commission. To assist and advise the commission, Reverend J. Owen Dorsey of Washington's Bureau of American Ethnology was brought in. He had an intimate knowledge of the Ponca situation, having converted Standing Bear to Christianity; later he had attempted to help the Poncas after Standing Bear was arrested at the Omaha reservation in 1879 by writing to Washington about their mistreatment.

The White House then instructed the Interior Department to bring White Eagle and his clan chiefs to Washington to speak before the Presidential Ponca Commission. James Haworth, an Indian Affairs Bureau inspector, and William Whiting, the new Indian Affairs agent at the Ponca reservation in the Indian Territory (a former Union army colonel whose name was confusingly similar to that of his disgraced predecessor), quickly brought White Eagle and his chiefs to Washington, where Indian Affairs denied them independent interpreters and sealed them off from the press and from Standing Bear, Bright Eyes, and Tibbles.

Carl Schurz then moved to circumvent his opponents. Before the chiefs could testify in front of General Crook and the Ponca Commission, Secretary Schurz personally interviewed them in private over two days, on Christmas Eve and then on December 27, supposedly to allow them to air their grievances. For these meetings Schurz used Oto interpreters in the pay of the Bureau of Indian Affairs who'd been brought up from Indian Territory by Agent Whiting. To show the press how magnanimous he was, on Christmas Day Schurz had the members of the Ponca delegation brought to his Washington home to meet his family.

On December 27, at the end of the two-day interview, White Eagle and his colleagues, exhausted, brow-beaten, denied access to lawyers or other advisers, and told by Schurz that the government would never let them go back north, caved in and agreed to stay in the Indian Territory and sign away their land in the north if they were paid compensation, had their children returned to them from Carlisle, and were provided with a school and other facilities. Secretary Schurz swiftly issued a press statement, saying the Poncas had signed an agreement freely giving up all claim to their Dakota Territory land and expressing satisfaction with the Indian Territory reservation. As Henry Tibbles had feared, Schurz railroaded White Eagle and his people into signing away their homeland and consigning their future to the Warm Land.

In a diary entry on August 10, 1880, Lieutenant John Bourke described Carl Schurz as "that spindle-shanked Mephistopheles presiding over the Department of the Interior." In the medieval legend of Faust, Mephistopheles was one of the seven chief demons, second only to Satan. Helen Hunt Jackson, who corresponded with Schurz in 1879–1880 about the Poncas, described Schurz as "that false souled man" and accused him of "astounding and wholesale lying."[266]

Chairing the president's commission, General Crook ignored Schurz's Ponca agreement, considering it acquired under duress, and proceeded to take fresh evidence from White Eagle and his chiefs, this time using a Ponca interpreter. He took his commission members to Indian Territory and the Niobrara so they could talk to the Poncas at each location and see the situation for themselves.

Standing Bear had no doubt about who was to blame for the Poncas' miseries. Testifying to the commission when its members visited the Niobrara, he said, "If the Secretary is sick or foolish, I hope you will act as physicians and heal him. I mean the one who speaks German."[267]

In late January, Lieutenant Bourke worked day and night in an office at the War Department writing up the commission's report. That report found that the Poncas had been removed without lawful authority and advocated returning all the Poncas to the Niobrara who wanted to go. Crook didn't want to be seen as forcing the Poncas back to Dakota Territory after Lone Chief and Standing Buffalo had told the commission they would be happy to stay where they were; that would only be a continuation of the heavy-handed government treatment of the tribe. To give Poncas in the Indian Territory time to consider their options, the report recommended allowing tribe members a year to decide where they wanted to live. The commission also recommended allotting land to individual Poncas at both reservation sites, depending on where they chose to be, and paying compensation for their mistreatment.

As Bourke was writing his report, it came to light that one commission member was writing a minority report. The odd man out was not the Indian Bureau's William Stickney, as might have been expected, but Walter Allen from the *Advertiser*. In his minority report Allen made much the same recommendations as Crook, but he went farther, discussing the causes of the Ponca injustices and strongly attacking the role of the government and Secretary Schurz in particular. Point by point, Allen challenged Schurz's claims about how he'd handled the matter and about the legitimacy of Interior Department actions since 1877. He also challenged the December 27 agreement signed by the Ponca leaders from Indian Territory, declaring that free will had played no part in it; Allen, like Crook, knew that Schurz had pressured the Poncas to sign it.

On January 24, General Crook went to the White House to present the commission's majority and minority reports to the president. After Hayes took possession of the reports, he told the general that he would shortly present them to Congress. He then stunned Crook by informing him that he would also be attaching a copy of the agreement signed by the Indian Territory Poncas, which Carl Schurz had rushed to him on December 27; this was the document declaring their contentment with the Indian Territory reservation and their desire to remain there.

There is no record of what passed between the two men in this White House meeting, but it seems that Crook informed Hayes that the Poncas told him that Schurz had worn them down until they saw no option but to sign the agreement. Hayes retorted he could not believe Carl Schurz would be a party to such pressure tactics. Ignoring Crook's protests,

Hayes said he would be passing the new agreement on to Congress with the Ponca commission reports and commending all three documents to the Senate and the House.

When Crook met up with Lieutenant Bourke shortly after leaving the White House, he appeared devastated. Bourke was fit to explode after the general told him what transpired in his meeting with the president. That night, an embittered John Bourke confided to his diary that he considered a two-faced President Hayes guilty of duplicity and treachery, for what he was about to do to the Poncas.

President Hayes duly presented the commission's two reports and the chiefs' agreement to Congress in the first week of February, declaring that the December 27 statement clearly indicated that the Poncas in the Indian Territory were healthy, comfortable, and contented, and recommending that Poncas who wished to stay there should be allowed to do so. In taking the Interior Department's line, Hayes rejected Crook and endorsed Schurz and his actions. Perhaps he felt he must stand by a senior member of his cabinet and a friend. Perhaps he suspected that Crook had inspired Walter Allen to write the minority report with its scathing attack on Schurz as a way of getting at Schurz without breaking his word to the president that his report would not criticize individuals; after Crook's behind-the-scenes role in the habeas corpus case this wasn't impossible. If Hayes truly suspected Crook of trying to outflank him, he used this tactic to put him in his place.

Although Crook was quite caustic about others when he later wrote his autobiography, he rarely uttered an unkind word about anyone and always overcame slights and reverses. His friendship with the Hayes family ultimately survived this rocky episode.

Hayes was to leave office on March 3, having previously decided not to run for reelection. He left the Ponca problem to the next Congress and his successor in the White House, fellow Republican James A. Garfield. John Bourke later wrote that as far as the Ponca tribe was concerned the only positive outcome of the Ponca Commission was that "members of the band who had returned to the mouth of the Niobrara were permitted to remain there unmolested."[268]

One of the recommendations of Crook's report was that all Indians should be able to appeal to the courts for the protection of their rights and property, and this theme was promptly taken up in Congress. A Republican senator, Samuel J. Kirkwood, sat on a Senate select committee that held its own Ponca inquiry through February 1881 using the Crook commission reports and the December 27 statement as its starting point. Determined to continue to influence events and defend his position, Interior Secretary Schurz took the unprecedented step of sitting with the select committee and questioning the committee's witnesses. This select committee was not subjected to the restrictions that Hayes had imposed on Crook. It also looked into the killing of Big Snake, although it was subsequently unable to lay blame for the death of Standing Bear's brother.

Consequently, on March 3, 1881, the last day of the Forty-sixth Congress, Kirkwood pushed through a Ponca bill of his own creation. Much like the Crook recommendations, the Kirkwood bill gave Poncas in the Indian Territory the right to go home to the Niobrara but allowed those in the Indian Territory to stay there if they chose, allotting 320 acres per man for Poncas who made their home in Dakota Territory and 160 acres per man for those who remained in the Indian Territory. Parts of the Ponca reservation on the Niobrara not allotted would be taken over by the government, but the tribe would be paid $53,000 a year for five years in compensation.

The Kirkwood bill was not perfect, but it was the best news yet for the Poncas and their supporters. None of the provisions could be acted on until the Sioux voted in favor of officially ceding the Niobrara land to the Poncas, but the new bill required the Interior secretary to implement that vote before year's end. On the strength of the Kirkwood bill and the success of the second Webster-Poppleton legal challenge before Judge Dundy, General Crook allowed Standing Bear and his Poncas to transfer from the island at the mouth of the Niobrara to land on the northern-western bank of the river, in advance of but in expectation of the Sioux vote being put into effect.

Back north of the river for the first time in almost four years, Standing Bear pitched his family's tent and made plans to build a simple wooden frame house. Other Poncas in Dakota Territory did the same and looked forward to all tribe members coming home from Indian Territory and being reunited in their homeland. But the bulk of the tribe was too frightened to risk it until the authorities said they could all go home. The killing of Big Snake had convinced many in the Indian Territory that they would suffer a similar fate if they tried to go against the Bureau of Indian Affairs.

The Interior secretary, who was now required by law to arrange for the Ponca tribe to have their land returned to them by the Sioux, was no longer Carl Schurz. When President Garfield took office in March, he didn't retain Schurz as secretary of the Interior, although Schurz had lobbied for a cabinet post in the new administration. On March 7, Carl Schurz left the Interior Department and moved to New York to become editor of the *Evening Post*. He was never brought to account for the misery he visited on the Poncas and other Indian tribes in the name of expediency, but his reputation was so stained that he never again held a government post, nor was he elected to another public office. Till his dying day he claimed to be a reformer who fought to end government corruption. Yet, tellingly, a friend and admirer, politician Henry Watterson, remarked, "Truth to say, Schurz never wholly adjusted himself to political conditions in the United States."[269]

The new Interior secretary was a Republican politician who resigned from the Senate to fill Schurz's empty chair—Samuel J. Kirkwood, the same Senator Kirkwood who put through the new bill in support of the Poncas—and he set up the machinery enabling the Sioux vote to be taken by the Indian Affairs Bureau by the end of the year.

That spring the crusaders went home to Nebraska again, this time convinced that their struggles were nearing an end. After consulting Iron Eye and the One Woman, and with the weight of their two-year battle seemingly lifted from their shoulders, Henry Tibbles and Bright Eyes quietly informed their friends that they would marry in the summer.

Henry Tibbles's autobiography includes no reference to his romance with the little Indian girl fifteen years his junior, fearing an accusation that he and Bright Eyes had begun their affair while he was married. For the same reason, he did not mention Bright Eyes's early pivotal role in the Ponca campaign. Despite Tibbles's attempts to camouflage their relationship early on, there is little doubt it was purely platonic prior to Amelia's death. Both Henry and Bright Eyes were deeply religious, and the very thought of an extra-marital affair in those straitlaced times would have been abhorrent to them both.

It's possible that Tibbles fell in love with the spirited young woman while his first wife was alive but kept his feelings to himself. After Amelia's death, Bright Eyes became an emotional backstop for Tibbles, just as he had already filled that role for her.

On July 23, 1881, wedding guests gathered at the little stone Presbyterian mission church on the banks of the Missouri on the Omaha Indian reservation. They had come to witness the wedding of Thomas Henry Tibbles and Susette Bright Eyes La Flesche. It was to be no marriage of convenience; there was genuine affection between the pair. Harvard ethnologist Alice Cunningham Fletcher, who traveled with the newlyweds on a visit to the Omahas, Poncas, and Sioux in 1881 described the loving couple in her diary, calling them "Mr. and Mrs. T." In her company they shared intellectual jokes and were as playful as puppies with each other.[270]

So it was that guests joined the bride and groom at the Presbyterian church on the Omaha reservation in the summer of 1881 to participate in their wedding, officiated by Reverend S. N. D. Martin.[271] There is no record of the guest list, but Bright Eyes's parents, Iron Eye and the One Woman, would have been there, and her siblings, including her sister Rosalie, who the previous year had married the Omaha reservation's industrial teacher Edward Farley, and her sister Susan, home from medical school for the summer. Susan was to become the first Native American woman to graduate as a doctor of medicine. Tibbles's mother, Martha, was probably at the wedding, together with his daughters, Ida and May. General Crook would have been there, and probably John L. Webster and his wife and other Omaha Indian Committee members. Standing Bear and his wife, Susette, would have been there, along with other members of the Ponca band from the Niobrara, including medicine man Buffalo Chip and his wife. By this time a total of 130 Poncas had fled Indian Territory and joined Standing Bear at the Niobrara.

The bride, who was dwarfed by her tall, broad-shouldered groom, would have worn a simple, full-length white dress, the groom, his Sunday-best suit. As Bright Eyes became Susette La Flesche Tibbles, Henry would have looked at his new wife with pride. In two years she had gone from a shy but determined young lady to one of the most famous women in America, although she disliked every aspect of her celebrity apart from the fact it gave her the chance to speak out on her people's behalf.

As for Henry Tibbles, in many ways he was a different man from the rough-and-ready frontier newspaperman Bright Eyes had first come to know. Time among the elite of the East had given him a little polish, although not enough to erase his western charm. Shocked by his first wife's death and pummeled by the slings and arrows of two years of arduous campaigning for the Poncas and Omahas, Tibbles confirmed the prediction made by Boston orator Wendell Phillips. He had said that Tibbles's hair would turn gray before the laws were changed to benefit the Indians, and over these past two years, Tibbles's thick, jet-black hair turned very gray. In another two years it was totally gray and eventually turned snowy white.

Henry Tibbles's many enemies were unimpressed by the marriage. "I fear poor Bright Eyes has made a mistake," Deputy Interior Secretary Alonzo Bell wrote from Washington to his former boss Carl Schurz in New York shortly after news of the wedding became public. "But I am willing to forgive her if the act has effectually disposed of Tibbles." Bell hoped that Bright Eyes's "sacrifice" would give the country "a rest from the vexatious borings of the Tibbles school of philosophy."[272]

Mr. and Mrs. Tibbles were not sure what they would do in the long term; both had already tried their hand at writing books and articles, and Bright Eyes had also taken up painting. But they agreed to go on one last eastern speaking tour starting in December. With the Poncas almost certain to achieve the security of tenure that Standing Bear had fought for, the Omaha and Boston committees asked the crusaders to undertake one final tour to push for land ownership and citizenship rights for all Indians.

Standing Bear also agreed to join the latest speaking tour, although he could ill afford to spend time away from his struggling little farm, where his wife and daughter labored in the fields at his side. He had already piled up the lumber to build his house, but as he returned to the Niobrara following the Tibbles wedding he would have been convinced the tour was the right thing to do. Other Indians, including Bright Eyes, were committed to extending the campaign to all their Native American brothers and sisters. Standing Bear felt that of all Native Americans he had the most to be grateful for now that he was living unmolested on the land of his fathers, as he had hoped and dreamed. His house could wait.

This last lecture tour promised to open the door to rights for all Native Americans. The vote by the Sioux ceding the Niobrara homelands back to the Ponca tribe would go forward over the winter. The Kirkwood bill would then come into effect, legitimizing the Poncas' occupation and individual ownership of those lands. Other moves in Congress pointed to the Omahas being given title to allotments on their reservation; they too could then get on with their lives free of the threat of dispossession. That year 1881 was a positive one, a happy one, full of promise that all was sure to come right for the Ponca and Omaha peoples and their Indian brothers and sisters.

✦ Chapter 22 ✦

THE END FOR STANDING BEAR

IN THE THIRD week of May 1906, Lincoln-based historian Addison E. Sheldon made his way to Standing Bear's house on the flat beside the Niobrara River. He came in the company of an unidentified reporter for the *New York Times* and an interpreter. Sheldon brought a camera to record the image and a notebook to record the words of the former clan chief of the Ponca tribe. He was writing a chapter on Standing Bear in a detailed history of Nebraska published eight years later.

The *Times* reporter hoped to document Standing Bear's reaction to the death of former secretary of the Interior, Carl Schurz, in New York City on May 14. Papers nationwide were giving Schurz glowing obituaries. America had forgotten the Ponca case, and Schurz had worked hard to rehabilitate his reputation in his latter years by heading up a reform movement and writing well-received political biographies. Time and events had consigned the Poncas to a very small corner of history by 1906. Even when the fight for the Poncas and Omahas was at its zenith in 1881, sensational events pushed the Indians out of the news—the assassination of President Garfield and the Standard Oil scandal. After that, political dramas occupied the headlines, not to mention an economic depression and the Spanish-American War. But the *Times* editor hadn't forgotten the Poncas; he wanted to know what Standing Bear thought of his onetime foe.

Standing Bear, now in his seventies, thin and wrinkled with short white hair, obligingly agreed to be photographed outside the humble little farmhouse he built on the flat prairie in the 1890s. For the first photos he wore his farm clothes. Because Sheldon wanted to include a classic image of an Indian chief in his book, eventually Standing Bear agreed to strip to the waist and be photographed holding his "peace" pipe. And he put on the last remaining emblem of his days as a leader of the Ponca tribe, his bear-claw necklace.

Once the photographs had been taken and Standing Bear put his shirt back on, he sat talking with his visitors, puffing on his pipe as he reminisced about days past and the men and women who peopled his life. Many of his friends, those who helped him become a person in the eyes of the law back in 1879, were gone now. Iron Eye, last chief of the Omahas, his good friend, died in 1888, still a comparatively young man. General Crook died in 1890 at age sixty. He was struck down by a heart attack while lifting weights in the Chicago hotel where he'd lived since becoming a major general and succeeding General Sheridan as commander of the Division of the Missouri. Standing Bear would have heard that many Sioux and Apaches wailed in mourning when they learned of General Crook's passing.

The general's loyal aide, John "Ink Man" Bourke, passed away six years later, just short of his fiftieth birthday. Judge Elmer Dundy died that same year, 1896, and was buried on Staten Island. Lawyer Andrew Poppleton was in his grave too, going blind before he died. Helen Hunt Jackson, unofficial fifth member of the crusading team, nationally famous in 1884 with *Ramona*, a best-selling novel about California Indians written after she served on an Indian commission in California, had only a year to enjoy her success, being claimed by cancer in 1885 at age fifty-four.

So many good people had been taken, and too many of them too young. Saddest of all, Standing Bear had lost his dear friend Bright Eyes three years back. Bright Eyes, his speaking tour partner until they finally gave up lecturing in 1883, died at forty-nine; some said of consumption, others, of cancer. She and Henry Tibbles tried farming near the Omaha reservation before leasing out their little property and becoming reporters. For a few years they were Capitol Hill correspondents in Washington, D.C., before returning to Nebraska when Bright Eyes's health began to decline. Tibbles edited a Lincoln paper for a time, even going back to his old Omaha stomping ground and rejoining the paper in which he launched his Ponca crusade. It had a new name now; in 1889 the *Daily Herald* merged with a new Omaha daily, the *World,* becoming the *Omaha World-Herald.*

In her last years, Bright Eyes wrote magazine stories and painted. She assured everyone she was quite content. She and Henry did one last speaking tour in 1886–1887—a heady year in England and Scotland, meeting royalty, lecturing five days a week. The British called her Princess Bright Eyes. She continued to visit with New England literary friends, occasionally speaking in public, but she was happy to retreat from the limelight.

Bright Eyes died disappointed and estranged from her brother Frank. He achieved his goal of graduating from law school and became like a son to ethnologist Alice Cunningham Fletcher, who found him a job at the Bureau of Indian Affairs in Washington as a clerk. The determined, imperious Fletcher personally led land allotments to individual Indians in the 1880s, starting with the Omahas in 1882. Too late, Bright Eyes realized that Fletcher and many like her were not true friends of the Indian. They set out to destroy Native American culture, forcing Indians to embrace the "civilized" white way. By breaking up reservations into thousands of little farms they broke up the tribes' communal way of life and then redistributed millions of "excess" reservation acreage to whites.

Was Standing Bear disappointed? In 1889 a majority of the Sioux finally voted to restore the Niobrara land to the Poncas, and in 1890 Standing Bear and 166 other Ponca males who had returned to the old reservation were each given 320 acres. The government sold the balance to white settlers. By now, that land was in Nebraska, after Congress moved the state line north to the 43rd parallel in 1882, chopping 400,000 acres from what became South Dakota. Not that such tinkering with lines on maps meant anything to Standing Bear; he had kept his promise to his son, burying Bear Shield's bones with those of their ancestors. He had brought his family home to the Niobrara. He had gained legal title to a slice of his homeland.

So, disappointed? No, but things were never the same as before. The Poncas had become two tribes—those who remained in the Indian Territory, the Maste'Pa'ca, or Hot Country Poncas as they called themselves, and those who returned to the old homeland, the Osni'Pa'ca, the Cold Country Poncas. Occasionally Standing Bear visited his relatives and friends in the Hot Country, and once the parting was so painful he even thought seriously of staying down there. But he had come home to the Niobrara. This was where he wanted to die. He was happy enough.

Puffing on his pipe, Standing Bear told Sheldon about the Poncas' past, of the time before the treaties changed everything, of the days of skirmishes with the Sioux, of the annual Sun Dance and buffalo hunt. All gone now—the holy tent, the sacred pole, the dances, the ceremonies, the Soldier Lodge, the tribal way. Now only a few, like Standing Bear, remembered the rituals, the words, the steps, and soon he too would be gone. For Sheldon's benefit too, for the first time in many years Standing Bear retold the stories of the terrible trek of the chiefs in 1877, the tribe's forced removal to Indian Territory, the death of Prairie Flower and Bear Shield, the desperate escape back to the Niobrara, the anguish of his arrest.

After Standing Bear finished, the *New York Times* reporter asked him if he remembered Interior Secretary Schurz. The old Indian nodded slowly. He had never forgotten the Interior secretary, the one who spoke German. In 1880, when he was returning to the crusaders' hotel in New York, a newsboy showed him a cartoon of Carl Schurz by influential political cartoonist Thomas Nast in the latest *Harper's Weekly*. Buying the journal, Standing Bear took it back to the hotel, and in the hotel barber shop he borrowed a pair of shears and cut out the caricature. He asked Henry Tibbles to paste it into a scrapbook for him, and for years he would take out that cartoon and look at it again. It always made him chuckle.[273] So, yes, he remembered Carl Schurz well enough. Schurz had been responsible for much of the ordeal his people had gone through, he told the man from the *Times*.[274]

The reporter then informed him that Carl Schurz was dead. Standing Bear dragged on his pipe, thought for a long time, and then he spoke the one word of English that he now used with any regularity. "Good," he said.[275]

Two years later, on September 3, 1908, Standing Bear died at home. He was buried on his little allotment beside the Niobrara, on his own land, the land of his fathers. His greatest wish was fulfilled: "Let our bones be mingled together with the earth where our forefathers lie, and on which we lived for so many years and were happy."[276] Standing Bear would not walk alone in the afterlife.

EPILOGUE

1884

John L. Webster and Andrew L. Poppleton represent Omaha Indian John Elk, who has separated from his tribe and has sought to register to vote but has been refused. Based on the precedent of the 1879 Dundy decision, they are suing the voting registrar and the U.S. government to have Elk's right to vote confirmed. The government is represented by District Attorney Genio M. Lambertson. Justice Gray finds against Elk.

1887

The General Allotment Act, also known as the Dawes Severalty Act, sponsored by Senator Henry L. Dawes, is passed by Congress. It provides for every Indian head of household to receive a small allotment of reservation land and for citizenship to be granted to those landholders—subject to approval by state law. Indian reservation land not allotted is to be confiscated by the government.

1890

Congress declares that every adult male Indian in the Indian Territory is eligible to enroll to vote—legislators are keen for Indian Territory to become the next state of the Union, but they need a set number of enrolled voters to qualify. Few Indians enroll.

1901

To increase the number of voters in the Indian Territory so that it can gain statehood, Congress declares that every Indian adult male is a registered voter. It will take another seven years for voter numbers to reach the level required for the territory to become the new state of Oklahoma.

1924

The Snyder Act grants the vote to all male adult Indians in the United States who do not already possess it. But the act must be ratified via complementary legislation by the states. Many states do not pass the necessary legislation.

1926

A congressional investigation into the operations and repercussions of the Dawes Severalty Act reveals a catalog of woes and wrongs. The allotment process has been a disaster for Native Americans, breaking up tribes and families, creating enormous financial and social problems.

1934

The Indian Reorganization Act sets out to correct damage caused by the Dawes Act. The allotment system is abolished. Over 2 million "surplus" acres are returned to tribal control. Members of the Ponca tribe in Nebraska are given back eight hundred acres for tribal use.

1945

The U.S. government announces a policy of abolishing some Indian tribes to reduce the cost of subsidizing reservations. The Ponca tribe is not affected.

1948

After lengthy court actions, the last states to legislate to grant Indians the vote, Arizona and New Mexico, finally do so.

1962

In a bill sponsored by Senator Frank Church of Idaho, Congress officially abolishes the Ponca tribe of Nebraska. The eight hundred acres previously returned to the tribe are confiscated.

1988

After years of agitation by the Northern Ponca Restoration Committee, the Nebraska state legislature officially recognizes the existence of the Ponca tribe of Nebraska.

1989

Nebraska Senators James J. Exon and J. Robert Kerry introduce a bill into the U.S. Senate calling for the restoration of the Ponca tribe of Nebraska.

1990

The Ponca Restoration Act is passed by unanimous vote in Congress. President George H.W. Bush signs the act into law. The Episcopalian Church, which owns the 160 acres on which the old Ponca agency building sits, cedes the land to the Ponca tribe of Nebraska. To prevent the tribe from gaining tax advantages, the federal government declines to give the area federal reservation status.

1993

Helped by dancers and drummers from the Ponca tribe of Oklahoma—which has retained many of the dance customs of old—Standing Bear's people, the Ponca tribe of Nebraska, hold their first dance festival, a pow-wow, in 114 years, beside the old agency building.

TODAY

There are now more than 1,300 members of the Ponca tribe of Nebraska and 3,000 members of the Ponca tribe of Oklahoma. Next August, as they do every August, the Ponca tribe of Nebraska, the Ponca tribe of Oklahoma, and the Omaha tribe of Nebraska and Iowa will be holding their annual powwow festivals. All are welcome.

NOTES

CHAPTER 1

1. Bourke, *On the Border with Crook.*
2. Bourke, *On the Border with Crook.*
3. Bourke, *On the Border with Crook.*
4. He was the lowest ranked West Point graduate promoted to major general.
5. Bourke, *On the Border with Crook.*
6. Bourke, *On the Border with Crook.*
7. Brown, *Bury My Heart at Wounded Knee.*
8. Crook, *General George Crook,* editor's note.
9. Bourke, *On the Border with Crook.*
10. Bourke, *On the Border with Crook.*
11. Tibbles, *Buckskin and Blanket Days.*
12. Tibbles, *Buckskin and Blanket Days.*

CHAPTER 2

13. McDermott, *Excerpts.*
14. From an interview given by Agent James Lawrence to the *Indian Herald* in February 1877; reprinted in the *Arkansas City Traveler,* March 4, 1877.
15. Lawrence, interview. While Standing Bear put the number of students at fifty to sixty, Lawrence said the number was seventy-five.
16. White Eagle, testimony to the Senate Select Committee concerning the Removal and Situation of the Ponca Indians, 46th Congress, 1881.
17. Bright Eyes, testimony to the Special Commission to the Poncas, 1881.
18. Standing Bear, testimony to the Ponca Commission.
19. Standing Bear, testimony to the Ponca Commission.
20. Charles Morgan, interview, *Omaha Daily Herald,* April 1, 1879.

21. Various sources provide slightly different lists of the chiefs involved. This list was provided to the *Arkansas City Traveler* when the chiefs were in Arkansas City and was published in the *Traveler* on February 21, 1877. The *Traveler* referred to Little Chief as "the Chief."

22. According to Charles Morgan, the interpreter at the Ponca agency at the time, Charles Le Claire and his brother David sent Washington a petition calling for the removal of agent Arthur Carrier and his replacement by their friend Lawrence. Morgan said that the Le Claires included names of chiefs who later claimed to know nothing about it. Once he had the job as agent, Lawrence made Charles Le Claire the official interpreter.

23. Tibbles, *Ponca Chiefs*.

24. The Poncas knew and trusted Reverend Hinman. One of the clan chiefs, Standing Buffalo, even named a son Hinman, after him.

25. White Eagle, testimony to the Senate Select Committee, 1881.

26. From a report on the Ponca chiefs' visit, *Arkansas City Traveler,* February 21, 1877.

27. *Arkansas City Traveler,* February 21, 1877.

28. White Eagle, testimony to the Senate Select Committee, 1881.

29. Standing Bear, statement, in Tibbles, *Ponca Chiefs.*

30. White Eagle, testimony.

31. This episode is based on Standing Bear's statement. White Eagle told a similar story, but with less detail and without crediting Standing Bear with the leading role; he also failed to mention the detachment of the older chiefs.

32. *Arkansas City Traveler,* February 28, 1877.

33. Tibbles, *Ponca Chiefs.*

34. Tibbles, *Ponca Chiefs.*

35. Tibbles, *Ponca Chiefs.*

36. Edward Kemble, testimony to Senate Select Committee, 1880. He said the telegram was sent on April 12.

37. In his statement, Standing Bear says he was taken to Yankton, but all other sources say it was Fort Randall, which was opposite the Yankton Sioux reservation. There may have been an error in the Standing Bear translation.

38. Senate Select Committee, 1881.

39. Bourke, *On the Border with Crook.*

40. Brown, *Bury My Heart at Wounded Knee.*

41. The size of the military force was later confirmed by Interior Secretary Schurz.

42. The $4,000 estimate was by Tibbles, *Ponca Chiefs,* as was the journalist's wage. The $25/month house rental was advertised in the *Omaha Daily Herald* in May 1879.

43. Tibbles, *Ponca Chiefs.*

44. Alice Cunningham Fletcher, *Fieldwork Diary.*

45. *Omaha Daily Herald,* May 2, 1879.

46. Testimony to Senate Select Committee, 1881.

47. Charles Morgan, *Omaha Daily Herald,* April 1, 1879.

48. White Eagle, testimony.

49. Tibbles, *Buckskin and Blanket Days.*

50. Howard's report is included in the U.S. Commissioner of Indian Affairs, *Report for 1877.*

51. Standing Bear, testimony to the Ponca Commission.

52. Standing Bear, testimony to the Ponca Commission; White Eagle, testimony to the Senate Select Committee.

53. Bourke, *On the Border with Crook.*

54. Bourke, *On the Border with Crook.*

55. White Eagle, testimony.

56. Standing Bear, testimony.

57. Tibbles, *Ponca Chiefs.*

58. White Eagle, testimony.

59. Hayt, letter to Schurz, in Tibbles, *Ponca Chiefs.*

60. Tibbles, *Ponca Chiefs.*

CHAPTER 3

61. He did not approach his son-in-law Shines White, identified by Standing Bear as the husband of Prairie Flower. According to interpreter Willie Hamilton (in testimony to the habeas corpus hearing of May 1, 1879, reported in the *Omaha Daily Herald,* May 2) Standing Bear's two grandchildren were orphans—both their mother and their father were dead. Either Shines White was not the father of the two children or Hamilton was in error. According to the *Arkansas City Traveler,* Shines White was alive and well in the Indian Territory in 1880.

62. Standing Bear consistently used the name Chicken Hunter for this clan member. In the April 4, 1879, petition for a writ of habeas corpus, he is called Little Duck, apparently a translation error.

63. Charles Morgan, interview, *Omaha Daily Herald,* April 1, 1879.

64. Bourke, *On the Border with Crook.*

65. Tibbles, *Ponca Chiefs.*

66. Special Order no. 33, reprinted in Tibbles, *Ponca Chiefs.*

67. The above special order made provision for the quartermaster to supply the horses and mule team. No specific mention is made of a military ambulance, but this was a common form of army transport. General Crook loaned Henry Tibbles a military ambulance from Fort Omaha when he took Alice Cunningham Fletcher

to the Omahas, Poncas, and Sioux in 1881. With its spring suspension, it was considered more comfortable than a wagon.

68. Tibbles, *Ponca Chiefs*.

69. Tibbles, *Ponca Chiefs*.

70. Morgan told of his absence in the *Omaha Daily Herald,* April 1, 1879. Young Hamilton told of his role as translator during the arrest in his testimony to the habeas corpus hearing of May 1 reported in the *Herald* of May 2.

71. Tibbles, *Ponca Chiefs*.

72. Tibbles, *Ponca Chiefs*.

73. No documentary evidence exists for the March 29 meeting between General Crook, Bright Eyes, and Iron Eye, or the presence of Bright Eyes and Iron Eye at Crook's subsequent secret meeting with Henry Tibbles. Crook's autobiography never reached the Ponca affair, while Tibbles deliberately failed to mention Bright Eyes's early involvement in the campaign, to protect her and to prevent anyone from inferring that he and she were close at that time, since he was a married man. In his books and diaries John Bourke mentioned nothing of Crook's involvement in the behind-the-scenes activities on behalf of the Poncas, including the clandestine meeting between Crook and Tibbles in the early hours of March 30, to protect his general. What Crook embarked on with Tibbles was nothing less than a conspiracy against the U.S. government, a conspiracy to which Bright Eyes was a party. I steadfastly believe the meeting between Bright Eyes and Crook took place on March 29, and that this meeting spurred Crook to act on behalf of the Poncas within hours, early the following morning, after the prisoners had been on his doorstep at Fort Omaha for days, since March 27. The following Monday, March 31, Crook declared, a little impatiently it seems, "I have heard all this story before. It is just as they represent it." He could only have heard the entire story recently and from an insider with intimate knowledge of the case. Reverend Dorsey and Reverend Hamilton had no comprehensive knowledge of the Poncas' mistreatment, and young Willie Hamilton, the interpreter, confessed he didn't even speak to Standing Bear or the others after they arrived at the Omaha agency in March 1879. Crook could not have heard the story from Standing Bear or another member of the Ponca tribe as he hadn't spoken to any of them prior to March 31. Bright Eyes is the obvious source of his detailed information. Her pro-Ponca activities, some of them illegal and clandestine, prior to and following the arrest of Standing Bear, show that such a mission to General Crook is the sort of thing she wouldn't have hesitated to carry out. Only one hint about her secret trip to see Crook and then Tibbles at Omaha made its way onto paper. Addison Sheldon, in his book *History and Stories of Nebraska,* for which he interviewed both Standing Bear and Bright Eyes, wrote of Bright Eyes and Standing Bear's Poncas, "She visited Omaha on their behalf. While thus engaged she became acquainted with Mr. T. H. Tibbles."

CHAPTER 4

74. See Chapter 3, note 73, for a detailed discussion of the role of Bright Eyes and Iron Eyes in this meeting and the earlier meeting with General Crook at Fort Omaha. The fact that Crook left his visit until the early hours of the morning is telling. He didn't wear an army uniform as a rule, so he could have slipped into the newspaper office unnoticed at an earlier hour. But Indians in the streets of Omaha in March 1879 would certainly have turned heads; while Bright Eyes may have passed for a white, Iron Eye would not have. The 1:00 A.M. meeting time was obviously chosen to ensure they weren't seen, and, more importantly, not seen in Crook's company.

75. Harsha proved to be an active supporter of the campaign for the Poncas. He became so wrapped up in the affair that he wrote a novel, *Plowed Under* (published in 1881 under the pseudonym of Anonymous), which purported to have been written by an Indian chief. He even managed to have Bright Eyes write a foreword for it. Critics soon realized that Harsha's overwrought tale of injustice could only have been written by someone with an outsider's knowledge of Indians, not by a Native American.

76. Tibbles, *Buckskin and Blanket Days*.

77. Tibbles, *Buckskin and Blanket Days*.

78. Tibbles, *Ponca Chiefs*.

79. Tibbles, *Buckskin and Blanket Days*. General Crook had secretly asked Tibbles to go to Spotted Tail, chief of the Brulé Lakota, and urge him to reject proposals that would soon be put to him personally by the Indian Affairs commissioner, proposals that Crook considered against the Brulé's best interests and contravened promises Crook had made to the tribe. Of that incident, Tibbles wrote in *Buckskin and Blanket Days*, "I gladly accepted the mission, agreeing to Crook's firm demand that I should be very careful not to let anyone, either white or Indian, learn who I was or what my purpose was."

80. Tibbles, *Buckskin and Blanket Days*.

81. Tibbles, *Buckskin and Blanket Days*.

82. Tibbles, *Buckskin and Blanket Days*.

83. Tibbles, *Buckskin and Blanket Days*.

84. Tibbles, *Buckskin and Blanket Days*.

85. Tibbles, *Buckskin and Blanket Days*.

86. Tibbles, *Buckskin and Blanket Days*.

CHAPTER 5

87. Tibbles, *Buckskin and Blanket Days*.

88. Tibbles, *Ponca Chiefs*.

89. Both Tibbles and John Bourke (in his diary) wrote that Morgan was a full-blood Omaha, but other sources, including Mathes and Lowitt, *The Standing Bear Controversy*, say he was an Iowa who lived with Iron Eye's family on the Omaha reservation for a time. Iron Eye's mother was part Iowa, his second wife a full-blood Iowa; Morgan may have had a family connection with Iron Eye through one of them.

90. Bright Eyes, testimony to the Senate Select Committee, 1881.

91. Tibbles, *Ponca Chiefs.*

92. Tibbles, *Ponca Chiefs.*

93. Tibbles, *Ponca Chiefs.*

94. Tibbles, *Ponca Chiefs.*

95. Tibbles, *Ponca Chiefs.*

96. Bourke, *On the Border with Crook.*

97. Bourke, *On the Border with Crook.*

98. Tibbles, *Buckskin and Blanket Days.*

99. Tibbles, *Buckskin and Blanket Days.*

100. Bourke, *On the Border with Crook.*

101. Tibbles, *Ponca Chiefs.*

102. Tibbles, *Buckskin and Blanket Days.*

103. Speeches made by Buffalo Chip and Standing Bear were reported in the *Omaha Daily Herald*, April 1, 1879, and, with slight variations, in Tibbles, *Ponca Chiefs.*

104. *Omaha Daily Herald,* April 1, 1879.

105. Tibbles, *Buckskin and Blanket Days.*

106. Tibbles, *Buckskin and Blanket Days.*

107. Tibbles, *Buckskin and Blanket Days; Ponca Chiefs.*

108. Tibbles, *Ponca Chiefs.*

109. Tibbles, *Ponca Chiefs.*

CHAPTER 6

110. Headlines from *Omaha Daily Herald*, April 1, 1879.

111. Tibbles, *Ponca Chiefs.*

112. Tibbles, *Buckskin and Blanket Days.*

113. Andrew J. Poppleton, *Reminiscences,* said he was certain the idea of the habeas corpus challenge started with Crook.

114. All these Omaha attorneys advertised for new clients in the *Omaha Daily Herald* in May 1879, at the time the Standing Bear hearing was taking place.

115. Tibbles, *Ponca Chiefs.*

116. Tibbles, *Ponca Chiefs.*

117. Unlike the Omaha attorneys described at 114, Webster did not advertise for new business.

CHAPTER 7

118. Tibbles, *Ponca Chiefs.*

119. During her interrupted speech at the Omaha Presbyterian Church the following September; Tibbles, *Buckskin and Blanket Days.*

120. Tibbles, *Ponca Chiefs.*

121. Tibbles, *Buckskins and Blanket Days.*

122. Tibbles, *Ponca Chiefs.*

123. Tibbles, *Ponca Chiefs.*

124. Tibbles, *Ponca Chiefs.*

125. Tibbles, *Ponca Chiefs.*

126. Tibbles, *Ponca Chiefs.*

127. Wakely, *Omaha.*

128. Tibbles, *Ponca Chiefs.*

129. Tibbles, *Ponca Chiefs.*

130. Bourke, *On the Border with Crook.*

131. Bourke, *On the Border with Crook.*

132. Tibbles, *Buckskin and Blanket Days.*

CHAPTER 8

133. Tibbles, *Ponca Chiefs.*

134. Hayt, letter to Schurz; in Tibbles, *Ponca Chiefs.*

135. Hayt, letter to Schurz; in Tibbles, *Ponca Chiefs.*

136. Hayt, letter to Schurz; in Tibbles, *Ponca Chiefs.*

CHAPTER 9

137. Bourke, *On the Border with Crook.*

CHAPTER 10

138. Bourke, *On the Border with Crook.*

139. Tibbles, *Buckskin and Blanket Days.*

140. Bourke, *On the Border with Crook.*

141. Tibbles, *Buckskin and Blanket Days.*

142. The *Republican* story was also picked up and run by the *Arkansas City Traveler* on May 21, 1879.

143. Standing Bear related this to Sheldon, who included it in *History and Stories of Nebraska.* Also cited earlier in Jackson, *A Century of Dishonor.*

144. *Omaha Daily Herald*, April 1, 1879.

145 Tibbles, *Buckskin and Blanket Days*.

146. From the Dundy judgment in the Standing Bear case. Dillon, *Cases Determined in the United States Circuit Courts for the Eighth Circuit*.

147. Dillon, *Cases Determined in the United States Circuit Courts for the Eighth Circuit*.

148. All quotes from the hearing come from the lengthy verbatim reports of proceedings that appeared in the *Omaha Daily Herald* on May 2, 3, 4, 6, and 7; also in Tibbles, *Ponca Chiefs*.

CHAPTER 11

149. Tibbles, *Ponca Chiefs*.

150. Tibbles, *Buckskin and Blanket Days*.

151. Tibbles, *Buckskin and Blanket Days*.

152. Lambertson's arguments are reconstructed from Judge Dundy's judgment and from A. J. Poppleton's rebuttal of those arguments, which appeared in full in the *Omaha Daily Herald*, May 4, 6, and 7, 1879.

153. Poppleton's summation and Lambertson's interjections appear in full in the *Omaha Daily Herald*, May 4, 6, and 7, 1879.

CHAPTER 12

154. Tibbles, *Buckskin and Blanket Days*.

155. Tibbles, *Buckskin and Blanket Days*.

156. Tibbles, *Buckskin and Blanket Days*.

157. Tibbles, *Buckskin and Blanket Days*.

158. Tibbles, *Buckskin and Blanket Days*.

159. The report in the *Republican* was used by the *Arkansas City Traveler* on May 21, 1879.

160. This was how the *Boston Advertiser* described Bright Eyes's speaking voice on October 30, 1879.

161. *Omaha Daily Herald*, May 2, 1879.

162. *Omaha Daily Herald*, May 2, 1879.

163. Repeated in the *Arkansas City Traveler*, May 21, 1879.

164. Tibbles, *Buckskin and Blanket Days*.

165. Tibbles, *Buckskin and Blanket Days*. In his May 3, 1879, *Omaha Daily Herald* report of Standing Bear's speech, Tibbles didn't include this emotional climax. Perhaps he thought that with its accusatory tone it might antagonize Judge Dundy, the last thing he wanted to do, if he ran it. Tibbles merely wrote in the *Herald*, "After a few more remarks he closed." Tibbles included the full closing in his later life story, long after the judge handed down his decision.

CHAPTER 13

166. From the Dundy judgment in the Standing Bear case. Dillon, *Cases Determined in the United States Circuit Courts for the Eighth Circuit.*

167. Repeated in the *Arkansas City Traveler*, May 21, 1879.

CHAPTER 14

168. *Omaha Daily Herald*, May 15, 1879.

169. Tibbles, *Buckskin and Blanket Days.*

170. Bourke, *Diaries.*

171. *Omaha Daily Herald*, May 15, 1879.

172. Bourke, *On the Border with Crook.*

173. Reported in the *Arkansas City Traveler*, May 21, 1879.

174. Letter of May 20, 1879, from Sherman to the secretary of war; included in the record of the Senate Select Committee looking into the removal of the Poncas, 1881.

175. Tibbles, *Buckskin and Blanket Days.*

176. Tibbles, *Buckskin and Blanket Days.*

177. Bourke refers to the bag of bones around Standing Bear's neck in *On the Border with Crook.*

178. Tibbles, *Buckskin and Blanket Days.*

179. Tibbles, *Ponca Chiefs.*

180. Tibbles, *Ponca Chiefs.*

181. Tibbles, *Ponca Chiefs.*

182. Tibbles, *Ponca Chiefs.*

183. Tibbles, *Ponca Chiefs.*

184. Tibbles, *Buckskin and Blanket Days.*

185. *Omaha Daily Herald*, May 15, 1879.

186. *Arkansas City Traveler*, June 11, 1879.

CHAPTER 15

187. Tibbles, *Buckskin and Blanket Days.*

188. *Cheyenne Daily Leader*, April 26, 1877.

189. Tibbles, *Buckskin and Blanket Days.*

190. Tibbles, *Buckskin and Blanket Days.*

191. Tibbles, *Buckskin and Blanket Days.*

192. Tibbles, *Ponca Chiefs.*

193. *New York Observer*, January 1881.

194. Senate Select Committee, 1881, Senate Executive Document 14.

195. Senate Select Committee, 1881, Senate Executive Document 14.

196. Senate Select Committee, 1881, Senate Executive Document 14.

197. Senate Select Committee, 1881, Senate Executive Document 14.

198. *Arkansas City Traveler,* June 18, 1879.

199. Arkansas City Traveler, May 26, 1880.

200. Tibbles, *Buckskin and Blanket Days.*

201. Tibbles, *Buckskin and Blanket Days.*

202. Tibbles, *Buckskin and Blanket Days.*

203. Tibbles, *Buckskin and Blanket Days.*

204. Tibbles, *Buckskin and Blanket Days.*

CHAPTER 16

205. Tibbles, *Buckskin and Blanket Days.*

206. Tibbles, *Buckskin and Blanket Days.*

207. Tibbles, *Buckskin and Blanket Days.*

208. Tibbles, *Buckskin and Blanket Days.*

209. Tibbles, *Buckskin and Blanket Days.*

210. *Boston Daily Advertiser*, August 6, 1879.

211. Tibbles, *Buckskin and Blanket Days.*

212. Tibbles, *Buckskin and Blanket Days.*

213. *Boston Daily Advertiser*, August 6, 1879.

214. Tibbles, *Buckskin and Blanket Days.*

215. Tibbles, *Buckskin and Blanket Days;* the entire conversation. Phillips later wrote a dedication in *Ponca Chiefs.*

CHAPTER 17

216. Tibbles, *Buckskin and Blanket Days.*

217. Tibbles, *Buckskin and Blanket Days.*

218. Tibbles, *Buckskin and Blanket Days.*

219. Tibbles, *Buckskin and Blanket Days.*

220. Tibbles, *Buckskin and Blanket Days.*

221. *New York Times*, August 23, 1879.

CHAPTER 18

222. Hayes, *Diary and Letters.*

223. Hayes, *Diary and Letters.*

224. Tibbles, *Buckskin and Blanket Days.*

225. Crockett, *Davy Crockett's Own Story.*

226. Tibbles, *Buckskin and Blanket Days.*

227. Tibbles, *Buckskin and Blanket Days.*

228. Tibbles, *Buckskin and Blanket Days.*

229. Tibbles, *Buckskin and Blanket Days.*

CHAPTER 19

230. Senate Select Committee, 1881, Senate Executive Document 14.

231. Senate Select Committee, 1881, Senate Executive Document 14.

232. *Arkansas City Traveler*, December 8, 1880.

233. *Arkansas City Traveler*, December 8, 1880.

234. Hairy Bear, testimony to Senate Select Committee, 1881.

235. Joseph Sherburne, testimony to Senate Select Committee, 1881.

236. Hairy Bear, testimony to Senate Select Committee, 1881.

237. Hairy Bear, testimony to Senate Select Committee, 1881.

238. Tibbles, *Buckskin and Blanket Days*.

CHAPTER 20

239. Tibbles, *Buckskin and Blanket Days*.

240. Tibbles, *Buckskin and Blanket Days*.

241. Tibbles, *Buckskin and Blanket Days*.

242. Tibbles, *Buckskin and Blanket Days*.

243. Tibbles, *Buckskin and Blanket Days*.

244. Tibbles, *Buckskin and Blanket Days*.

245. Tibbles, *Buckskin and Blanket Days*.

246. *Boston Daily Advertiser*, November 2, 1879.

247. *Boston Daily Advertiser*, November 2, 1879.

248. *Boston Daily Advertiser*, November 2, 1879.

249. *Boston Daily Advertiser*, November 2, 1879.

250. Tibbles, *Ponca Chiefs*.

251. Tibbles, *Ponca Chiefs*.

252. Tibbles, *Ponca Chiefs*.

253. Tibbles, *Ponca Chiefs*.

254. Manifest Destiny, a doctrine attributed to journalist Cora Montgomery (real name Jane Cazneau) and first espoused politically by Democrats and later adopted by Republicans, held that the United States should and inevitably would expand its national boundaries, initially west to the Pacific and then beyond.

CHAPTER 21

255. *Arkansas City Traveler*, January 7, 1880.

256. *Arkansas City Traveler*, January 7, 1880.

257. Bourke, *Diaries*.

258. Barnard, *Rutherford B. Hayes and His America*.

259. Tibbles, *Buckskin and Blanket Days*.

260. Washburn, *The American Indian and the United States*.

261. Hayes, *Diaries and Letters*.

262. Hayes, *Diaries and Letters.*

263. Hayes, *Diaries and Letters.*

264. *Arkansas City Traveler,* December 8, 1880.

265. Colonel George W. Manypenny, a former member of the board of Indian commissioners.

266. Jackson, *Indian Reform Letters.*

267. Standing Bear, testimony to the Ponca Commission, 1881.

268. Bourke, *On the Border with Crook.*

269. Watterson, *Marse Henry.*

270. Fletcher, *Fieldwork Diary.*

271. The date shown in *Buckskin and Blanket Days,* provided by Tibbles's daughters, is incorrect. County records and newspaper articles noting the wedding confirm the 1881 date.

272. Schurz, *Speeches, Correspondence, and Political Papers.*

CHAPTER 22

273. Tibbles, *Buckskin and Blanket Days.*

274. *New York Times,* May 27, 1906.

275. *New York Times,* May 27, 1906.

276. Standing Bear, testimony to Ponca Commission, 1881.

BIBLIOGRAPHY

American Nonconformist. Indianapolis, Ind., 1893–1895.

Arkansas City Traveler. Arkansas City, Kans., 1877–1881.

Army and Navy Register. Washington, D.C., 1891.

Barnard, Harry. *Rutherford B. Hayes and His America*. Indianapolis: Bobbs-Merrill, 1954.

Bell, William Gardner. *John Gregory Bourke: A Soldier-Scientist on the Frontier*. Washington, D.C.: Potomac Corral of the Westerners, 1978.

Boston Daily Advertiser. Boston, 1879–1880.

Boston Post. Boston, 1887.

Bourke, John G. *The Diaries of John Gregory Bourke*. Edited by Charles M. Robinson. Austin: Texas A&M University Press, 2003.

_____. *On the Border with Crook*. New York: Scribner's, 1891.

Brown, Dee. *Bury My Heart at Wounded Knee: An Indian History of the American West*. London: Barrie & Jenkins, 1971.

Catlin, George. *North American Indians*. New York: Viking Penguin, 1989.

Cheyenne Daily Leader. Cheyenne, Kans., 1876–1877.

Chicago Times. Chicago, 1879.

Constitution of the United States of America.

Council Fire. Washington, 1879–1880.

Crary, Margaret. *Susette La Flesche: Voice of the Omaha Indians*. New York: Hawthorn, 1973.

Crockett, Davy. *Davy Crockett's Own Story, As Written by Himself*. New York: Konechy & Konechy, 1992.

Crook, George. *General George Crook: His Autobiography*. Edited by Martin F. Schmitt. Norman: University of Oklahoma Press, 1946. Republished, with a foreword by Joseph C. Porter, 1960.

Cutler, William. *Andreas' History of the State of Nebraska*. Chicago: Western Historical Company, 1882.

Dillon, John. *Cases Determined in the United States Circuit Courts for the Eighth Circuit*. Davenport, Iowa: Egbert, Fidlar & Chambers, 1880.

Fletcher, Alice Cunningham. *Camping with the Sioux: Fieldwork Diary of Alice Cunningham Fletcher*. Washington, D.C.: National Anthropological Archives, Department of Anthropology, National Museum of Natural History, Smithsonian Institution, 1881.

Fletcher, Alice Cunningham, and Francis La Flesche. *The Omaha Tribe*. Bureau of American Ethnology, Twenty-seventh Annual Report. Washington, D.C.: Government Printing Office, 1911.

Foreman, Grant. *The Last Trek of the Indians*. Chicago: University of Chicago Press, 1946.

Giffin, Fannie Reed. *Oo-mah-ha Ta-wa-tha*. Lincoln, Neb.: Self-published, 1898.

Gray, E. Jane. *With the Nez Perces: Alice Fletcher in the Field, 1889–92*. Lincoln: University of Nebraska Press, 1981.

Green, Norma Kidd. *Iron Eye's Family: The Children of Joseph La Flesche*. Lincoln: Nebraska State Historical Society, 1969.

Green, Rayna. *Women in American Indian Society*. Broomall, Pa.: Chelsea House, 1992.

Greer, Emily Apt. *First Lady: The Life of Lucy Webb Hayes*. Kent, Ohio: Kent State University, 1984.

Harper's Weekly. New York, 1880–1881.

Harsha, William J. *Ploughed Under: The Story of an Indian Chief, Told by Himself*. Introduction by Susette Bright Eyes La Flesche. New York: Flords, Howard & Hulbert, 1881. Initially published anonymously.

Hayes, Rutherford B. *Diary and Letters of Rutherford B. Hayes*. Columbus: Ohio Historical Society, 2003.

———. *The Diary and Letters of Rutherford B. Hayes, Nineteenth President of the United States*. Edited by Charles R. Williams. Columbus: Ohio State Archeological and Historical Society, 1922.

———. *A Message from the President of the United States Transmitting a Report of the Commission Appointed December 18, 1880 to Ascertain the Facts in Regard to the Removal of the Ponca Indians*. 1881. South Dakota State Archives.

History of the Ponca Tribe. Niobrara, Neb.: Northern Ponca Housing Authority, 2001.

Howard, James. *The Ponca Tribe*. Washington, D.C.: Government Printing Office, 1965.

Indian Herald. Osage Agency, Indian Territory (Oklahoma), 1877–1880.

Jackson, Helen Hunt. *A Century of Dishonor: A Sketch of the United States' Dealings with Some of the Indian Tribes*. 1881. Reprint, New York: Little, Brown, 1900.

———. *The Indian Reform Letters of Helen Hunt Jackson, 1879–1885*. Edited by V. S. Mathes. Norman: University of Oklahoma Press, 1998.

———. *Ramona*. Boston: Roberts Bros., 1884.

Jackson, Helen Hunt, and Abbot Kinney. *Report on the Condition and Needs of the Mission Indians of California, 1883*. Washington, D.C.: Bureau of Indian Affairs.

Lauter, Paul, ed. *The Heath Anthology of American Literature*. 4th ed. Boston: Houghton Mifflin, 1998.

Mathes, Valerie Sherer, and Richard Lowitt. *The Standing Bear Controversy: Prelude to Indian Reform*. Urbana: University of Illinois Press, 2003.

McChesney, Lea. *American National Biography: Mary Porter Tileston Hemenway*. New Haven: Yale University Press, 1998.

McDermott, John D. *Excerpts from General Crook's 1876 Campaign Report*. Sheridan, Wis.: Frontier Heritage Alliance, 2000.

Morton, J. Sterling, and Albert Watkins. *Illustrated History of Nebraska*. Lincoln, Neb.: Jacob North, 1905.

New York Daily Sun. New York, 1880.

New York Observer. New York, 1881.

New York Times. New York, 1879–1881.

Ponca Commission Report, 1881. U.S. Senate Miscellaneous Documents, 1880–1881, vol. 1, doc. 49.

Ponca Tribe of Nebraska: Community Environmental Profile. Niobrara: Northern Ponca Tribal Council, 2003.

Poppleton, Andrew J. *Reminiscences*. Lincoln: Nebraska State Historical Society, 1915.

Pratt, Richard H. *Battlefield and Classroom: Four Decades With the American Indian, 1867–1904*. New Haven: Yale University Press, 1964.

Red Man. Carlisle, Penn., 1900. Carlisle Indian Industrial School newspaper.

Roberts, David. *Once They Moved Like the Wind: Cochise, Geronimo, and the Apache Wars*. London: Pimlico, 1998.

St. Louis Republican. St. Louis, Mo., 1879.

St. Paul Pioneer Press. St. Paul, Minn., 1879.

Schurz, Carl. *Speeches, Correspondence, and Political Papers of Carl Schurz*. New York: Putnam's, 1913.

Sheldon, Addison E. *History and Stories of Nebraska*. Chicago: University Publishing, 1914.

Sicherman, Barbara, and Carol Hurd Green. *Notable American Women*. Cambridge, Mass.: Belknap, 1980.

Tibbles, Thomas Henry. *Buckskin and Blanket Days: Memoirs of a Friend of the Indians*. 1957. Reprinted, with an introduction by F. P. Prucha. Chicago: Lakeside, 1985.

_____. *Ponca Chiefs: An Indian's Attempt to Appeal from the Tomahawk to the Courts*. Boston: Lockwood, 1879. Republished as *Ponca Chiefs: An Account of the Trial of Standing Bear*. Introduction by Kay Graber. Lincoln: University of Nebraska Press, 1972.

Topeka Daily Commonwealth. Topeka, Kans., 1879.

Towl, Edwin S. *Judge Elmer S. Dundy. Proceedings and Collections*. 2d series, vol. 5, 1902. Nebraska State Historical Society.

U.S. Commissioner of Indian Affairs. *Annual Reports*. Washington, D.C., 1877–1891.

U.S. Senate. Executive Documents 14, 30. 46th Cong., 3rd sess., 1881.

Utley, Robert M. *The Lance and the Shield: The Life and Times of Sitting Bull*. London: Pimlico, 1998.

Wakely, Arthur C., ed. *Omaha: The Gate City and Douglas County*. Chicago: Clarke, 1917.

Ward, Geoffrey C. *The West: An Illustrated History*. London: Orion, 1999.

Washburn, W. E., ed. *The American Indian and the United States: A Documentary History*. New York: Random House, 1973.

Watterson, Henry. *Marse Henry*. New York: Doran, 1919.

Wilkerson, J. L. *A Doctor to Her People: Dr. Susan La Flesche Picotte*. Kansas City, Mo.: Acorn, 1999.

Wilson, Dorothy Clarke. *Bright Eyes: The Story of Susette La Flesche, an Omaha Indian*. New York: McGraw-Hill, 1957.

Winfield Courier. Winfield, Kans., 1881.

Wooster, Robert. *Nelson A. Miles and the Twilight of the Frontier Army*. Lincoln: University of Nebraska Press, 1993.

INDEX